WITHDRAWN

GRAVE OF LIGHT

GRAVE

NEW AND SELECTED POEMS 1970–2005

ALICE NOTLEY

OF LIGHT

WESLEYAN UNIVERSITY PRESS   MIDDLETOWN, CONNECTICUT

WESLEYAN POETRY

PUBLISHED BY WESLEYAN UNIVERSITY PRESS

MIDDLETOWN, CT 06459

COPYRIGHT © 2006 BY ALICE NOTLEY

ALL RIGHTS RESERVED

PRINTED ON ACID-FREE, RECYCLED PAPER

IN THE UNITED STATES OF AMERICA

LIBRARY OF CONGRESS CATALOGING-IN-PUBLICATION DATA

NOTLEY, ALICE, 1945–

GRAVE OF LIGHT : NEW AND SELECTED POEMS,

1970–2005 / ALICE NOTLEY.

P. CM. — (WESLEYAN POETRY)

INCLUDES INDEX.

ISBN 0-8195-6772-8 (ACID-FREE PAPER)

I. TITLE. II. SERIES.

PS3564.079G73 2006

811'.54—DC22

2006015712

From *The Descent of Alette* by Alice Notley, copyright © 1992 by Alice Notley. Used by permission of Viking Penguin, a division of Penguin Group (USA) Inc.

"Would Want to Be in My Wildlife," "One of the Longest Times," "As Good as Anything," "Choosing Styles—1972," "I Must Have Called and So He Comes," "The Trouble with You Girls," "Hematite Heirloom Lives On (Maybe December 1980)," "Mid-80s," "Sept 17/Aug 29, '88," "1992," "Lady Poverty," from *Mysteries of Small Houses* by Alice Notley, copyright © 1998 by Alice Notley. Used by permission of Viking Penguin, a division of Penguin Group (USA) Inc.

"Circorpse," "Help Me Corpus Sagrada," "The Islanders Remember That There Are No Women and No Men," "Red Fish," "Enuma Elish," from *Disobedience* by Alice Notley, copyright © 2001 by Alice Notley. Used by permission of Viking Penguin, a divison of Penguin Group (USA) Inc.

Selections from *Alma, or The Dead Women* are used with permission of Granary Books.

Selections from *Close to me & Closer . . . (The Language of Heaven)* and *Désamère* are used with permission of O Books.

Selections from *Margaret & Dusty* are used with permission of Coffee House Press.

Selections from *Waltzing Matilda* are used with permission of Faux Press.

The author expresses her profound gratitude to Ed Foster of Talisman House, Publishers, who published *Selected Poems of Alice Notley*.

CONTENTS

My publishing history is awkward and untidy, though colorful and even beautiful. A number of smallish books and chapbooks came out in the early years which didn't find their way into subsequent, dignified "collections." I found, when I began to edit this selection, that organizing the text according to my "books," and interspersing previously unpublished poems, would entail an apparatus of titles and title-pages making for a choppy reading experience.

On the other hand, I've explored sequential and long poems since I first began writing: as chapbook-length and book-length entity, as epic poem, and as quasi-autobiography. Increasingly, the long and/or serial form has become how I write. Such works cannot be represented without overall titles.

Thus, when I decided to present *Grave of Light* in chronological order, I dismantled previous collections to present poems by the year in which they were written, but kept poems from sequences together since they were written at the same time. Unpublished poems also appear chronologically. The larger headings in *Grave of Light* are meant to designate sequences or long poems. The years printed at the bottoms of poems or extracts from sequences are the years of composition not of first publication. The book now tells its own story.

In the back of the volume may be found a list of published books with the titles of poems selected from each beneath, as well as the titles of unpublished poems appearing here for the first time.

I expect my unconscious models for the construction of *Grave of Light* have been *The Collected Poems of Frank O'Hara* and the earlier *Selected Poems* of William Carlos Williams, both of which marked me definitively. I mention them because my book is necessarily so different from theirs. I invoke and thank the spirits of Williams and O'Hara, nonetheless. And I heartily thank all my publishers past and present.

ALICE NOTLEY

GRAVE OF LIGHT

FROM *LOVE POEMS*

2/?   Saturday

    Shadow

      of pen & fingers on paper

Shadow

Window

        divides into sky
              window & brick

    & overlay

        of old rain stains

      & see through lights

I divide

      into man boots small size baggy
                pants

    rough red shawl

      & guest face   I guess

             I see
                         little bones hands

      Aura of you

           dissolves into

                         in the window

      Leaves aura of me free

      gets up to get

                         just warm

FRIDAY MIDNIGHT EXACTLY

      I heard the knock though I thought
      possibly it was the drum in the phonograph
      I open the door it is the girl upstairs
      will ask me for a knife to open her lock
      she forgot her key or to turn down the
      phonograph I open the door I start & shake
      all over an embarrassing little spasm
      there is someone there after a week's
      waiting it isn't you it's the girl up-
      stairs asking me to turn down the
                                    phonograph

COLD POEM

Cold Poem coffee gone cold

Merrill coughs a throb in my head

& I'm sleepy now

     not a moment too soon

Weep ye weepers especially

Suzanne is coming

with pills at midnight right & I won't weep

   But

    I won't dance

   if I can't dance with you

I HOPE I'M NOT HERE NEXT YEAR

I'll say

the one nice thing about that apartment

was how my desk was

Desk?

Shit it was an orange crate

But right in front of a window

in a stream of

dazzling 3 o'clock light

Even in February

the sun there was almost too much

for me

reading William Saroyan & me

[1970]

1.

I dreamed of a clipper ship
Gold on blue THE CHASEY ALICE
Until he'd seen which Captain You said
He'd seen nothing. I woke bold
Chased you to get caught in the hold
Back to sleep 2 nightmares
Solid ones down not to be told
Woke not wanting to be in life
Wasn't, outside warmed
To my blood clean cold quickened
On the way to town for food and
Back for you, though I was still
A little sulky & grim
So you fucked me back in

4.

New the curtains wall desk beer
Black Label old jealousy
Through which I try to clear
This house came gratuitously
Christmas new friends their

Summer house
Jealousy keeps
To stun from where
To escape I speak
Always suddenly there stable
Times jangling rose
Energizes me, sleep disabled
Keeps me on my toes knows
To fasten my 2-year love
To shake me up my hands prove

15.

Time of, dress warmly, 3 A.M. walk
Coat over sweater, shawl over
Hair, boots over slippers, snow
On & over all, I forgot
To mention I'm drunk (martini
& piece of toast) I think
Our traffic signal's remarkable
In the air, 2 wires & 2 streets
Cross exactly there. I cross
On green, the snow, making tracks
To a white beach, a long time's
Sliding into bed, reaching
To feel you, in place, in place I
With snow, on my hair, on the sheet

22.

I dreamed you brought home a baby
Solid girl, could already walk
In blue corduroy overalls
Nice & strange, baby to keep close
I hadn't thought of it before
She & I waited for you out by the door
Of building, went in
Got you from painting
Blue & white watercolor swatches
We got on a bus, city bus
One row of seats lining it & poles
It went through the California desert
Blue bright desert day

[1971]

DEAR DARK CONTINENT

Dear Dark Continent:

                        The quickening of
the palpable coffin
                        fear so then the frantic
doing of everything experience is thought of

but I've ostensibly chosen
                            my, a, *family*
so early! so early! (as is done always
as it would seem always) I'm a two
now three irrevocably
                        I'm wife I'm mother I'm
myself and him and I'm myself and him and him

But isn't it only I in the real
whole long universe? Alone to be
in whole long universe?

But I and this he (and he) makes ghosts of
I and all the *he*s there would be, won't be

because by now I am he, we are I, I am we.

We're not the completion of myself.

Not the completion of myself, but myself!
through the whole long universe.

[1972]

INCIDENTALS IN THE DAY WORLD

You and baby you know me and I am
my ankles and angles and cavern-
haired particular whim

a bank of violets devours
deposits itself again and again

in the flame boa heap with the diaper pins
the Chanel for the monthly bath and the invisible Rodins

Our moving cars through the rain
I'm grabbing the road
trees can turn fish or rock
underwater   (or city like toad)
our compacted gyre, common load
setting out to win a face
child was is me, and me, and no one
spangled with charm apparently flesh
you in me with me mean mind clear and fleshed

Lovely and wise in a number I

poignance is a spear in use bossed, with dew
numerical I overcome Sansjoy

numbers are my face when I am flow
when I perform a number I'm in num-
ber's silver clean, exalting hollow
"Thought it was the Reader's Digest but
it was Life": number's deepening deepening hum

Their arts they move they escape clean
I serpentine invent my luck
I marry you world, my stolen heart
dispersed into the fray of clothes
I'll get back by wearing everything

it's a number like any other, one
I'll wear my death my baby gives away
I'll wear my death like anyone like day

Not undoing: I must love the glassine eye
caves being minor matters violent-
ly velvet, the crystal sphere rod strip screw
no magic bone, disjointed forces a block
a construction to men-ladies lent
a true Oscar's a candle a standard
stage in the Little Sailor's Home, meant
as an Eve blossom, space's form, hard
to loosen, warm milieu, sugar now coffee heart

Here's a world for today:
Killing and not dying   fantastically not lying
know a humble etiquette
                    assuming everything
          to encompass a gold ring
     spiraling outward to include every-
thing (will she)   spaciously running
like a silver animal for a quarry:
unfleshed air, of a day when some of its motes are starry

"A square chest is trying to attach it-
self to my round one" my round self
my most faithful and tender friend and prick
the scenery the coffee is a shelf
but I don't believe in an elfin self
or brilliance before radiance: "Nothing
monstrous about that violin" that clef
and I'm cleaving
to a bottle a cylinder glass not undoing

Hot, and everyone as if what it
is high serpent stretches
vegetable spears
                    the stars' web sticky
to caress me ripe peat will lick

bunches of knot grass ringlets,
clime feeling suffocant

sucking wetness overtakes the cool level-eyed sets

You take my old time and space I wanted
having set out and won another's face
wanted it back or wanted a new it
a bold blind face
little baby extend my space   the rent
is extensive tho space for a whole heart
marriage has a bold blind face

but our birth rent me from an easier part

"Marriage like the car is an invention"
curled interestingly
you stare and wonder and wait and don't, cun-
ning is its not yours it might be a felony

my magnet, shimmer of the formal sea
colors of men are drawn to its clothes
colors flesh all, for all, when flashed as clothes

I wish I could stay awhile longer
if the world weren't anything but poems!
flawless spined strung longueur
and it is and I'm not, a woman
a small palm offers its leaves to the wind
with the rock that also tears it: a man
an actual measure exists in
measures my span on our wall by his span
(Cézanne) ended perfected before me always begin

The drive to radiate light of the broil
when the blood is vintage we'll
chat over coffee holding hands and foil-
ing flirt the stately music, sunny chill
from peak to sea and they laugh at the not too brill-
iant; cumbrous light tore my shade of
freely blank and yield and wind

my form he came from I come from his again

Adorned with fruitful entities all around
dead centers: steel graters or stars
I ordinarily build a sphere's ground
the Prince's stolen heart might be here
with a baby, emblazoned with thick red air

thick as love you too must come here
with hair and claws I have no death
I claw into being all of our puissant birth

That I pray to with steal and charm, for you
square the circle to fuck it
in instant needs and breath brazen to
innocently olive and dark take it
to you, with breasts and meddling intent
I despise innocence I have so
little I forget everything, innocent
new, I drink and pause, my favorite so
you may be yours too, and comfortable, our row

My body becomes boat, water
which can't hold back my knees
my artifice
uncanny at the ceiling flies off
drunken flying knees; the flesh's tryst scoffs
          stars
to make it whole—you understand
simple sparks and trapezes
in the grit of your knowing of it and
. . .

Syllables
my neck breasts knees open bare
not describable but perceptible words
as the haunted blood's gentle dear
I'm not at all completely sincere
untaken, emblazoned with thick red air

restore the other half of a pair
here's the palpable air of earth, the earth of air

You knee my desert clarity
my sea in porcelain
my nothing knees ecumenical balmy
up around you in curls
or I must make howl
ellipsoid elliptical mongoloid

  the paper white must avoids:
a callous steamer maturity tryst in the world

Careless of my stealth and of my fame
I take a serpent shield from flower sun
and, would for anything be blamed
accepting anything all and one

disgraced disarmed disarming graced
our pottage hundreds of crushed suns

jewels: such attitude our clothing's face
such show becomes then the center's force, of our race

If my most beautiful ape
is ugly my most beautiful knee is miraculous
its completely palpability, nape-
sexy behind its pillar's unselfconscious-
ness, the cunning adulterant rapes the face
but
what you don't kiss won't sing less

in the wind, awkward but, coolly, cold

Thinking of three
I mostly say I
we feel mingled in perfect sanguinity
in me on sherry secretly dry
circling and twining so
lively so like the void is silly
light will mass and dry, sly
will fake will coyly
pose and refuse but I won't fear the incident I'm

In our moving cars through the rain
unlacing lofty crest for outgrown bangs
you play me fair as gold blown
or over each branch and its blossom hangs
air of honey and boomerangs
"a salvage beast embost" in splinters
every object a phone rings
rings into gold contract
wedding ring blinding messy air made more compact

We spell spell "spell," I spelled it: knew
from deadly danger was loose from
and light in, now dress for my sphere to
rest my person where I nest from
back black clear
the meaning of my face
that velvety intersection's bloom
with no fear of the compass
or my incident   I encompass

Another walk with my seeing it
my fancy if it's a personal oyster
soft as a mat to a tumbler's must
the sky seems as kind as a teamster
do I get out of the cave guitars of
my mortal slime my billowing senses
                                a scimitar

through to a wondrous darkness
but cylinder sphere and cone I the spherey earth press

I embrace all the dead
voices instruments waters medicines

their furious loving fits made wind
strange phantoms in pleasure's valentine

my dead and my ghosts my atoms fine
by these rent reliques speaking their plightes
(Spenser, I feared so the other side of my sight)

Alone mixing skin with sheet
pigeon rags windowed mirrors wrath and flesh
sipping a pale, human's aperitif (air)
keep its hardened lovely must or
the world away you left worshipless
cold and hot she laughs—we laugh—walls
feeding on city cliffs coast dress

inchoate, I'm still always choked with bells

[1973]

YOUR DAILINESS,

                                    I guess I must address you
begin and progress somewhat peculiarly, wanting
not afraid to be anonymous, to love what's at hand
I put out a hand, it's sewn & pasted hingewise &
enclosed in cover. I'm 27 and booked, and my
grandfather

my grandfather, I begin with, played dominoes
called them "bones." Bones is a doctor on Star Trek.
Black, intensive, rectangular solids starred
with white dots, and laid end to end. Mysterious
perfections, like flowers, but all, all as we can
know, give, take down address of, felt in the (bred
in the) bones. Loose cloak with half-mask
worn to conceal identity, esp. at masquerade, whence
dominoed
which I am
I saw it in a movie THE BLACK KNIGHT, with Alan Ladd
and Patricia Medina
                            the rooms of skulls of the
sacrificed at Stonehenge, wearing silky wigs blond
as Victoria's our visitor's hair. We intermingle.

That night I dreamed of my grandfather, playing
dominoes, and my mother my aunts—dreams are not
brightly lit—a brownish dream. Once, I dreamed
of the in perfect happiness, a motion not too fast
through space with one with whom I was completed.
Tetherball, skull and strung bones, my nightly fantasy
when an aunt died, blond and mad, I was six so I'd

something great to tell everyone. My father's best
friend died, I was twelve and excited, my

aunt died. I saw her in dying wasted down to her
bones, the most pitiable animal I'd ever seen so I
cried without thinking, though didn't grieve
I cried til there were unnaturally huge shadows
way down to my cheekbones and my cousins were
astounded and impressed. With them her death was for
us to hold close. I heard an elegy for Paul Blackburn

read by a friend today, and cried, for the beauty
of the work, his and his, don't quite catch the
whole implacable rectangle. Those last two lines?
And for Ezra Pound: "In that palace they will
dwell forever / and guard the mystery of the world."
So I mismanaged my first love affair, I botched it

humiliated, one sunset, eighteen, and I'm flooded with
the I have to die. It lasts a year. I take it
everywhere. I take it home. One whole night one
night I awake control every single breath I take
in case I might stop breathing. Victoria returns
from a walk with my baby
                              The next morning I'm
different. A halo of will, my grandfather's name.
He plays solitaire and whittles out how "when you
go you go" sky roofless. I never kissed him, once
had to my grandmother, didn't want to, wrinkles
tasted dusty. She has cat's eyes, hates doctors,
didn't kiss Will before she married him

                                    she told me,
me too. I lay awake at night in the girls' dormitory

and hug death to me it fills my body with will. I
can't watch horror movies until suddenly last night.
I've watched my husband cry for the death of Jack
Kerouac, for his grandmother's, for Allen Ginsberg's
Elegies for Neal Cassady, and for the latter,
knowing neither, for the nobility of the poetry I
cry too. I cry last night at the end of Star Trek

the Captain rematerializes from the other, ghost
universe and Bones and the Vulcan are friends.
My husband's mother doesn't die as simultaneously
Paul Blackburn does. Thin wounded tough animal. Now,
she complains overweight and sends me love I'm
blank but can summon a rectangle for her a letter, is
that how I love? A few months later, in the same

heavily natured town where we heard the Cassady
Elegies So many colors flowers that sit and flowers
that fly and that girlishly dress and talk, I'm told
by letter my grandfather Will has died. I cry

comfortably, as comfortable as this year for Picasso
they were both in their nineties. I go to the museum
to pay homage to the Picassos (Chicago) and for the
first time, in a year of trying, I miraculously really
see EXCAVATION by de Kooning
bypass the Picassos, some angel's around, is it Picasso?
Once I dreamed him exactly, corporeally, but young
(from photos) in a house of ghosts "What nonsense!"

Picasso and I said, in shrug language, to each other
meeting in the green hallway. Two days after my
grandfather letter, afternoon between waking and napping
I dreamed he came to me in air, like a baby in a

white nightgown, then flowed away. I just fed the
baby for the third time today, I must do these things
daily.
          Several months before I met my husband
I began to concentrate on ghosts, that they were there,
there here, and I, I might see one, if anyone why
not as with anything, I? I waited every night. I
went to bed and turned out the light, though no longer
lovingly hugged the dark, to see if it would appear,
the ghost. For three months. Nervously fell asleep.
I told my friend Mary she said Why not just see it?
I didn't want to be one who saw ghosts. I waited
waited. Then I dreamed

                              a woman a poet spoke to me
out of a drawing on my wall, spoke what? Spoke.
The ghost would appear, and in a shower of gold, he
appeared and he was Rory Calhoun in his corniest
grin and loudest plaidest with shoulders sportscoat.
We embraced.

An enormous domino impenetrable of ghosts and also
evil perhaps. I wrestled with the ghostly, to emerge
real, and I wrestled I think with evil for it must
all be in me all of all in the world, kill, kill
yourself. A few weeks after Grandpa showed me himself
as a baby, my son was conceived.
                              10 minutes before
birth a shot of sodium pentathol: then I woke from
deepest black to where it was green, like my dream of the
room where everyone at all of each's significant
ages for me, everyone I knew in one warm dark room
assembled in intimacy with me, a child. My child's
my secret name, Libby.

There's the son you wanted
the nurse said. I cried and told her she was a skilled
and wonderful nurse. A person I don't know

poet Ezra Pound part of my life dies he dies not that
part. I dream in order to participate in "the ceremony"
I must be decapitated, head placed on plate, with others,
at a white table. I awake and it's I have to die,
all over again, not I but the baby will never die and
he, husband, and I will, not together. A wax-like
substance slow combustion ordinary temperatures luminous
in the dark, I fall dizzy to the floor

a week later, think I'm dying. Find I wouldn't be
ready. But I don't die death the unconceivable horror
so why not why not do the bad things the worst
things in life? Why am I not one who's suicidal or
who's evil? I wait as for the ghost but I'm haunted
by knives, and I work I write. I'm dizzy in the
museum but I grasp on to worship Cézanne, Picasso.
Weeks earlier I'd dreamed of poet Ed Dorn, in a lovely
greenish light, with a book a sequence of poems heavy
rectangles each they grant you comfort in the
territory where overlap life and death, not comfort
they grant you life in it. I dream I'm a blond

girl Samson in a pink prom dress, and I dream of
Ozymandias. Anonymous stone enormous stone head,
conveyed particle by particle from a place to a place,
but, says the Professor, useless to the conveyors
because not from *their* place. This is my place

In England we live in the country. A friend in
New York City has actually jumped into death from a

window, so palpable in my mind he might enter the room
and tell me again color preferences their meanings.
Blond . . . fair, person with such hair & skin; silk
lace of 2 threads in (hexagonal) meshes (orig. of
raw-silk color). Colors their flowering I wait
for my evil the monolith is me inescapable, that I am not
evil, thread life and death. I waited six months
and wrote and wrote "I'm well and whole" to be so.
England's so old that layers of death

pervade beautifully the beautiful countryside.
Last Sunday I walked barefoot through the cemetery,
came home and wrote ". . . And the dead the golden
warm & shady earth / I'm comfortable with / . . . Sights
& insights endless as the dead . . ." Intimacy with
all, spreading, Your Dailiness.

[1973]

BUT HE SAYS I MISUNDERSTOOD

He & I had a fight in the pub
5 scotch on the rocks 1 beer I remember
Only that he said "No women poets are any
          good, if you want it
Straight, because they don't handle money" and
"Poe greater than Dickinson"
    Well that latter is an outright and fucking untruth

6-line stanzas

                              Open though some?
And he forgot to put my name on our checks
            However,
He went to get the checks however
He had checks to deposit in his name
            Because
He's older & successfuller & teaches because
When you're older you don't want to
            scrounge for money besides it gives him
            a thrill he doesn't too much acknowledge,
                  O Power!

                  So I got pregnant
I hope not last night now
I'm a slave, well mildly, to a baby
Though I could teach English A or
            type no bigshot (mildly) poet-in-residence like him
Get a babysitter never more write any good poems
            Or, just to
Scrounge it out, leave him. All I can say is

This poem is in the Mainstream American Tradition

                  [1973]

I

                Pregnant again involucre

                              (sounds gorgeous)

Pregnant

       not the repast of news or psychological

                            though arithmetical

(stars, filth)

        I ingeminate

        I dream
        of a compost
        into whose composition paper
        can go

        and which itself
        composes the paper
        but literally
        how, do you suppose

        the wonders
        that would be facts,
        from dreams,
        get lost

reflex you refractor old saw you
thought
     you'd got swisher,
          craggy, from the Chinese, more masculinely
feminine, only refined
when wanting to be startling,
          emeralds sacral putrid but
you're just cavernous
     round a foetus
          and true

A dream hole
in tower wall
to admit or
mirth music
the holes let issue

Mohaves coffins flowers jealousy

"What's great is three Irish
whiskies—we have to wait for the grill

to heat up—to get masterfully
irritable and declaim from the fitfully lit

up clouds above the table that their
sole interest is their sexual

power at age 19; though it might conceivably
be experientially satisfying

to be a man, one by definition attracted
to, in love with them by definition you jerk!"

And so pay for having been yourself
                            such a girl
Fuels Shakespearian
                Old style shrink
That every movement naturally produces
                                    noise
                which attracts, pursues, tears to pieces,
                                            utensil and wing,
                        the thing

                        til she lives

Like a mirror irritation
                        the fabric of reality is stretched
to the breaking point or point
                        the orgy of patternless vitality

            "This isn't *me*, Mommy!"
                                        —all night—
pinpoints your arc light
                        you're a global stretch from
her, who you're now
                and the breaking point   .

                    is lack of stretchability
                    you're compacted utility
                    fabric sewn up into globe

[from *Songs for the Unborn Second Baby*]

                    a galaxy
            consents to be an ear-
            lobe out of rumored curiosity
            and the echelon day of the time it is

                            when you conceived singsong

Everything must have been precariously certain self the socks the
stars the spring of the bedsprings unmatching
                                    the making then the
taking of
        off-balance,
                    you tripped
                            drunkening
over
        your hopefully whorish heels

                        and now you're still lying here comfortably

                        only the stars could be reeling
                        only the flowers, crocus
                                        velvet-brodded
                        could be unreal

                                they're not drinking this
dark ale are they?
                    to beat the devil
                                as does my hysteria
urgency of base metal
                        is preferable to
                        your gold standard encomiast
                        of God the Cork

                                    [from *Songs for the Unborn Second Baby*]   **29**

"To flesh is to incite

            by taste of blood"

                      You seemed

  calm and fresh

           and that seemed blood so I was fleshed

and thought so to be carnal

               paper flaunt

but I had to flesh and, flesh, be fleshed and flesh again

raised to morbid heat

                  You, you kind of anagrammatic puzzle

                              enter into this name

with my offenses committed of hurts and thoughts

              which some call quibbles and some, redolent

of a fiscal though fabulous opera

                  My God
                  is that I've
                  stolen already
                  breast and pit
                  from and for it

                  everything that's "out

                  of equilibrium, except
                  all of it" like my

                  growing
                  belly with my knees

I live dangerously another
                          What almost bothers me
is this shit I keep coddling on paper like loving
                              "an ugh to love" that love
I bulge, curl up, pucker with

            caused by fungi and attributed to dancing
            also accounted a strange incidence, marvelous
            progress or fabrication, a faithful fib organ

                                        I consult
the dictionary as if it's its
If the oracle is just another barnacle at least the slink
        blow with one's head does pearl and storm!
                                    cup-handed
    crocus mid the "wrong" compost
                            with cream-washed purple petals
            and in their straight, strict, orange
                        center
                    the true oracle.

The pistil is the female organ of flower
to piss is to make
water in a cyclone
the dictionary
                gives me fumble fever
                only displays my hydra heads?

Had love such largesses giving joy to me
and "pooled myself" about it,
I care not a bean about.

May God the Chosen have His Joy
if *that's* what he wants, anyway

Give me good issue
whom no fencing can avail it, for

The flambeau between my ribs and hips
is its own flair

                        when it's born I'll have
to "have" mine. . . .

[1974]

"ALICE ORDERED ME TO BE MADE"

intricate ship

Thing well
in my heart

"Alice ordered me to be made"

Waltz to Repel Invaders

machinery was in use by carving jade

bolts of silk instead of memory

at first they made only small,
ritual chopsticks

old rags to supplement advice

the heartlands and the furniture

the mist tiny human
bloodties study the first
porcelain

throughout the rose
to prominence

lilaceous bus of the Missouri
or an injury, lights and darks reversed

tend to attract affection, the
shaft of a column constricted part-
tooth to caress in love
a body useful in combination
how could you? and durability
of its figure or timbre or
profane the pardon with
cosmetics outside the rings,
an act of shocking outskirts

Sound of a word tic waters.
Of certain fabrics surface so
formed, fine hair, downy, any
of several American
gooseflesh. A plain de-
tached window openings.
And saved to be sewn to-
gether. And West Africa
And black. horse. Angle
round

and tell me the
twist amorphous
flesh or dust to muscle, I
mean if the leaves plant
the Trojan War does the
key wide true does the
pretender smell God?

Yes.
As the twig is bent
I nestle
to retrace the radiant
puddle of all remarks. Ravish

raw hay thaw the theater
Preposition
He was presumptuous enough to call
the president by his first name:
lost leaves. I had an impulse to
strike all vaccinations
but I leak too many burning
stars
of human affection

as warriors take position
thousands of them
as leaves and flowers appear in their season
hearts burning to break them
singers without memory
curved sea wandering the wild
hearts
where silver is first begotten
a thing shameful but bringing joy to the enemy
me.
Colorful utter foolishness and utter sense
supposedly work well miracles together.
A miracle: not that the crown jewels
are forbidding, but that per-
sonally who stars

I wicked as a lens or wine or legendary queen

shimmering lets fall a light
tear. Did this ever happen?
She who is only a little thing

first. The shining wine and
pleasuring the heart. Divine
salt to lighten the ship, sacro-
sanct, we are all held in a
single honor, light as the
strip. But around my own
shelter and beside my black ship
I think.

Well.

A libation to
the divine Dawn, the
lovely-haired flashes, the
inward heart, circle and
spear; the stars have
gone far on their course

sounds rose
Dawn rose
the wearisome goddess
incessant rose
difficultly wrought iron
storm of
dust rose

the fire's rush

Single one sheer. Bless
darkness and brazen slumber.

The sea stood apart
rejoicing

She bewitched her
shining eyes. Shamefastness
and lovely with a veil: pattern-
pierced zone

tears like a dark running

sheer is my heart

my love loves me

Near my father dying in hospital
April 1975

"THE VIRTUE OF UNCREATEDNESS"

?

immediately create

Roses beautiful

               when I look at you
           your leaves against
       what a lightful and formal baby-
               blue volkswagen!
                               touches the roses
           in the window plane
                   though one street width away

           What is watching? a

                   peddlar of insects
                   a figure, possibly god impersonator
                   a rain charm probably
                   a flowers music dance
                   a slit-drum head
                   a kneeling figure, figuratively
                           from Duck River, Mississippi
               "I'm in my sin"
                   a standing figure fetish
                   wood paint nails cloth leather beads shells
                   arrows twine nuts
                   a Maiden spirit mask

                           totally uncreated!

                       Here

       take this mess it's yours it falls away into

       A silver truck just drove into, and stopped,
                   the entire window

            falls away into
                        dot dot dot

Dot Lamour
Dot in Oz
Dot Parker.

            [1975]

                ENDLESS DAY

        O me being me
                        designed
        to satisfy the gods feeling it
            just as one

        need not know it that
        every experience is a mystical
        one
            the sun
        shines the lamp shines the Albers
        glows
                What a nice day!

                        the
        doors open and shut and when they
        shut you're either in or out
                        right

in a supreme mental clarity
though its validity often
appears in doubt to you not
to mention Art in America
who thought up this vocabulary one
day
in our air! I say

                    music is an emotion month
                    poetry is an emotion bird
                    painting is evident

                    O John Covert

          I was trembling
                          like a gallows
          I was sopping wet with
          every bit of God knows nothing
          what I was trying to hide a
          lack of an abstract mystical expression
for
          His world His Ringling   Her world Her Ringling
          Brother His world   Sister Her world
          the life of a saint!   the life of a saint!

The world is the saint
                    Honey Sweet
Swete Herte
the world is as
fresshe and free as its
heart of yours

olive
    black
        "aggressively anti-illusionistic" I'll bet
  brilliant
      sparkling
Criseyde
mourning and fucking
with gestural looseness with
regal tension with
          feathery
beautifully
      fleeting visions

  in praise of the dead

     O you in your frames each

  splash that is alive forever

as the white light's a salt shaker

  a splash alive forever

a rosary is so pretty

  a splash alive forever

"which are perhaps a little dull"

  a splash alive forever

clashes from wall to wall

a splash alive forever

a small courteous gesture

a splash alive forever

do I believe? I'm busy saying

a splash alive forever

crevice for love to enter and fill

a splash alive forever

riding the billows selves to the waves

a splash alive forever

[1975]

30TH BIRTHDAY

May I never be afraid
          especially of myself
                              but
Muhammed Ali are you telling
the truth?
          Well you're being true aren't you and

you talk so wonderfully in your body
        that protects you with physique of voice
  raps within dance
          May I never be afraid

     rocked and quaked
             the mantilla is lace
             whose black is oak
But if I'm dark I'm strong
       as my own darkness
my strength the universe
       whose blackness is air
       only starry
       lace
But if I'm alive I'm strong
      as life
Strong as the violets
in Marlon Brando's fist
     his dissemblance flourished into truth
                  She

took them
I'd take me too
    I do
    and my Ali I see you
         a hard bright speck of me
the savage formalist
     authentic deed of gossip

  a kind body

[1975]

JANUARY

Mommy what's this fork doing?
                                    What?
It's being Donald Duck.

What could I eat this?
                              Eat what?
This cookie.
                    What do you mean?
What could I eat it?

Does he bite people? That fish is dead. That fish got
dead today. That fish gets dead today, right?

These are my silver mittens Mommy
No, it's gold, they're gold mittens

On myself
I put my black
hat
and my mit-
tens,
myself.

Edmund. Edmund. Edmund. Maaaah. Lodle lodle lodle

Daddy, the doctor did put a wart on you,
right?

I touch the purple petals
She says Hey!

        The flower says, we are purple,
together
    they touch purple it keeps purple
    purple means us, here.
    The air moved a person, I like people
    because they're as serious
    as I am. Being purple is very serious.
    It's dense and still.
    It's a matter of fact
    but light seems it.
    I seem the light
    makes me feel purple.
    A petal is crumpling I've done
    before
        I sleep in the bulb.

    Being purple is long.

Crumpling is not as serious
as being purple

    (I may disagree)

I'm not not serious not smiling.
I'm smiling
as crumpling
only a little now.
I'm mostly staying serious purple now.

Do you remember when you were like Edmund?
                                        Yeah.
What did you do?
                    crawled with him.
Do you remember last year?
                            Yeah, Mommy what did you
do when you be Anselm?

    The jacket is furniture.
    I have to fix, Mommy.
    I have to fix all the tools.
I'm in the snow and my feet go in the footprints.

I'll look up "love" in the dictionary. They're beautiful.
Bodily they're incomprehensible. I can't tell if they're

me or not. They think I'm their facility. We're all about
as comprehensible as the crocuses. In myself I'm like a
color except not in the sense of a particular one. That's
impossible. That's under what I keep trying out. With
which I can practically pass for an adult to myself. Some
of it is pretty and useful, like when I say to them
"Now will I take you for a walk in the snow to the store"
and prettily and usefully we go. Mommy, the lovely
creature. You should have seen how I looked last night,
Bob Dylan Bob Creeley Bob Rosenthal Bob on Sesame Street.
Oh I can't think of any other Bobs right now. garbage.
It perks. Thy tiger, thy night are magnificent,

it's ten below zero deep deep down deep in my abdomen
It pulls me up and leads me about the house. It's got the
sun in the morning and the moon at night. It does
anything in the world of particulars without wanting.
The anyone careless love sees that everything goes, minds.
The melody was upsidedown, now the melody turns over.
One note: my feet go.

       30 years old married 4 years 2 children
       is the same little girl in the yard
       until dusk and into night
       in air with myself, others
       has a mother and father
                        nature (courage)
       smiles frankly at the camera don't
       blot your anonymity your littleness

child you are is the source of all
honestly bliss at dusk in Chicago
is face you've ever been
                              and almost before
dusky the child air you are
handsome you're head-to-toe

It's too early. It's too dark. If I can't watch T V I'll
turn on the light and look at stars.

I see 2 full moons.

I walk.
I am big.
I can say
what they
say. It's
fun to
sound. I
walk. I am
big. I finally
get the blue
and red container
of . . .
sneezes!

the trees have no leaves they lean
like her over the snow and green
wire fence of the school
                    the sky
is white low low low
                    Greggy Ruthy
and Jill are there

Daddy tomorrow we'll have donuts and chocolate soda
and my birthday party and eat snow and throw snow and
make snowmen.

He'll take off your wart tomorrow and you won't be sick.

My armpits smell like chicken soup. But really I hate them
because of their tacky and unchanging book collection. My
head weighs too much on the pillow. I have to sweat. I'm
crying free water don't worry. Under your tongue looks like
pussy. You seem to bloom. The colors are brighter but I
think I'm deaf.
                    I'm remembering all my dogs.
One was taken away because he howled too much and my
parents said he wanted to fight in World War II and so joined
the army. All things considered there's nothing to say for
Chicago. I dreamed you led an army of empty pieplates

against another one. I dreamed you had a baby. I despise
someone. I have to sweat. I need you to stop this train.

I didn't lose any weight today
I had clean hair but I drove
Ted nuts and spanked Anselm on
the arm and wouldn't converse
with him about the letter C. And
didn't take Edmund out or change
the way the house smells or not
drink and take a pill and had to watch
John Adams on T V
                and fantasized
about powers of ESP when on LSD—
there is no room for fantasy in
the head except as she speaks.
The Holy Ghost is the definitive
renegade like in the white falling-out
chair stuffing, 2 chairs
                    asking me if
I liked my life. I thought she
meant my life and said
                  how could
you dislike being a poet? and having
children is only human
                but
she meant my chairs. The
trouble is the children distribute
the stuffing to the wind. It's

soft and pliant and they can do it
intimately together.
There are 4 green sunbursts on the
curtain. Oh it is a cold night but
the jade plant will handle it.

Came in from the snow and melted on
            the floor. There's
Glistening where Jill and Ruthy's feet
Sat Ruthy with braids and colored
Yarn in her hair, a girl
Beauty cars go by to hitch
Away on
            Is it their rumble
That comforts? Or this room full
Of everyone who's sat making
Stuffing appear from the
Chairs, and flowers too last years

They just want to do their yoga too. I guess so. I try
to call up Casey Gold. Some money comes by anyway; the
day brightens, Casey Gold.

I don't appreciate the simple
war of nerves
                    my courtesy
rewarded with a goring
                              is it boring
the toro rhymes, what else do
children have to think about?
well if the cape is all wet it won't
blow in the wind
                    but I have to check
something
                    You're still in no condition
to fight a bull
                    But he found his own . . .
What a glistening golden
baby!
                    Enough to make one woozy. Matador,
I am with the wind and unwinding
am wonderfully useless to you.

[1976]

HOW SPRING COMES

            Toys and rose   The zoo body zigzags
I think fish too
                    but I'm a polite
social being, I'm a Ladle Lady or purple

and blue I write green letters and gold
editorials for the Krystal Oxygen Company
I have one hip as far as I can see, that
I see as I write say

          white tee-shirts
            upsidedown
         turn em around
         & put them on
             your muscles
             my angels

   or

       a semi-colon
         is blue window
        to me
is that a haiku? I fly over San Diego in some one or
another real despair and ask you to comfort me. You
more or less do, you aren't even there
      my best me my wordly me
      my taste of spring my continuance my
      comfort will you comfort me?
I offer you my heart over Tucson
           I can't use it
     take it to comfort me
              free
     me be it take it take it to
     be it
which apparently you don't or take you help provide
me it I think, that
happens among true people, that poem I was writing
no good poem
       but Moment framed the Pleides

The garnets ring more beautiful the longer you
                    are waiting for me in them,
                    where Deity makes me friendly there.

But who put on all the tee-shirts in Hunter's
Point? Well we're all good boys my son said so.
A semi-colon is a semi-precious garnet cluster
telegram; what we love are such depths between all
the messages. Pass the salt; Ladies of the Tang,
bubble of night; this book about Harry Truman is wonderful.

I see the Gulf Moon Rising every night. I'm familiar
with the zonked starfish. I've the sheen on under
the fire-escape railing all streetlight-lit. The
hollow suddenly appeared to enlarge and fill with a
bright light. Wild with the taste of wine it does not
remember the despair of an hour ago, which was true
that is of a true woman. She was somehow hating her
position on the round earth in the dusky sky on a
harsh Sunday. On the ground forgotten flowerlike
firmaments. She addressed in uneloquent hatred
SMUG LIFE
                    the one who soothes one's foolishness the
Great Face Construct who loves you for your kinks child
anyway, the Guru God:

         Oh I will come back a knockout tomorrow
              Useless to you!
                    You're not it you smug face
         I'm not doing your yoga not wearing
         Your moondrops using your cream
         Rinse letting you fuck me Exquisite

Like I was one of the Ones With Brains Too!
Intelligence in panties with peekaboo
holes—

No I'm coming back raw
I'm getting drenched in the rain
It's rain and it's wet I'm soaked I'm
Chilled and I'm coughing the air's raw
To my throat, which is raw from
Coughing, coughing so strong
Coughing and coughing
So strong from killing you!

Etc.

She didn't kill nothing.
& I don't get to share
no secrets with the stars. I make chow. I contemplate
semi-colons. I despair as a mother. I scream at that
kid I'm gonna crack open your big walnut if you don't
go to sleep. Theories of grace, that it implies no
surprise no shock. Ukrainians sudden on Sunday speaking
Ukainian, the cross not Christian but Gracious
and when I want to cry or cough violently
it must diffuse back into my embassy; hard, that takes
hard. And if it weren't for you . . . not you smug life
face, but real you. Please play cribbage
Pass the salt.
Think of a garnet-black cabbage, a
Ukrainian is selling it on 7th Street in honor of our
marriage. A Spanish fan opens in my abdomen
I have Spanish dancers in my stomach

they're my arching striving in dance where it's black
red flowers darken to be huge pleasuring the
        severe, tried Angel who meets transition,
    transport, as abruptly as necessary
                for everyone's are apt

Says the Unassuming Graceful
Whose down-hip-ness
Is that window
The dancers' sensuous flaw
That admits Spring,
Contingent upon our personality
Spring is for the worldly
                        Just like the HaHa Room
            Just like dearest rockbottom
                            suddenly gone buoyant

        To be black geese to be
        strenuous dancers
        is not to dignify a passion but to
        grip it.

            Not saints but always pupils
pupils dilated fully black in full achievement of
gut-feeling. Joy.

[1976]

LITTLE EGYPT

A wave composed in
smoke, wine & peridot, white accessories of the sea
the evening sky shines me with stars, like mistakes
that will attend my eventual dismissal, or numerous
branching waterways. Closely at the wrist a domain
thunders, that of the cosy little worker of
defective thing   into a shrub engine idea, it is
sweet music at right angles to expectation, even mine.
Who dismisses? a gesture
The sea is a sphere, or glued to one, I cup
it but can't throw it

                        that's not what I care about
anyway. I want all my stars, that are were reflections
Like a half-gesture is a gesture
And so they
              frighten me out of my wits, all the side events
so close to reality as to be it. If I were
        an Egyptian, I'd be
buried with all my mistakes and halfnesses, and not
in the interests of proper perspective, but for that static
that commits the body to life. Picture
an Egyptian princess walking out to, what else? fuck Apollo
which isn't quite transpiring, my ornate golden breastplate
cannot be gotten on to be gotten off just right, Apollo
a sort of Dudley Doright made out of light, softly, green
        woods, her serpentine coronet
I cannot explain my untoward behavior.

Apply the geranium lipstick, and deviate

                                        O Arjuna
I will indeed make known to you my manifestations; but
I shall name the chief of these, only. For, of the lesser
variations in all their detail, there is no end.

          I am a verbal agreement to be operative: I
          complete one revolution of the earth each day.
          I am a musical composition: I hum then I feign
          death when in danger, a pause exactly timed.
          Among opiates, I am Poppy, that little exhibitionist.
          Make of me what you will: I'll take them all.

          I flavor time and devour its ribbon-shaped pasta.
          Of sense-organs I am the sponge. Among mountain-peaks
          I am of the murmurless others, though I might not
          mind being the moon. I am the spirit of fire, for
          I burn. Among waters I am lapse into breath. Though
          fragmented, I am the loud insistent tone. Black
          Label. I am water among waters.

          I am courage inspired by friends, I am the Old
          English for "by hook or by crook." Ancient Greece
          gives me Texas Fever; Divine Glory makes me a case.
          I am a haphazard construction. Wherever I go I will
          return if I go ten thousand miles.

          I am the length of a bridge then a river. I apply
          to intangibles, all of them. I am the incurable
          bumpkin, I like that. I am on the hoof, among horses.
          I think this is getting boring in passing. Pay
          all my bills and get me off the hook.

I am a contemptible person like a woman of great
insight. Whatever in this world, is powerful,
beautiful or glorious is an organ of mine, also called
legend. I am in one's own person, I am an engrafting,
I am the traffic for several hours. I am expressing
affection in handiwork. Among jerks, I am "her
version of story."

I am your kindness. Thus, in this world, nothing
animate or inanimate exists without me. I am always
a passing look . . .

                    A series of vessel, from each of which
a liquid successively overflows to the next. Male self
is the enabler, and I will seize this liquid
and it will be hard as nails, hard as stars.
And it will not be I
                    To cross winds
                    Deposit on the piece

                    I must tell you
Her back finally on frontward
                    I must tell you
The particular, meandering Egyptian purpose
To play at Greek,
                    yet to collect and bury
Yet to shift, song-like, with the minute. Yet
Time is a great big sparkler, crackling
                    I must tell you

                    [1976]

SONNET

The late Gracie Allen was a very lucid comedienne,
Especially in the way that lucid means shining and bright.
What her husband George Burns called her illogical logic
Made a halo around our syntax and ourselves as we laughed.

George Burns most often was her artful inconspicuous straight man.
He could move people about stage, construct skits and scenes, write
And gather jokes. They were married as long as ordinary magic
Would allow, thirty-eight years, until Gracie Allen's death.

In her fifties Gracie Allen developed a heart condition.
She would call George Burns when her heart felt funny and fluttered
He'd give her a pill and they'd hold each other till the palpitation
Stopped—just a few minutes, many times and pills. As magic fills
Then fulfilled must leave a space, one day Gracie Allen's
        heart fluttered
And hurt and stopped. George Burns said unbelievingly to the doctor,
        "But I still have some of the pills."

[1976]

A CALIFORNIA GIRLHOOD

The Brothers Grimm grew weaker and flickered, blue light
        in the well. Hans Christian Anderson
and his tiny gossamer bride went to bed beneath a walnut shell

encrusted with every star, Copenhagen's
Sky, dreamed Louisa May Alcott, but when we awaken
       in New England my head will rest on
my cousin's shoulder, beneath *my* tree.
Anna Sewell, that the shining aren't suffered to continue to
       shine! though, old, he finds
his way home, Carolyn Keene's blue roadster
       cannot replace the young horse. There's nothing
left of her, Michael Shayne, but lipstick and
       fingerprints on a cognac bottle; Erle Stanley Gardner
knows the Chief will never pass cross-examination
       and on to ripeness, the breasts!
Where is orphan Canada, Anne of Green Gables?
       the smell of a white dress it rained on because
it was graduation. Frank G. Slaughter
       has given him hands that heal her after
she sleeps through rape by a snob. Frank Yerby
       pierces right through the membrane she cries
out triumphantly, one of the others, skim
       bunches of adjectives.
Margaret Mitchell moved to the eye which
       watered 3 times: that bright moon moves on. But
you can't strain hydrogen and oxygen out of tears
       or Raphael Sabatini out of life, Captain
Blood, the sword is worn
       against my tattered petticoat.
Charlotte Brontë is tense and comely as a first child.
Emily Brontë walks out to copulate with a
       storm. Indigo to emerald to
indigo, the Mississippi "better den rum darlin"; then
       Mark Twin gets hit on the hammer
and glowers a whole other lifetime. Anya
Seton sighed. "If only angels be angels and witchery

the fine art it is
I still have to
bother about something besides décolletage."
Gwen Bristow pulled the arrow out of her arm
and thrust it into the Indian's chest.
When a guy goes molten John Dickson Carr
orders the witch is nonexistent, yawn
Sigrid Undset loses her life and yet loses nothing
as a river in her bed flows beneath
the stained-glass leaves, thy breath is sustenance.
She wouldn't rollerskate through the Swedish palace,
Annamarie Selinko. Lawrence Schoonover
respects the first man to use a fork in Spain,
a Jew of Inquisition times,
she dances in little but castanets, Kathleen
Windsor, it's a scheming pussy wind
that ripples and funs with the bleak sea. Knowledge
of evil an inadequate knowledge, as
Herman Melville would say, read National
Geographic, for your first glimpse of nipples,
free maps, Arctic, Hibiscus. Jane Austen
sneaks a suspicion. You look like the
flash with the cash.
John Steinbeck. My name
is Rose o'Sharon
the gorgeous coarse prayer, as the sentimental horrors
encroach and recede, repeatedly. Edgar Allen Poe
is on purple alert. Alexander Dumas, fils, announces
My favorite song is Rainy Night in Georgia.
Daphne DuMaurier wept tiny drops of Dom Perignon. Did
Lady Brett Ashley copulate? did
Herman Wouk read between the lines?
T. H. White allowed one her manhood; Guinivere is

Jenny, but I know I carry a lance.
William Faulkner incomprehensible, an
        obsidian cliff, does the ballerina wear cleats?
She puts her ear to the delicate shell of Ernest
        Hemingway; hears
Willa Cather orchestrate her death. Victoria Holt
        is still, chastely, darkly in love.

[1976]

POEM

St. Mark's Place caught at night in hot summer,
Lonely from the beginning of time until now.
Tompkins Square Park would be midnight green but only hot.
I look through the screens from my 3rd floor apartment
As if I could see something,
Or as if the bricks and concrete were enough themselves
To be seen and found beautiful.
And who will know the desolation of St. Mark's Place
With Alice Notley's name forgotten and
This night never having been?

[1977]

WHEN I WAS ALIVE

When I was alive
      I wore a thin dress bare
shoulders the heat
      of the white sun

and my black thin
      dress did envelop me
till I was a shell
      gladly and breeze

ruffled and filled
      against good legs
the translucent fabric and my
      heart transparent

as I walk towards Marion's
      and Helena's as my
skirt fill empties and fills with
      cooling air

[1977]

AFTER TSANG CHIH

I was brought up in a small town in the Mohave Desert.
The boys wouldn't touch me who was dying to be touched,
        because I was too quote
Smart. Which the truck-drivers didn't think as they
        looked and waved
On their way through town, on the way to my World.

[1977]

TODAY

So gray, unseasonal as to be
        perfect
                in old newspaper
I carry it upright
        uncolored
            a flower
September's
        been bestowed, miserably
            to be not
temperate —
        wears not one color today, has
            no such skill.
Yet I smile
        as is necessary
            for I'll outlive her

But in my building as if mislaid
    as crimes are,
        the news that someone's
life has been brutally
    changed by
        those whose axis
can turn in any direction,
    who've no season
        no color no flower at all.

[1977]

YOU

By dust made beautiful,
Spun light of the window:
By bricks Lee sees are pink—
That deluxe sensation of them:
By all October rains
That contract to silvered puddles:
By fine grain of atmosphere
In which walkers' lone thoughts mingle:
By plies of wine-dark night
And the outlandish moon:
By these shores of light-washed blocks
Where one transforms in love
The squalid to the innocent,
Matter to its sparklet bits:
By this cubicle where I

Re-stir the dirt & make a song:
And by, brighter than believing,
The star I shine as here:
I conjure you to know me
As best of children best of women.

[1977]

THE GODDESS WHO CREATED
THIS PASSING WORLD

The Goddess who created this passing world
Said Let there be lightbulbs & liquefaction
Life spilled out onto the street, colors whirled
Cars & the variously shod feet were born
And the past & future & I born too
Light as airmail paper away she flew
To Annapurna or Mt. McKinley
Or both but instantly
Clarified, composed, forever was I
Meant by her to recognize a painting
As beautiful or a movie stunning
And to adore the finitude of words
And understand as surfaces my dreams
Know the eye the organ of affection
And depths to be inflections
of her voice & wrist & smile

[1977]

UNTITLED

My little boy's sick tonight
Oh get well while you're asleep
Honey, and we'll go out
Together at noon
Everything as always

[1977]

"IF SHE SAYS THAT SHE'S
THE GODDESS FORTUNE"

If she says that she's the goddess Fortune
Thus by definition riches & power
Are hers and one has them only on loan
                    Okay I concur

They not being what I long for, but if
So-called Muse withholds what's called inspiration
I'd kill if I might get back what's never mine
                    Nothing's anyone's

No talents abilities or genius
The day is so grey, but grey that's a color
Lovely, translucent, in & out windows
                    Which are us aren't they George

[1977]

THE WORLD, ALL THAT LIVE
& ALL THAT OCCUR

The world, all that live & all that occur
Within it, being the one organism
A monstrous life-death living not-dying
Caving-in upthrusting all over it-
Self like pits & mountains forever thing—
I was despairing one
Grey day a week ago
Cold, we having fought he
Having thrown on the floor say 3 large books
The way the Weather Angel was throwing
Just a handful or 2 of hard, tight rain
Out that morning: so thinking
About that organism, I disappeared
Into it—And I brought him, who is you,
A placatory copy
Of the biography of, as it turned
Out, poor Vivien Leigh.
Today, the weather exactly similar
And I again different, my tiny
Lights in a December tree and
Fingers happily black touching the pearl sky
A man crosses Avenue A
Customarily not thinking about the Universe.

[1977]

BUS STOP

The weather's at its coldest these
days, I'm happy I'm finally not
at the bus stop but sitting on the
crosstown bus. Then, at the next
bus stop he gets on, a man who
has said before the door even closes,
"How often does this fucking
bus come?" Why he is the young
Howard Da Silva! "Every fifteen minutes,"
the mostly inured brown bus driver says.
"Every fifteen years?" says the young
Howard Da Silva. I smell his
alcohol breath from across the aisle.
He, like me, is sitting in those seats
reserved for the elderly and handicapped.
At the next stop a youngish plain
woman, in glasses, vaguely reddish
hair, gets on sits down beside him.
"These seats are for the elderly and handicapped!"
the young Howard Da Silva says,
low, and scary, and she
crosses to another seat with her
miffed and timorous look. At the
next stop a lady gets on and drops a
chartreuse kleenex on the floor
between us, me and the young Da Silva.
The bus driver eyes it nervously, but
Da Silva and I have already seen it
and relaxed. We don't ever look
at each other in the mutual way.

At the next stop Da Silva gets up,
disembarks, the chartreuse kleenex is left
beautifully untouched, undisturbed.
I see him cross the street and
go on down ten-degrees-out Sixth Avenue,
his bright blue jacket unzipped, his
glove, black, sticking out of his back pocket,
his wonderful menacing cheekbones held high.

[1978]

JACK WOULD SPEAK THROUGH THE IMPERFECT MEDIUM OF ALICE

So I'm an alcoholic Catholic mother-lover
yet there is no sweetish nectar no fuzzed-peach
thing no song sing but in the word
to which I'm starlessly unreachably faithful
you, pedant & you, politically righteous & you, alive
you think you can peel my sober word apart from my drunken word
my Buddhist word apart from my white sugar Thérèse word my
word to comrade from my word to my mother
but all my words are one word my lives one
my last to first wound round in finally fiberless crystalline skein

I began as a drunkard & ended as a child
I began as an ordinary cruel lover & ended as a boy who
                    read radiant newsprint

I began physically embarrassing—"bloated"—&
                      ended as a perfect black-haired laddy
I began unnaturally subservient to my mother &
                      ended in the crib of her goldenness
I began in a fatal hemorrhage & ended in a
                      tiny love's body perfect smallest one

But I began in a word & I ended in a word &
                      I know that word better
Than any knows me or knows that word,
                      probably, but I only asked to know it—
That word is the word when I say me bloated
                      & when I say me manly it's
The word that word I write perfectly lovingly
                      one & one after the other one

But you—you can only take it when it's that one & not
                      some other one
Or you say "he lost it" as if I (I so nothinged) could ever
                      lose the word
But when there's only one word—when
                      you know them, the words—
The words are all only one word the perfect
                      word—
My body my alcohol my pain my death are only
                      the perfect word as I
Tell it to you, poor sweet categorizers
                      Listen
Every me I was & wrote
                      were only & all (gently)
That one perfect word

[1978]

THE LOCKET

She's been engaged several times. She's been
to Texas too, to attend college for the few
only months she can ever afford to. Her
favorite subject was philosophy, she says. She's
worked in a dime store and a school office.
She's been to business school, and is now
a bookkeeper, I think. She's pretty, in a
way that has to do with pleasantness and
openness of face and walk. Blue-green eyes,
thick, brown hair, large breasts, tallish.
She's given up her education, nearly
everyone has, in the 30s. It's casual,
to give it up—to leave that for a younger
brother or sister or whoever. It's a question
of timing, what you be. Of world timing.
I think she did give up something, truly,
with casual grace second to no other
entity of value. She's given up one of her
possible lives, though she remembers every
word the philosophy teacher said. She
gives it up—the world's a song of notes of
equal value. They will be those notes,
she will be this note.

Being at harmony in the world, she marries
a man whose tensions move her. He has
really black hair. He was the kind of poor
to quit school in the 10th grade. He's
fraught with feelings of inferiority and the
desire to express his knowing, best self.

He bursts out, makes speeches, to you as if
to someone else. Who?
                              I think she's willing to be
fascinated by his ambition—to be somebody, to
create a . . . it's a building,
filled with mysterious objects, and there are
people, people on both sides of a counter,
who know all the objects' kinds and ways.
The people have a manager, an ultimate knower
of the objects, which you get to be in a
long time from now after much will have passed.
Within it you will make it go as it should. A
parts store is a should, a complex should
of flesh and metal.

But he's a store floorsweeper now. He's a
year younger than she. At first he lied to her
about his age. They have fun and know
people named Babe. He has a gift for courtesy—
manners make you any person's equal, make it
possible to grasp the world. She has a
natural easy manner, he has manners—and they
go and see and do like marvelous innocents.
Common adventures involving bars and cars, I
think. They both have this sense of fun that's one
thing for both. And he doesn't read except
the newspaper, and she only handles machines as
she has to—but he studies the paper, really,
and she handles machines easily. He knows
her opinions can be dumb from lack of interest;
she knows that he's a fanatic. They are
loyal to each other's faults.

I think she's
fascinated by his ambition etc, but she loves
some him, that's all, a face she's seen and
loves forever, intransmutable. I think so. I
don't think he loves a her that way, I think
he has a need that way. But then, I don't know.
And I think the love and the need are of equal
nobility, or value, or reality. To need is to to
love, but not as happily as to love is, maybe.
And how happy is her love? Actually,
her love is only itself.

[1978]

SEPTEMBER'S BOOK

—bum & zoom. leaving & yet never this awful old
   this dark ocean life that hardly sees comes &
   flashes on the sofa sits as Ms. Missa Brevis—
   to go to try to find the rail between names.
   I've tried painted black in a basic baggage dress
   now ghost & jacket & engine now I'm surely going
   fresh from qualifications to the canal and
   the man in Texas I am a next
   horse to be west of the pebbles almost as if
   if again. I always get to change minutes.

—I'd like you to know I am very
   important vices. I insist.

—When I leave the bar post-storm it is
    a yellow sky & a fresh sidewalk.

—I am a man when I didn't
    know it then. We're all
    secret-bound
    made into a tight lawn out front
    & some man's & occasionally go immediately
    to Villain in G Minor there's the
    this bad thing your finger here
    offered me. Hear me world you
    frantic woman! Masts & lights await me!

—I am the famous crouching
    Aphrodite of Rhodes
    1797 to 1828 Opus 171 & shit.

—I like this strangely you know,
    this quite dark-eyed ship I will sneak on
    quietly as a dew drop & then away
    I'll be where the real *there* is, but
    women, sometimes I think they're
    not profound enough to die. Roll down
    the seriously favorite joke theory
    & raise up All in the Foggy Him He Stands.

—It's very interesting how I *am*
    the ship & my sea is and yet
    I must be seriously things, songs & forlorn
    little arounds sometimes. In his sleep as
    planned has agreed. Everything's look-blue
    with dark corners. The delicate
    dismals & pretty little looks.

—These typings . . .

—So?

—I am my type you know.

—Off the top of my waves I guess I know.

—Here we go.

✳

I am man who dazzles in the
regular schedule in the park
with glasses yet a good
solid Afro. I Central Blind Dumb Diamond
fiddle howling, salt thighs, yet playful

the kids playing leapfrog over the defunct
fountain, too short for me, it, or I'd
join impress & conquer them. This park's

short on pussy as well but a sweet wind cleans out
nostril & ear. On Sunday morning it supposed to
got done last night yet here I am again cheerful enough
I surprise myself.

Shall I sit next the prone limp body or the skinny
white mother? some choice. His beer's finished—could
amuse self by watching her *totally taut up* when I
say "Boo, lady, got a match a word those your kids
what you reading where do you live whatcher old man do—"

Why don't these dolls loosen up into a little roll
it on the tongue natural civility? Hey girl what
you scared of—I will masterfully perform with
you every caress tongue-loll thrust penetration &
complication described on page 192 of that book
you're reading, in lieu of the possibility of all
of which I will dally in words. It's a fiiiine
afternoon-morning, sister. Care for a quart
from the Superette? Naw, she won't, she wouldn't—
drink beer in broad daylight under a green tree
in front of the possibly baleful closed eye of
Mr. limp body slowly slidin down off the bench here?
Naw, no way—no fun for Mrs. white nose & skinny lips,
my only favorite caucasian fantasy lady of the
morning. Maybe I should prove to her *I* can read too:

> NO ALCOHOLIC BEVERAGES
> PERMITTED IN THIS PARK

                                        Hear that?

> DONNA'S PUSSY GOES STRAIGHT

                                What idiot thought of that?

The wind cools becomes a prickly sensation sweetness.
I'll betcha her right nipple just puckered closed in
& up against that cool little breeze, it surprised
her, ping! She looks at me as if she knows I know—
oh fuck she's staring at that this huge leaf just
blew in my face. She smiled at me. She's pretty
like a wan but yet all together & brown-haired &
small-breast thing. & that's as far as we get to
get, right? Right. So bye. *Bye.*

*

I America & the time eternal
being sound of mind
& of heart being in mild heat
but not quite become plainting Wyatt
no sighes no terys am just a girl in
a soft swoony semi-miasma cars
& shops go by & men who're like
gentle wildernesses & great poppies
& immense freighters & horizons
& swamps & tempers & brandies &
I get pleasurably weaker they
go by in the solids of their shirts
& have columnar necks &
intense looks capacity to melt
& faces that ripple with pleasure
at changes of flavor in flirtatious talk
from formal to risqué to mock-icy
to complimentary to tender to risqué to formal
so I'd become wild birds in search of
amusement but am too soft & lazy
& thick & go back & sit & think of
shirts & noses & hair & lovelily
delineated upper lips & hasn't
shaved today faces & affection-
imbued courtesies & possible
legs & backs especially backs &
warm seas & implications & atmospheres
how they enmesh & mutual sorcery
& old friendships & new fugues as my
poore true hart is
comforted much by the restorative fantasy
of sensuall love which
begetteth song & poem friendship & society

& sympathy & light & airy sleepers &
lovely ornaments & care in costume
all dissolving back into friendship &
acquaintanceship & fellowship &
all those ships as one changes from
this auncient lover to the idiom that
is oneself—what a muggy
September day! what a dream!
what a blanket!

*

—Drawn land day & tragedy of the jacket.

—I am a girl scow fumbling in the rain.

—Well I hate being a pill nigger.

—My pills are on ration. I could give you one but
  one never gets *you* anywhere.

—Agh. I can't stand it.

—How about some spaghetti & canned kidney beans?

—Nah, I have to go home & read this book. It's
  about a major-league first baseman who also solves
  a murder.

—Hmmm. I was wondering. Do you think you're a poly-
  theist by nature or what? Or do I mean a pantheist?
  Do you say excuse me when you bump into chairs?

—I stopped saying excuse me a long time ago when I
   started bumping into everything.

—(Yawning) It's about time for me to go get a Pap smear.

—I'll do it for you.

—Predictable. Why don't men have to have Pap smears?

—Predictable. I'll say yes to the spaghetti if you give
   me a pill.

—I'll not give you a pill if you do the dishes after
   I eat the spaghetti. You can still eat some.

—No, I have to go home & be a shambles so you can
   be a compulsive young-old horror & nervous wreck
   in peace.

—Ain't it so love? See you later.

—Bye bye, meanie. God will punish you.

—God is a chair I always say excuse me to.

—I'll put on a brown wig & saw a leg off the chair
   & then he'll punish you.

—Do you think a brown wig is enough?

—I'll cut a tangerine in half & stick them under
   my shirt.

—Well while you're doing that I think I'll get a
   teensy bit high & read some Dante.

—That does it! Good bye! See you tomorrow.

                              *

So sir you'll disguise me as a boy, so I can freely
move until I find out what I am must be, as my only
love my fellow-child brother now dead to me, who
else be but he, for he was we were certainly me, so
I'll go to the park in my jeans & T as he. I trust
your character with its sky of blue & clouds &
leaves to find me the man I will sing me to. For
I want to be found out as she, how funny that is!
want everyone to find out my nipples through the
white cheap cotton shirt. So sir, your light will
make my breasts not show then show as you will as
you know I need, sir.

So I meet an older guy like fall in with him, he's
got a house an extra mattress sometimes & a few
drug habits & drugs & in his house is where they
hang out, would-be's & already's in the constellation
of Arts. He sits in his chair see, & when he thinks
of it remembers he's in love with a lady painter,
an extraordinary & new & well, feminist type & proud
talented in hanging together gluing laying on summer
colors, disguised jewels of madonnas of love's colors.
I mean often he remembers her when not talking reading
listen to records write a poem he whom my secret soul
must now love, sir. He has insisted of me that I

attend her parties—she sworn to see & love only
women, till she ceases to mourn her first 30 years of
mother & father & men & understands who she is. So
I'm to attend her, it's good for me he says, she's
so queen talented I'm a kid would-be painter, I'm a
contact with her he's incidentally passionately in
love with. I'm his go-between assessor of situation:
why does she mourn with her women so long—but why
not to discover her heart?

But then I attend her parties, & right now she fancies
women, & I'm become this boyish-woman boy-woman little
girl butch oh it's me she fancies, how funny. I'm
inclined he might discover he loves me at some point
when I have enough presence assurance & true stature
as self to take off my T shirt—but then aside from what
I have to do about myself, shit! do I have to find
someone to occupy her? For she'd hate me for spurning
her whom I do admire, & more, he'd hate me too for
being loved by her. I need my boy lookalike the myself
I can't really be but that she really loves, that
stubborn she who refuses to cease to mourn her lost self—
and *he*, he has got to get addicted to me who am his
own counsel & friend & page-girl companion & sing
songs to him when he's sad—I'm his daily girl voice
though he thinks I'm kind of neuter though almost
sexy.

So what is it essentially I have to do? find my dead
brother self, sir, yes, when I find a real boy me I
can give him to her & then I'll have my chosen love to
myself, & also we'll all be friends together. Will
it really be what *I* do that makes everything fall

into rightful place? Is that how I'll know that I've
become myself? When I give my boy to her & my chosen he's
accepted my girl? For she's mourned so long & come
so far that any sweet soul of a boy will do—that
resembles me—why me? easy to find one, a dime a dozen
physically, but why me? That in court to her I'm
so nobly nice? being *his* emissary—but she won't see
him he's a man, so I've created the physical type for
her man. I'll find the guy for her tonight, scout
apartments bars clubs & bring him tomorrow as my friend
to her party, & somehow I know she'll know it's him
she wants. Then my love take what's been nicely at
hand & ever will be—me. Then I will proceed to paint,
which is the real business at hand. But now, sir, you
have to help me bury this intricate machinating I
must forget it so it will only be what happens, a comp-
licated chapter in the lives of some normal complicated
people. So sir, I'm off, lightly, to houses clubs
streets parties galleries & all of life. I know I'm
part him & part her & am me too & I'm doing this for
all of us, presumably they are too, sir, but I'm for-
getting everything in order just to walk, which is
what they prouder & older cannot. Walk about, a girl
half-disguised as a boy lightly happily through the
city, become free as a boy become free as my brother
would be, living & doing & walking under your sky.

*

They're always consolidating into artists
            and bragging. They
I won a spelling bee in Texas when I was

15. It was
thrilling. I say to her, I wonder
                    where I'll be
this time next year? She says right
                    in that chair—as
if it might be true. I only ask because
                    I'm an old woman
& am supposed to; if I didn't ask,
                    I'd be a saint, and
I'm a good Bible-belt Protestant, I'll
                    plaint & tyrannize til I die
if weakness of body, & near sightless & deaf be
                    tyranny, & in 3 more
years I'll be as old as he was when
                    he died. I don't
want to be older—I want to make it
                    all equal. Like
catch up to him, though maybe he never
                    caught up to me.
He didn't win a spelling bee, nor
                    marry a drunkard
nor, a woman, divorce a mate at the turn
                    of the century. His
wives died in childbirth each, & then he just
                    took another! I
gambled at 15 on a terrific drunkard, lost,
                    & then gambled on him. He
was good. If I die at an earlier
                    age than he, I figure
I used to know when I was younger what
                    he knew when he
was older, so it equalizes & we'll
                    meet in heaven

as peers & lovers & no ones—for I'm surely
                bodily, now, tiny as a no one.
No we won't know ourselves in heaven
                but since I barely
know myself now I don't mind
                if thinking of him
gets me up to mop the floor & eat my
                hamburger, why
the floor gets mopped the—things get
                done who else can
do them? I don't trust the others too
                much & I got to leave the
floors to them when I die? In heaven
                the floors'll be always
clean, & men fed, & thus no need for
                the sexes—they'll
ask me for my story & an angel tell it
                so I won't even have to
remember it, & he & I have no story, happily
                being no one together.

                    *

Do you think we men want only to be babies & women want
to be perfect old men? I'd be the baby of bliss &
she'd be the wrinkled canny old one. Because she thinks
I'm canny & I think she's golden, & she knows she's really
canny & I know I'm really golden. Because those are what
we can't say or appear to be. She doesn't believe in the
blue welkin, I do, but it's she who sees it & says it
since she wants it to be real, I don't see it I believe
in it, belief?—shit, there it is. So why say it? They'd

never let me be a baby, nor her the canny ancient. So
here we are. But we'll be them, the one same thing those
two are. She thinks I'm not thinking about it. She's
changing blouses for the third time before the dinner
party. Because all the blouses are beautiful, & there's
too much time left before we leave. I always answer
her truthfully which blouse looks best. She could do
with a new pair of jeans—could do to change her whole
style—skirts?—but then, jesus one set of specifics
is bad enough to live in—new mate new clothes new
details? Jesus Christ, what an awful idea! what an effort.
She's so pretty when she's reading & sleeping & laughing
at something delightfully stupid—she's pretty all the
time, but anyone's pretty. She's anyone. She even knows
it! that's why she tries on all the blouses. Fine
gradations of this anyone fascinate her. Which inch
of anyoneness be tonight? Which that no one notices but
she'll experience a slight change of color of the
spectrum. of anyone. Every morning after she's the
same old anyone. She has a hard time with party witticisms
except in her private mind, so if she gets one out
maybe she's more than anyone! but she secretly knows
each is so nothing. Each dinner party is a wrinkle
in the face of her canny old man & each thousand meaningless
witty things I say blend into the goldenness motes of
my baby. Every one I say is a wrinkle I cast off, &
every one she manages is a wrinkle as if in order to be
recognizable. It's so hard for her to say & then know
it's really nothing & I say so much nothing & get rid
of the hardness or evade it—because men must say
nothings importantly & well & everyone listen. We
both know everything, but I'm always saying it & she's
always surprised by people thinking it must be

said so she says a one & it's just a one thing said,
a nothing in nothing, a wrinkle in skin. She was born
an omniscient baby & I was born male thus an old man,
& we're always moving towards each other's origins,
where the circle connects. Now I think this whole
meditation I'll re-think it later, yes, with her to
become the baby, & me to become the wrinkled canny
old man. Hey, she's chosen her blouse! it's blue &
nearly transparent.

*

—It's me again, you'll remember. I keep wanting to
    address you in sweeter more graced words, but
    I'm other than that.

—(offstage) Nothing the engine, girl in a death.

—Who's that?

—A possibility. Or lots of men & women are bits of
    coals. Or I'm the blue sea my room.

—What is the source of light? Which things are
    razors?

—You are the source of light & the razor.

—Oh I am only a very old dowry of people's. Or that is
    a wordless thought in the day addressed as always
    to Sir Lady, Doctor Nobody.

—Which of us is he & she?

—(Reproachfully) You didn't mean to voice it.

—It's so beautiful in this room, white with the sky
   seeping in, blue or grey. Bricks lean in & say
   Hello, why don't you make tea?

—One time I dreamed that I was up here with someone
   It was just like it is.

—It's hard to keep saying the right thing in a perfect
   situation.

—Numbers & colors sing to the ear. I made that up
   myself. Maybe we should talk to each other in
   arithmetic. I say one plus one, you say why that
   equals two, then I say That's nice.

—Did you hear that girl & the Duke are officially
   cohabiting?

—I saw a photograph of a Greek statue yesterday . . .
   Oh yeah, I saw them buying a used rug & some wine
   glasses.

—I wonder what an interesting mind is.

—Probably a bother.

—Do you think women & men have kids in order to become
   immortal?

—I think they just sort of conduct an experiment. No
   I believe in the debt to nature, sex children death.

—This room is beautiful because of nature don't you
   think? It's just a tenement room but all charged
   with nature. Nature makes the walls airy white &
   you look so nice.

—That seems obvious.

—I made no claim to the interesting mind. Do you
   like morning glories?

—I guess I like leaves. But to get back to Nature,
   those bricks & this cup of tea, gee . . . I think we're
   now in another room. It's like a whole house on
   the fire escape in summer. Or a musical intersection.

—A what?

—Not with cars but with worlds.

—I thought you meant where the tubas stopped for the
   flutes to walk across the street. You mean the
   music intersects with your knowing, so you don't
   have to know it, what you know, I mean.

—Shut up.

—Okay. I think I'll watch you do that for awhile.
   It looks like it takes a long time.

—It's sweet hard work. Could you hand me that?

—Which?

—No the long one. Now where are those? oh there.

—I thought your store ran out of them forever.

—I found another store.

—What's that for?

—I have to repair them a little.

—And then you'll be all set to begin?

—Yeah. Except it's always all going on.

[1978]

A TRUE ACCOUNT OF TALKING TO
JUDY HOLIDAY, OCTOBER 13

Remember something you never saw
a real edelweiss, or Anne-Marie's lily
a throat-hollowsized shadow
lonesome for its cameo, golden
cobwebs hair, Judy Holiday
playing a sexy serene spook
in the haunted house we sit a spell
chatting & thimblefuls of giggle

there's a chest of antique thimbles
in the attic where

Judy's donned that Laurette Taylor dress
now but now I never saw the play
Bert Lahr played Lear in the same
production and
really Judy's playing Ms. Nobody
comprised entirely of outer nuances it
lets her be them for you as if
you're the casual voyeur in the corner store
that you are, "I am life a
thousands a walking millions nuances walking as
one, every wrinkle on Auden's face
on me as a crook of finger corner of
mouth up, cross my legs make a tiny light—
& the spook attic's the place where
we dispel the spooks by being them
of course, we put on a spook dress
& gossip. Laurette's dress" said Judy
"Well Laurette said quote
It's interesting to wear anything
& in which you remember who,
love, you never were & oh, love,
how well you do do remember! so
rapturously, Judy! Now you, Judy, put on this blue
ruffles fade number & let your
wrinkles you don't have show—it's so
sad & lovely to be lightly a hollow
encased by attic dust blue!
That's just what Laurette said" Judy said
"Do
I myself have to?" I myself then said, "Oh
a moment just," Judy sighed then giggled,

"Oh try it now!"
    Laurette's blue dress so light dust yes
    but I never saw the play, you'll remember
    I can't remember it, so what is remembered?
    Waves for ruffles & stars for dust
    on them, & I told Judy she said That's
    what we remembered too. That's
    what sad is, & everything else is.
    And that's what all of our dresses are.
    Goodbye Alice don't worry about whether
    you've just played me or I've just played you.
    And the least of your worries is who
    you are or what's your dress, every dress
    is lonely & expansive & — it's how best
    give your deep & light worries to your on-screen face
    that you be beautiful — beautifully present that is —
    and all human too. Oh just try to remember.
    I'll try to I'll try to remember I said.
    Then we vanished & I alone resumed,
    playing me for you.

                    [1978]

            POEM

        You hear that heroic big land music?
        Land a one could call one.
        He starred, had lives, looks down:
        windmill still now they buy only

snow cows. Part of a dream, she
had a long waist he once but yet
never encircled, and now I'm
in charge of this, this donkey with
a charmed voice. Elly, I'm
being sad thinking of Daddy.
He marshalled his private lady,
did she wear a hat or the
other side? Get off my own land? We
were all born on it to die on
with no writin' on it. But who are
you to look back, well he's
humming "From this valley," who's gone.
Support and preserve me, father. Oh
Daddy, who can stand it?

[1979]

THE PROPHET

They say there is a dying star which is traveling in two directions.
Don't brood over how you may have behaved last night. If you
Can't remember that much about it, don't ask anyone else about it
Except a little, in case you were wonderful in your abandon.
Don't gloat if you were wonderful, for you have a hangover, ass,
Soon you will be old and you will still be this childish.
It is precisely a tremulous April new day. Things that
Might be found in a pill bottle include a tiny photograph.

A sponge besides being an animal that looks & grows like a plant
Is a thing in your kitchen sink that comes to smell peculiar
& gets neglected to be replaced. Many things, like yourself,
Are often misleading, transformed, or elsewhere. In the morning
When you awaken, your body is already here for you.

Some things have been made easy for you, and some are easier
                    than they seem.
If you cannot open a door and it consists of two doors, don't
                    surmise that you are locked in,
You can sometimes open such doors by opening both doors at once
                    with long & widespread arms.
Many major things are not interesting. Things perhaps not interesting
                    include the drugs that we take, the decade
That we live in, & current political crises—they are X the Boring,
                    to deal with
Them constantly mentally is to dry-fuck or is it dry-hump?
                    not that
They have to do with sex. Everyone knows a recipe for something,
                    for example,
A peanut butter sandwich. A recipe may produce breakfast, but
                    I am not nourished by
Your recipe for my world—its cruelty is repugnant or its
                    benignity is like
Benignity rather than thoughtless invisible goodness. Shut your
                    brain up,
So I can wash my hair. Dignify the world by being beautiful or
                    seriously ugly.
There is sometimes a miniscule playing card on the floor, it is
                    facedown & blue with stars
And you will never turn it over. To complain of money will ruin
                    your conversation; if you do not
Complain of money there is probably something wrong with your life.

Perhaps you should
Call money "green zinnias." "For a few hundred more green zinnias
            I can fly to Rome at
The end of June." "Any spare petals?" "I owe the government thousands
            of green zinnias in back
Taxes; as you know they're not easy to grow in New York City."
            If you open
Your eyes & see double, you may choose to keep on doing so
            or maybe to wear
Glasses. If you discover one morning you are a drug addict
            or an alcoholic,
You are words. When you go outside it's different. No one
            is smarter
About another person than that person. Imperial Painting in India
            Between 1600 & 1660
Is at Asia House in 73 paintings through April 19.

To prosper step softly on new blades of grass.
Mind the corner where life's road turn. You have remarkable power
Which you not using like sonofabitch. For example, one way to
            get your name in
The papers is unknowingly to sit down on a toilet seat which has
            just been painted
With toilet seat surface. You will then be stuck to the toilet
            seat until the rescue squad
& the reporters come, and you will have plenty of time to
            flush the toilet.
To desire to get your name in the papers is ignoble
Unless you are a beautiful movie actress with such sublimity in your
            beauty that it soothes the world.
Your current crop of movie actresses, these guys are all effort
            no lift-off though that one she
Sometimes seems an exception. If you are sublimely beautiful, I for

one would appreciate

Your becoming a movie star. One is of two minds about the money part
of movies & stardom; try

To be of two minds as comfortably as possible this condition must last
A lifetime. Perhaps only Paul Blackburn has written naturally
& gracefully,

In his poems, of defecation. If you're certain you cannot be a great
movie star, perhaps

You might attempt to write well of bathroom things, at least for
as long as

You are stuck to the toilet seat. People from certain regions of
the United States,

Such as the Southwest, tend to have a sense of humor which is
preoccupied with

Toilets, defecation, etc. And everywhere men often tell spun-out
jokes about pussy, women sometimes say gossip

As if it were jokes, in short sentences. E.g. "He thinks women
with high cheekbones

Give better blow-jobs because they already look like they're
doing it."

Is it interesting to think about what two sexes means. Sigh.

Today, on a TV quiz show, a lady who's won nothing says to the host,
"It's all right. I just wanted to meet you. I've been waiting
4½ years." Is that disgusting or love, you

May ask. Is he as worthy of love as a medieval sex object,
who knows.

If the weather is rainy & muggy, but the man at the Chinese
Tiny grocery store says hello to you & your child, you might stop in
Tonight at his store for a Tsingtao beer fortune cookie & lightbulb.
Your fortune's pale yellow tonight & says "A woman's curiosity
Is as great as a man's." If the novel you're reading is depressing you
because the events in it are

Heavy & extreme and it feels like you sometimes feel yet do you
    can you believe it,
You might reflect detachedly on the curious relationship between a
    novel & reality.
Curios are found in Arizona. "It's just a novel" doesn't ring quite
    as true as "It's just a movie."
Does it. Two people are friends for life I know them. Do
    you take it
Do you take it friendship with you when you die. Which were
    the things that
Made his terribly tired face light up tonight? Why must your
Husband occasionally seem to think other women are more wonderful
    than you?
Why must your wife worry about someone else's terribly tired face?
A wife & husband are often two people who love & can't do without
    each other,
They have no idea why, they are fatalistic. It is possible that
    people who
Die young have a vocation for doing just that. Are there
    ideal forms in heaven for
Can't live without each other, dying young, susceptibility to
    hysteria,
Strange androgyne, disco, atrocious housekeeper, etc. Did a
Fucking mouse just chew through your superb job of sealing up
    his hole?
If you have two children you may have two sons, two daughters, or
    a son & a daughter,
If you are Leda and the swan apparently the possibilities
    are the same and you
Do not have a chance of having one human one swan, two swans, or
    two humans, or do you.
He wasn't a swan really, idiot, he was a story. Not half-breed
    swans but half-breed gods,

I seem to mean stories. Half-story half-true, like everything that's
                    some knowing.
You're yourself you're a story. You refuse to be a story. Your clothes
                    belie your lack of story.
Occasionally you must expect a case of the shakes. If you have
The shakes you'll probably stop soon but it's hard to
Remember that. When you have the shakes you're not the story of
Person with shakes. You're not your history of you with shakes
Until you stop shaking. The shakes are useful for sense of
                    timelessness but
Otherwise a pain in the ass. Does a hippopotamus get
                    the shakes? Is
Your life a continuous attempt to burst out of and yet construct
                    your story?

It's not a good idea to be a taxi driver if you don't drive
                    at all well. However
You can probably manage to do so for some months, before you
                    finally quit,
Without killing yourself or anyone else. It is not remarkable
                    that you are
Still alive since so far you have always been still alive.
                    It is not
Psychologically significant that you nearly perished, & scared your
                    customers shitless, dozens of times
While driving cab. You were not self-destructive, you were sane
                    & dumb.
You were perhaps being a burgeoning poet. Four months driving
                    cab is part of your
Story, whenever you remember it, whenever you seem to need a story,
And not just be in the explosive impressive present. It is always
                    time to
Defrost the refrigerator. Or wash the dishes, if you so choose.
Purchase a copy of *The Sophist*. Collect some Gracie Allen jokes.

If your child says, "When Mom dies we'll see her come back here
           & be a ghost,"
Don't indulge in being spooked. Be amused. If you're reading
           Plato, the part
Where he seems to say women are a lesser order of beings than
           men, don't
Stop reading. A character is speaking. If you've yet another
           downstairs neighbor who hates every
Step you take on your floor his ceiling, ignore him to the
           extent that you
Must breathe & walk about & have lots of fun. Send three dollars
           for our informative full-color
Showing of India carpets & exciting decorative ideas. If poor,
           cut out
Tiny photos of our carpets & then paste them on your floors.
           Choose from
A range of color ways: many carpets come in two, three, or four
Gorgeous color combinations to fit your decorating scheme. Don't
Let cosmology make you queasy. If reading about an open universe
           vs. a closed one suddenly
Makes you perspire & feel urgently pressured by the fact that
           you exist,
Make a cup of tea, drink it, & sweep under & behind the couch. Save
Cosmology for later, perhaps for your dreams, when you may
           be given
A guided tour of the exact center of the universe. In one
           person's dream,
It was said to be 20 miles long & yet thousands of years long
           to pass through.
The center of the universe was pleasant, even the corridor
           within it in which
One would cease to exist. The dream's color combination was blue
           & white &
Dark, with a touch of black. The goal of awakening is black coffee.

Why did the truck cross the truck? to get to the truck. If you
Have been riding on a bus in your dreams for at least two nights,
                    perhaps
You should not go to sleep tonight. If two pigeon feathers fall
                    from heaven
To your feet, in the springtime park, & your friend says "They
                    were fucking, up there,"
Don't believe him. I don't know why. The feathers fell perfectly
                    lightly yet parallel
To each other. If you are riding the bus tonight in your dream,
Get off & get on an airplane. Small sons awaken with bright
                    bird noises,
But oneself awakens differently. The goal of awakening is black
                    coffee. It
Would be nice to be perfectly slightly off-key. On the bus you
                    keep stopping at
Small towns in Arizona, you're with your mother, it's the other end
                    of the universe. There are
Tacos & colored vodka, the vodka you mistake for wine. When you
                    do the mistaking,
The taco-&-vodka man laughs wickedly. Never hesitate to go back to
                    the beginning.

At one beginning, when you are a baby you are or there are two, but
                    your mother
Is so hard for you to see, that she is simply the other in airy
                    heaven. If
Your mother is now say an auto-parts salesman who eats tacos with
                    you in dreams. If
She finds you a bit of a wastrel. It's important—well you
                    are each
Flawed, specific, & idiosyncratic in the eyes of the other,
                    yet you once

Shared a heavenly space, when you were the newborn, she the mother
And neither had characteristics to the other except for
                    love & there & ever.
There is another beginning without her where there is no you.
                    And where
Is the father in all this? the innocent pained beloved guy.
He's given you his face. When the dykey block lush
Is hinting for lush money give it if you have it but remember you've
Dinner & your own beer-maintenance to provide for on borrowed
                    money. Borrowed
Money is only money, but need for beer is need for beer buy her
                    a beer.
It is important to read *The Thorn Birds* as rapidly & feeling
                    as flushed
As if you were fifteen. When you lose your train of thought
                    because you go to the
Bathroom & come out, perhaps you're not such a great writer, perhaps
                    you are. If your husband
Says that the woman in the portrait of you looks like a
                    murderess so what.
If you see a lady have vertigo in the Guggenheim instead of you,
                    it's almost okay
To congratulate yourself. She didn't want to see the pictures as
                    much as you did, though
You'd be perfectly willing to have vertigo at the top of a
                    boring building
With telescopes to look at roofs & streets & buildings through,
                    that's what they do up there.
There is no place in America for heterosexual poets with children
Unless they practice another full-time profession, except for
                    in your house.
I mean that's where there's room. You've lost your fortune
                    you've found it behind

A Prussian-y blue cup it says "Never change when love has found
                its home."
It don't make no sense. Or do it. Some good advice is Take five.
                Not yet.

When you die there are two that merge. When you're dead you'll
Probably never have another attack of wit. Possibly some
                dead people are witty
By being dead. No examples come to mind. Maybe when
Someone wants to kill you & you're already dead. When you're
Peeling potatoes with a peeler not a knife the wispy peels may fall
                on your bare feet & between your toes.
"Linda Ronstadt sat on an orange crate eating a taco & sighing
                to herself,"
Is an example of a sentence containing a singer's name a color
                & a piece of furniture.
Yet the color is contained in the name for the piece of furniture,
                two simultaneous
Is nice. Barbara Bach is the new Charlie's Angel, she's announced
                she's not interested
In stardom only in being a working actress. See the outsides of
Her breasts in that dress over her breasts she holds a gun. She's
A girl from Queens. It is impossible to understand how
G.I.s keep their fatigue pants zipped yours automatically unzip
Whenever you sit down. Don't ask your husband how to keep them
                zipped he'll either
Make an obscene remark or tell you about basic training. Do ask
If you want to flirt or hear army stories. Remember not to
                discuss P. G. Wodehouse,
C. P. Snow, or W. H. Auden with English people. Don't tell your wife
More old-girlfriend stories especially the one about breaking
                the bed with
The woman who's now her dear friend. It's important to stay

Amused. If you should take up stamp collecting, what? You
                    musn't lick a lot of stamps
Before oral sex. You'd better get serious, kid, is some
                    good advice. Seriously
Almost everyone is luminous. Exceptions look as if made out of
                    negative stone.
In your story, the story of you, it's important that you be
                    luminous that's all that
There is to the story of a person. You must often luminously tell
The grossest joke you know to all those stiffs in the other room.
You may have to put pussy, blow-jobs, & turds in it too, in order to
                    be a good person.
A lot of people have ugly feet. Everyone sings songs sometimes.
Science has almost made it that you yourself hardly ever perceive
                    anything. Yes. You are drunk.
Perceive anything directly of, or just, the physical world (what
                    a funny phrase).
It is sometimes possible to put the fallen petal back
On the flower. You can make something be all right again, though
Men, realists, & pessimists may deny this, experience affirms it. He
                    smiled again you too.
You must not believe anything Science or It's A Fact or Documented,
                    unless, perhaps,
Wonderfully written or said. You should not drink too much except
                    when you should.
It is okay to be moralistic at 2 AM. You do not look like you do,
                    as you well know.
Some good advice, my dear, is to go to bed. Not yet.

You do not have to do awake what you do in your dreams. You are not
A latent anything, because everything's already happening etc.
                    You've forgotten
Everything, you remember everything that ever happened to anyone,

Vaguely. People disagree about what colors things are, & they're
Different colors at night, etc. Molly's busy be patient. Don't
        two-time anyone.
Everything's funny-looking. You're presumed to be aging. A
        lot of love
Is there when you relax. When you die there are two that merge.
Don't be afraid of your own mind, there's an ocean there you know
        how to swim in.
Don't flirt cheaply. I don't know what you mean. It's great to
        walk with
Shod feet through the streams in the street when they open the
        fire hydrants, the
First hot day in May. Do something about this poem. Or it's
        nice to be
An unreconstructed something or other. If you're shaking a little
        again it's the kind
Of shaking that keeps you steady. You can't cook an egg on a diamond,
        that's what the man
On TV says while the egg yolk drips from the woman's hand. You should
Settle for the diamond being a diamond, not want to cook on
        it too. People tend to
Want everything to be good for at least two things, not everything is.
Spurs slip past Bullets: p. 77. UCLA Still Chasing Green.
Besides a diamond is too small to cook an egg on, but again
        you could cut out
A tiny cooked egg from a photograph & paste it on your diamond
        if you insist on
Seeing a cooked egg on it. A little art can solve a lot of problems,
Especially ones that have to do with strange desires. It is only
When dreams lose their importance that the dirty business of
        evil begins.
There's little to do this lifetime but fiddle around the sweet shape
Of the heart. Moonlight seems to go away fast. The bionic man is not

Stronger than the bionic woman. All of us know each other. Please
Take it easy & take care of yourself. Do not die in a
                    monument, like
Cleopatra, unless like for Cleopatra it's the only place left to
                    go. Be a
Noble girl, whether or not you die in a monument, whatever your
                    sex. Do not generally
Go about giving advice. That which is everybody's business
                    is nobody's
Business. Let thyself become undeceived through the
                    beauty & strangeness of
The physical world. It is almost possible to believe that if you
                    look at it really see it be it for yourself
You will be free. They say it will be cloudy tomorrow but they
Are often wrong. There's a lot to say about two & one. Your life
Is not small or mean, it is beautiful & big, full of
                    planets clouds skies and
Also your tiniest things of you. One is you & all this & two & yet.
                    You must never
Stop making jokes. You are not great you are life.

[1979]

DESERT FOR ALL OF MUSIC TO TAKE PLACE

Only time in Catholic church, empty in afternoon
There was red-rhinestone light
Well that was once.

Often are shacks with silver windmill & salty trees
Or the one inhabitant of Arrowhead Junction
Renowned for his filth of person
& of establishment where brown boards fall down.
When I grow up to be him
I'll feel a little funny.

Trucks & trains go east in 4 AM sounds & river air
Also therein cars of wildness go apart from me
He has green eyes
The movies give full love
Comparable to nothing else ever to be
And I know that

Flies wings airy hands
Does somebody grow up did a man child die live
He will inhabit America & his body forever
His eyes are blue
He's the guy who calls up every day just to
Tell you it's raining.

He's disinterested in music and's
The only one who knows how to whistle
Gas station attendants stay up all glamorous night

Red horses dawning air
Mountains shrink closer up you get
Monuments & landmarks being large deformed rocks
He wants to speak educated as a matter of courtesy & in
Assertion of superior breeding of sons of poor widow-women
I could become awhile too stupid to love a person for that
He has brown eyes with light coming through, his sorrow center
Seems above them mid-forehead
Am I just an occupant?
I dwell in air, I take up air, I hold possession of my air
Am an accuracy but whose, or rather what's?

Everyone drives off.
The library's upstairs from
The jail guys flirt through the bars of
With a fat dusty girl.
I consider flirting with them too they
Seem to have vast appreciative powers
There being nothing else at the moment for them to have,
But I go on upstairs. Strangely,
Gas station attendants stay up all night.

Boys gas station guys
Unrequited loves objects undead
I'll always still wish they would love me
Yellow mesquite flowers thy praises appear, or
I love the landscape because I love these guys

& also the movies. This big
Desert landscape flowering guys movies feeling
Is love, every one & kind at once.

Here's a dark in bed song:

Tarantulas & black widows & all kinds of spiders
They bite & crawl around your room
They're very poisonous
You'll get it when you know you get it right now
I think I'll sing the whole song
Love is all you need when you're getting in love when
It's time to
So when you get around love it gives you a hand
For time's running out
You'll get what you trout
Time & love in space is the end of this song.

They say my cousin Mike has a tender heart.

· · ·

How come Mohave men & women
Are used to each other getting fat?
It's part of how they are
It's part of how they're big

Big faces & features hair where each hair is a feature
Their feelings would be shapes big solid shapes things
That might be held up in two hands
The "white" Indian woman's blue tatoos about her mouth
They have a Cry House that burned down & all the dogs.
An other-world Navajo couple pass through town
All in conchos & velvets & hairdos
Maybe they're going to go into,
Where so many mysteries go on,
That green-painted-glass front walls place
Named so funnily, in red letters, SNOOKER BILLIARDS.

I'm accurate diamond white hollowness
An aching for something to be true that won't quite come through
To being an ultimate holding or knowing
Of a mountain or a gas station or a love moment
Through that hollow of one's does blow the best blue wind
Underivative, unworshipable.

Or am I an impostor?

The important erotic events of my time transpire tonight
At green-black watered-moon river's side
Whether inside or outside of cars.

Desert verbena momentarily purples dust,
Yucca blossoms a second's cream in the year car goes past.
Herman, the official town crazy man:
Somebody goes to his funeral.
I guess I've been in hopeless love with every man in town
Since I was 4.
His mistress ties her hair back with a purple ribbon
But his dead wife had a pince-nez & a pilot's license
Rivers mountains sky
Endless cross-ties & poles & stars
If you peel off another layer of air & another
Your eyes still can't possess these things
Yet they're so clear, but in so much space, which is air
I say "I can see air!" She says No you can't
I tell her it's all these little dots, dots of air.
Air has to be seeable I'm sure it is
& how can the surface of silence, the sky, be a color—blue?
& how can all the secrets be in something that's a color?

I'm not one of the 15 towheaded Walters kids meant
For their kind of trouble, nor
One of the 2 Wheeler kids meant for their
Kind of trouble, nor a Mejia, nor one of the several Garcias
Whose lot is a little more tragic, for everyone to marvel at
At dramatic Mexican funerals—
I'm one of the several Notley kids destined for their kind of.

There's one I never tell anyone hardly even myself that
I have a crush on,
Because he's the creature most like myself, thus
No consummation imaginable
I just love him for years every day.

But I know I'll always be this me now,
& it's almost only air,
& other me's horizontal layers of air
On that one flat detail of the original, almost only air me.
No, no that's not it. They'll tell me about it in time.
Hah, they will?
Hah.
        I'm a wide dust earth &
Mountains & river & a sky of blue that gives back nothing.
To me that's not to be strong, but to be just that.
Is anyone else in America that?
Is everyone?
Fill it with loves & movies & take it by car,
But only at night in playing-at-romantic river time.
The daytime blue sky gives back nothing.
I reflect the nothing time,
& love the romantic time too
At which I'm not just peeking
At which I'm singing love with you.
The lovers in cars aren't movie stars, and
They're so tacky. Or maybe,
They're not love, & there's no love, except
There's a big, big shape like a feeling

You can hold it up in your two hands, practically
And present it to the sky.

.   .   .

Marilee Downer brown gleam eyes
Flinging up her skirt
To prove to everyone saying she didn't
That she did wear underpants. Pink.

In the car at night they see a meteor vision something
"Light up the whole sky" a few moments
But I'm lying down in the back seat.
Alone I see a sidewinder on the sidewalk,'
No one ever believes me.
No one ever finds a peacock feather near the
Date-palm & peacock farm.
Inside me a person is playing the piano perfectly
While I play notes.
I can hear inside me it being how it's supposed to be,
Or else I'm mostly pretending that my music makes you love me.
An opening 3 notes of a piece are almost enough
Play them over & over, for all of music to take place.

[1979]

Clouds, big ones oh it's
blowing up wild outside.
Be something for me
this time. Change me,
wind. Change me, rain.

[1979]

FLOWERS OF THE FOOTHILLS
& MOUNTAIN VALLEYS

Compassion is pungent
& sharply aromatic. Small
yellow heads in late summer.
Love & hatred are
delicate & fragrant.
Around a yellow disc.
Glory is found along the shores
intoning "I change but in death."
Sincerity has delicate &
feathery leaves. Dignity is
fragrant & looks like a little
brown nail. The leaves
of hidden worth are deeply cut;
a 19th century American
artist & inventor. Sir
Thomas Campion blooms in July
pinkly with notched petals. The

clearest of gins taste of
bluish protection, lovely
Mary & little Jesus found
refuge, in Egypt, in gin.
Hid from sight in
the bark of the cinnamon tree
a light flashes on & off,
dazzles, whistles. Remembrance
is the most fragrant, love is
the most dark pink, courage
is grey-green growing wild.

[1980]

WORLD'S BLISS

The men & women sang & played
they sleep by singing, what
shall I say of the most
poignant on earth the most glamorous
loneliest sought after people
those poets wholly beautiful
desolate aureate, death is a
powerful instinctive emotion—
but who would be released from
a silver skeleton? gems
& drinking cups—This
skull is Helen—who would not

be released from the
Book of Knowledge? Why
should a maiden lie on a moor
for seven nights & a day? And
he is a maiden, he is & she
on the grass the flower the spray
where they lie eating primroses
grown crazy with sorrow & all
the beauties of old—oh each poet's a
beautiful human girl who must die.

[1980]

WALTZING MATILDA

For Jennifer Dunbar

12/2/80

I am an exhausted not-that-chrysanthemum Oh brother
Nothing's funny nothing's pretty, all the jokes
& gems collided at Gut Corner & then they did that
you know rolled over & over down the hill to the bottom of the
            tin-can gully,
And then there's me you know I that am like a stomach sick of.
I miss Barbara Nichols & the death of Apollinaire.
And can't live up to the presence of a flower or of
Anything else. Her dress. It was stunning. Very

Low-cut around the tits & black velvet she was
The cut flower for sure. He said her tongue felt like
A live animal. A lot of up to her panties & then I
Put that magazine down & take your temperature. 101.
Get under the covers honey. Okay? 'kay.
Real-life juxtapositions are the most tasteless. 'Cuz
Pretty soon I'm gonna take your temperature again & then
Back at the text she was naked. She was naked & in her hair,
Positioned enticingly on the table amongst his pile of
Law reports. I'm sick of this, this dum-dum logistics of it
all. Mom I don't think I'll throw up a, if I make a
peanut-butter-&-jelly sandwich I won't throw it up
this time. I guess it's really raining. Didn't you
Hear the thunder before? it was thunder in the kitchen.
How do you free? Why didn't they have a democracy
On Prospero's island? Something smells funny it may be
My socks or a fragrant flower. It's my socks they smell like
A rained-on tree that smells like feet. I don't re-
member what it's like to be a tree, but there's some people seem to.
She was naked but she got up off of the law reports
she said she was absolutely ripped on an old-fashioned
hallucinogen, she said all that paper recalled to her
her tree self but that was either after or before her feat of
radiant concentration which changed all the law-report words to their tree-
language equivalents so when he looked at the pages
he saw in brownish yellowish reddish green such verses as

> Bark must not
> do potato, tomato
>
> A leaf is local
> only when falling.

"What? like a gavotte?"
        the common evergreen rustle:
        hours & regulations & so on . . .

But what about my throbbing member? he said & began to
chase her round the table & when he almost caught her by the
                before he even
felt it her pubic hair was become soft moss on bark. Mom
                why don't
people read in the dark? They can't see the words in the
dark. I can. Please go to sleep now. Please, honey.

~

12/3

Next day sunlight smashing into the pine boughs & orange peels. December sun
blinding white cup of water germ. Temp. 103 degrees. Face of white mum also
turned intelligently towards TV. Somebody's dog & some elves are in prison. Contin-
ues. This kind pine has clusters of needles at end of smaller branches of branch, like
glossy little whisk brooms. Sun moves, I'm not so dazzled now. "He was one of those
guys not Little John—the pie or something"—"The friar?" "Yeah. I saw that with Eli-
nor with Bloody Pie or something"—"Captain Blood?" "Yeah."—"The Greeks' great-
est heroes & stuff. Like that. I liked the whole thing. Somebody like Jason came by,
& he knew this trick—the thin guy kicked you over the cliff when you washed his
feet—& I think the thin guy got kicked over." "Ow, ow. Ow, ow." "Why was Edmund
saying Ow?" "'Cuz he was copying the thing of what Tom said." "How'd he lose his
momma?" "His momma went out & Tom stole the egg." The sun moves too fast, I'm
cold, there's my panties on the floor as usual, as usual my most colorless pair, "Ma,
hand me my water." "Here." I'm not coming through. And I know it's right next to
me. If I say I'm two pine boughs that's cheap, that's cheap continuity, "With a guy
named Hans & that lady's being attacked by a dimetradon, & he throws a hook in the
dimetradon's throat. And Alex gets thrown into a tree." "And gets naked." "Oooh he's
smelling garbage." The green needles now have a grey gloss to them, their shadows

streak the white of the cup, the orange peels will never be rearranged, I'm not quite losing it, I wonder who this is all for, I picture a shadow sort of courteous man bending over my shoulder & saying quietly, "Don't forget the seed & that it was really a tangelo, not an orange, would you like me to rub your neck a little? You're guilty as hell but you're only a thin wafer of light my dear I know that's not or is scientifically correct note your cloud sample skeleton and all that remains, the bright smile, the sample babble, a marble bubble. It's getting sombre in here it's time to cook supper, goodbye my dear, (I cook too, I'm making eggs orientale in G minor with real midnight truffles & chicken soup.)" His wing. One wing. "You kids want jello & chicken noodle soup again tonight?" "Yeah, I'll have some." "Hope I can eat it & not have to throw up."

~

12/4

I remember so much that I generally don't ever
want to talk about it But first will you answer if I
ask, I said something like, he was as good as the
best, And she looked at me between loyalty & me
All right you dumb broad ex cathedra infallible bull-
shit in ex domine & the rest of it forget it, 100 degrees and
Yes she admitted, he's a real one, he's as great as I'm glaring at you
& this jackass was already falling on the floor talking about
parataxis & parthenogenesis, he lost his hardon for the
scene &
            be generous, It's all
yours. We're still all sick but there's his shut-eyed
theory of the great crocodile of the or whenever in
this too cold life fork it over anyway it's all fun
& tired & sad, how to live, read the mail, & that
that looks like it's got things called leaves but didn't
even say so itself, I'll see you then oh my, til Sun
boy oh boy, Alice hey can I have one of copies?

Sure I gave to life all that I had it's cold like
'cuz even if you look you must miss it, that makes
me think I did something of our own before the next
fucker whirlwind & meanwhile if your name is
Nell & you sign the note Nellie the world
is improved a whole lot at least mine is
& put stamps on with masks on them from Tlingit & Bella Bella

Did I give him enough aspirins? 101 degrees?
Well night the last hmmm He started the boiler-making at 5:30
I'd like to take this opportunity to say
I drank too much but couldn't vomit at 3 AM when
he flung handfuls of white crosses at us & so I
woke high as a kite at dawn & everything was as
fuzzy-looking as usual for a myopic person in bed but
behind my eyelids it was something else the
clearest-cut of mind-boggling fleeting pictures
½ spring ½ shrimp salad sandwich ½ terror excursion
so I went back to sleep & got up today
& still lived in the same house etc. what an
amazing fucking life you see I recently had this
dream that these various Chinas were on the march & in
the great primeval World War after I got tortured by
the bad Chinese when they tied me up in sort of fine
barbed wire well after that & when the vast good
Chinese horde had won & I'd found that my torture was a
dream you see it was also still my information
so I still had to tell it to Arab Chinese leader lady in black
& when I told it indignant & righteous & this is the point
of my speech now, when I told it to her righteous I felt I
was being more righteous than it had hurt really
though I felt I was telling in tone & way appropriate to
human being, so, so, I mean how much does

it hurt, it hurts, but it hurts me sorts itself out from
so much that you must be & then you have to learn
to be indignant or you won't ever tell her about it
the world has sorted itself out in the oddest way
You see? The lady was kind & offered food
to be eaten with the hands in a
room like a cave all torchlit full of musicians
dancers & populace all brown all of them all over

~

DEC. 5, 1980

Dear Adviser,

This is my problem I think. My husband is mad at me & the heat's off it's about twenty-five degrees outside. I plugged in the space heater & blew a fuse but I fixed that I'm so handy. I am having troubles with my writing because the words aren't jostling each other glitteringly in a certain way & they all have referents I think if that is a trouble. Now when my husband left the husband I mean house this morning shouting at me due to provocation on my part via tone of voice & inability to say the right nouns that would wake him up so he could fulfill a professional engagement involving a friend of ours, this gets tricky here, when he left shouting at me he shouted words to the effect that he was beginning to realize he should start batting me on the head more often when he felt like it that was all there was to it. Adviser I am of many minds to bat on about this. I feel like getting a provocative tone of voice again or being very grave & saying he's gone too far in speaking of batting me on the head or forgetting about it simply & lazily but should I let talk of batting me on the head simply pass by is it wise to forget it but it is certainly the easiest thing to do & it is so cold. Meanwhile I would like to point out that my husband has never batted me on the head or come remotely close to doing so & I would like to point out that his sentence to me, "I should start batting you on the head more often . . ." seemed to imply that he had. Do you suppose my husband woke up thinking he & I were two other people I mean not ourselves but say Reginald & Felicia or any two other names, or do you suppose he was momentarily gaga as I believe they say in England and imagined he had once or twice batted me on the head? Or do you suppose by "more often" he meant that after ten years it was probably about time he started, I am disturbed about all this you see because my husband, you see it's all about usage of words & to say what you intend to & he has always in the past been excessively careful with words, we both read L=A=N=G=U=A=G=E magazine. Do you think he has another wife or woman somewhere in the city that he bats on the head or do you think he has one of those peculiar "lexias" one reads about here & there but a speaking not reading kind & would that make it a "lalia"? Or do you think he simply got mad & spewed out some words any words Dear Adviser? It's getting colder in here so I must end this letter & do something to get my circulation going as they say perhaps walk downstairs & see if Poor Old Crazy Diane as my friend Molly calls her is arranging the garbage cans neatly & in straight lines even though it's cold out. Do you think my husband wants to bat me on the head because I indulge in such frivolous pastimes as Poor-Old-Crazy-Diane-watching while he is out teaching & fulfilling professional engagements & making the money that doesn't go far? Could you answer me preferably before five o'clock today?

Yours,

Anonymous

P.S. Or do you think by "bat on the head" he meant something loosely metaphorical? Then again.

P.P.S. Poor Old Crazy Diane wasn't out so I came back upstairs & swept the floor & chatted with my sick son whose temperature is a little over 97 degrees now. I took my own for kicks & it was exactly the same as his—it's cold, man.

~

Dear Anonymous,

Glad you met me at the old saloon
It's that your husband just was shone on by the gypsy moon
I give the same advice to everyone for everything
But it always sounds as different as, that every time you sing
A song you sing a different song because you're tone-deaf
At least I am. When the gypsy moon shines then there's this sheaf
Of people that each become a fallen-apart sheaf, even
If it's morning, the gypsy moon can shine, even if it's heaven
In the corner of the room in your brain where you read
The book of Crystal or Murky while you walk about & lead
Your life & lead it to the bathroom & the coffee & stuff.
"He likes Jim Carroll's songs" oh that was advice for someone
           else some rough-
Spoken creature whose husband threatened her with a carrot
In an orifice or up it because she hated it while he worked at
The realization of his favorite artifice a song that would combine
The virtues of the shoe & the pillow, King Kong & the helicopter,
           the pine
& the leather orchid: a song to be called "Language on Vacation: Haiti"
Well even I your Adviser a most distracted individual see that
           obviously that's another story.
"Why didn't she give me phone numbers for all those millionaires?"
I'm distracted again, forgive me, I liked your poem "Western Wind"
           & all those airs
Of yours that others sometimes call "immense horseshit, goddammit"
(I can't even tell if I'm getting anything done oh shit.)
As for the gypsy moon, it has no definition or explanation
It's a useful phrase for when there's free-floating fuckup & the one
Thing was then that shouldn't have had to be—It's a concept

That saves shrink bills, makes love affairs still be affairs, you bet
Instead of just love, & promotes friendship & heals the sick
At heart & gives glory to those that ain't making it, thick
Mantles of moonbeam sunshine that people wear as they sigh
& say "Last night was my worst, I must reconcile myself, I
To being not only a half-assed minor painter but a half-assed minor
Practitioner of fellatio & a periodic psychopath or
Social seismograph like a person in the papers which
Do not a one of them believe in the phenomenon the comfort the magic
Of the gypsy moon that when it shines for you & no one knows why
Or why it shines also for some seemingly random others, I
When it is I, absolutely weird myself out Oh boy."
"Gypsy" because you've wandered off into the woods with the silver-
        ware or boy
Or girl baby person self of someone else or something like that;
& as for "moon" well you must know why, as for where it's at
This gypsy moon, it's up in the sky, but you only know it's yours
After you've done what you did. So if down on you & your husband
        it pours
The light that wreaks temporary change the kind that distresses
Remember it's not psychology sociology numerology history or you, it's
        the gypsy moon's shivery long dark white tresses.

Best wishes,

Your Adviser

P.S. My own temperature is a perpetual 101 degrees.

*

Probably that's the only beauty you can have anyway. The kids got better yep. Generally you like to believe that people behave in other ways on such occasions. During the readings man it was so super. So I mean you know. I don't know where they came up with the figure. I do have it but putting it right next to my bed here. Right. That's the stuff that sticks into you. I fought for the South in that one. I'll forward a few to you you ought to enjoy them. No man he had this money thing on his mind—Jesus that's funny that's okay it was that night otherwise he'll have another one tomorrow. That was a little magic incident too. She even enjoyed puking, ha ha you guys are horrible. It was great. They went the next night too, I mean it's different here now. Past histories etc, but when you do it's you you're not *for* anything or against anything, I was really happy about it, & she told me she was really pleased, & the beam of attention from you made a world. You look & you listen. You gave an honest day's work for an honest dollar. & the other so for the sake of saying that. I had some opinions too given I was in X situation also I did know you wouldn't be in a snowbank dead. Man we'll do this again & we'll do it somewhere else again too. This was one of them I thought. You showed up at the right place instead before everybody else. Because I asked you. Right. Holy shit. Right. What's happening Baby? Were you sober by then? Thank god for that, if you've got some piece of identification that shows you're something. And the times the cops handcuffed you & threw you in the car. All you did was take a turn too wide or too narrow. And hit a tree & fucked up your life for nine years. Hey wait a minute I presume you might find twenty-five dollars, oh great. No it's not no it's great, I read a little piece it said this guy should be hung. Yeah well that was part 2 you know in New Hampshire snowed-in anything. And after that you were a little hard to find. Who's being asked, who's giving, who's not? I'm just doing the calling & asking. But the personal voice thing is better but I'll talk to you soon I gotta fall apart you know. See you.

~

12/9

All I can say it's too pretty damned
bad. Bless Ringo's heart he just got
on an airplane & came there.

Gee whiz it's all fucking heart-
breaking,
                    What did Judy say?
She said, Shit.
                    It's grey what
can you say? Everyone in New
York's staring at the newsstands
thinking what you were think-
ing & thinking that every
person on the street's thinking
the same thing,
                    They're very good
at choosing who to shoot,
they're very good at choosing the
one whose death makes you
feel most killed—or most
culpable—
& the Mayor & the President-Elect
have to make idiot speeches about
gun legislation—because a reporter
asks them—either for or against,
& state their "position," when what
they both want to say is If I
had a gun in my hand right
now I'd shoot that sonofabitch dead—

what's the noise?
                    that's a kid—
it's all so commonplace, it's all so
like us
                    Daddy you said he had a
good life,

                    Why should a guy with
            a five-year-old son have to get that?
            Ringo looked like my uncles at
            my father's wake—& my mother
            could hold herself together, but
            every once in a while one of
            my uncles would come out on
            the porch & push his hair
            back from his face—all
            the men in my family do that
            when they're worried or hurting—

            That guy was in our life.

                              *

It can be later the same evening not the way I had it to begin with. One of them was
& to no purpose. I can't I can't lose it quite simply, this minute this quite simply this,
even though I can't quite I almost finished this quite cheap way of getting it which
is answering some other person's that or philosophy. And then pay some more, let's
go find him in Maggie's whorehouse & take the bottle away. Your play, quite simply
your Fate says, I don't know what that means. The handout child long ago Beauty's
Other, I don't know what that means. Fuck 'em. Look just give me about five thou-
sand. Then we guarantee the beauty be taken care of, I just realized I don't know any
rich people. Man just give me the fuckin' rent money, it's for someone more beauti-
ful than me, the other me, the need glee depressions feeling, the beautiful homosex-
ual I used to be. It's much too late for me to be up worrying about this, children get
up soon, my panties all unwashed, I something something my tits & said no green-
grey clarity all day dammit poseless in a turquoise nightgown inside from a silky rain.
There's no one more beautiful than me though, no. Jesus this poor girl, she really
fucked old Shep, she got the inner ear scene for which there is no cure & I don't
know whether to give her a B or a C. Fuck her inner ear. I give her C.

                              ~

DEC. 11, 1980

Dear Adviser,

I'd like to ask you about yesterday
where should I start? I had a blister
in my eye, that's what it looked like & my
husband got a check in the mail so it
occurred to me, after three days of staring
at this blister, that I could actually
consult an eye doctor, my eye doctor.
The nurse said come at four but I went early
spent 20 minutes in Bloomingdale's
staring at Chinoiserie & jewelry
people were complaining about how long
it took to get waited on, a man said
"I want to buy a single gold bracelet."
I coveted some amethysts & left.
The doctor said I had a virus in
my old eye-operation place & shouldn't
wear my left contact lens for about a week.
So Dear Adviser I'm now lopsided.
Meanwhile my husband & I went to Hoboken
last night where he read his poems in a
restaurant place & I got drunk on wine
& Peggy's damnable bottle (Peggy's
my friend). We came home whence I took up
residence on the bathroom floor
I sat & laid there & groped for the toilet
tried unsuccessfully to vomit
I was very sarcastic to my husband
"Can I help you?" he said "Oh *sure*" I said
"Wouldn't you like to come to bed now?" "Oh
sure," I said, "just like *you* did the other

morning." He said I said that enigmatic
sentence, he said I said sarcastic things
to Steve, our babysitter, about Steve's
ex-wives. He said I said I'd written a
voodoo poem, set in New Orleans or
somewhere, for which I'd surely be
assassinated just like John Lennon.
Now, Dear Adviser, things get tricky—he was
having fantasias & nods, due to fatigue & drugs,
when he told me about how I'd acted last night,
early this morning. I am *not* working
on a voodoo poem, set in New Orleans,
though who knows what I said? and he retold
the evening from Dreamland, & room upon room
of other worlds of things that hadn't exactly
happened—these rooms we did walk through Dear Adviser—
as he told of the three famous poets we
met on the streetcorner, & Rosella in the hotel
this Rosella said something & there was a
car ride to another city & every five
minutes he'd say—Peggy having shown us
her first two real poems—"& Peggy's two poems were
pretty damned good!" Well they were & I re-
member that, & whenever for five
minutes we were vaguely somewhere we weren't
or hadn't been he'd suddenly say "Peggy's two
poems were pretty damned good!"
About 9:15 this morning he e-
merged from that state of consciousness & said
that when you were in that state you noticed
that people hated you for it & that
you noticed that people's everyday con-
sciousness was characterized by how they
felt so righteous. Then he slept for two more hours

then went to work. I have felt hungover
& chagrined all day. Dear Adviser I'm
not sure what my question is except
I don't mind my having flailed around on
the bathroom floor, & having been mean &
sarcastic, & having accidentally
broken the alarm clock face's glass cover,
which Steve had to sweep up, & never
being able to vomit, & my dream
of Steve feeling me up briefly under
my gown & saying "I just like to keep
sure my friends are all right," after which we
each ordered a meal in the cafeteria,
I don't mind my husband's amiable cosmic rambles,
I don't even mind my hangover, but
I truly hate the thought I might have said
that stuff about the voodoo poem & how I'd
be assassinated & all. My question
is, Dear Adviser, fourfold: 1) do you
think I said it? 2) do you think
there's something odd about my priorities
& values? 3) do you think I'd have had
more fun if I'd been fucked up like my
husband was not like I was or do you
see little difference between us?
4) why do you think I mind I might have said it?

Yours,

Anonymous

P.S. Later. We made love a little while ago & my husband said it was better than both
Picasso *and* Judy Garland. But I guess that's just bragging not relevant.

~

Dear Anonymous,

To answer your questions in order. 1) Did you say it? Of course you said it, you either said it outright or said it in his imagination, but either way you were saying it. Do you think you own yourself? Ha. Ha. Which isn't to say you aren't free, but you never know where on earth or in heaven you're going to be being free. 2) Your priorities & values, something odd about. Actually I rather like them. Sarcasm & meanness & inability to vomit etc., they just occur, & the husband or the babysitter they can then go fuck a duck if they're perturbed. What's odd about your priorities & values is that you don't see that about voodoo in New Orleans, assassination, etc.— saying that just occurs too. What you seem to hate is whatever you don't remember. Oh let go let go, dear Anonymous! Just imagine what you're doing & saying in *my* amiable cosmic rambles right now! You just told a drunk panhandler on 3rd St. you had the best breasts in the neighborhood & so didn't & wouldn't ever owe talentless him a penny; you just told one of your sons that you love him so much that you were lost forever, lost forever, you repeated the phrase trying to find it out; you just told your husband that you were writing a voodoo poem set in New Orleans or somewhere, but you said that with the rain you occupied a white scared sidewalk there. 3) I see little difference between you & your husband—you're both big and awkward sentimental truthtelling fuckups though you each have a different cover story. Do not envy your husband the cosmos because you put in some time on the bathroom floor; the positions may interchange next time. 4) Why do you mind so much? Because you had to mind about something because you're alive & a string of words was the easiest thing to mind about, it was just an object. So what if you're obsessed? So what? The wind is beating at the windows & it's cold & trying to tell the truth is boring when there are only two possible truths to tell: A) that your life is subject to the manipulations of the rich & powerful & acquisitive & the interferences of the mannersless & suspicious & judgmental & desperate; B) that you are this minute catching yourself at aging, loving, baby-sitting, being vain, washing the dishes, being complex, etc. Now I suppose you're asking why B) is boring. It isn't

except when you can't tell it because there is too much of A) going on in your life.
So buy yourself a Fischer-Price Activity Center, some glue & scissors etc. & get on
with it all.

Sincerely,

Your Adviser

P.S. My wife says "better than Beethoven & Patti Smith in their garterbelts."

~

12/20

Here's another scenario: He says
What we don't need in America is peace & harmony
What we need is strife & revolution
But what he doesn't realize is you need whatever peace &
Harmony you can get because most of your life *is*
Strife & revolution. What if he did distort the facts a
Little he didn't distort them too much but he had a
90 thousand dollar house & that ended it with us
Right there. But *him*, when he's confused
He says I'm confused & asks the advice of
A penniless bum poet, a poet whose poems he doesn't
Really like, & whatever boy he's sleeping with. That's
Sense. Well we can settle down for at least a half hour now.
Are you in a position to sell ten? Go call Johnny.
I like society again, I think it's all like in Charles Dickens
I'd been thinking too long it was like a Christopher
Isherwood book. Now I know I don't have to save
The queers from the rich people just myself from the rich
                people. Poetry
Is totally bad for the brain. When I talk that way I can't

Stand myself. I have hysteria. What the hell's gonna

Happen tomorrow or any other day? I'm afraid I

Just blew my chances at the Nobel Prize. I won one

Of the prizes *I* give out. Do you think he

Still has fun? He has fun going for walks, say

On the way to the Ear Inn. He sees a girl's dress

Fall off her & a dog run away with it in his mouth. You know

The kind of thing he sees, then he has fun.

What

Did you say?

    I think most

Electrical appliances can be repaired via nipple,

Christmas tinsel & same old angel. You can't

Do yourself right by yourself. No white

Shall ever see the tears of a Menominee. It was a full

Moon at 5 PM & pendant in the sky which wasn't

Dark over the park, the same park where in

My dream of this morning the Martians landed.

A silver cylindrical aircraft that I knew was the

Martians because it could lower & raise itself

Absolutely vertically, so I ran into Marion who was rushing

Along looking happy Wait I said there's the Martians

& I ran over by the bandshell & grabbed the kids

But then the spaceship really landed the Martians

Landed. Then I woke up. It was a good dream

Because it was the next day. The Martians had landed. I

Got up & ate a bialy & made myself a pot of coffee.

~

12/21

So what if I'm no longer Valentine Venus? I want to address you somewhere beyond
whether or not you "buy it," I want to decline the magicianship in order for you to

be present, right here. The door opens the cat leaps to the floor, "Aaah, what happened? I just thought of something funny but it can't be it must be a coincidence, forget it. That guy doesn't understand that the world is all hooked together like whole series of clocks, he just ain't serious enough & that's what Kathy had against him too." If I had to choose between being reflective or showing you my garterbelt I'd rather show you my garterbelt if I had one. We can do anything we want we can fly by flapping our arms, Oh Dear, I want to address you without saying pompous things about garterbelts. So did you go to the bookstore? No it was closed. Hell, he seems to have very little beyond ambition & that's not enough, My god, me I just heard the word spatula & went waltzing Matilda. But everything's such chaos, she's trying to make our life more difficult. But it's still terrific of her to think of it. Matilda of the steamed clams, the stew, & her hali*but* with the *butt*er sauce, my darling who finally taught me you can't try to change without try & change world or rather be in it differently not in oneself differently so much well I'm too old to be publishing such kindergarten revelations but this one requires that and that I'm sorry your Matilda tape's broken & this song won't exactly replace that song but won't you go a-waltzing Matilda with me if I at least show you my garterbelt. Which one? That one, that's the one that's the manic Christmas lights flashing on & off. If we don't have to wait till after the showdown at the bank or what, you know where I meet with the priests of Mars, and how can I ever clean this up? Or should I mess & blur beyond all recognition until I become a magnificent suffix or something, Well then I made a Christmas Tree & sat down, no one's gonna believe my story except you & him it's just gonna be "my version" & for two months I'm gonna be the one who went on too long as if everyone already knew the limits of everything unmade & undone yet as if love & homage & process & time were doled out like short strings of spaghetti or doses of medicine to get you through having to take & be on the medicine, but I was laughing & the hillside was streaming with light & then the storm translated my mood into its own work & the oaks were palpitating with vitality & no one could seek repose at the expense of my heart because it's their heart their spirit their character, Matilda, whether they ever know it or not.

January 3, 1981

All my life,

since I was ten,

I've been waiting

to be in

this hell here

with you;

all I've ever

wanted, and

still do.

[1982]

POSTCARDS

Feb. 17

Dear Barney,
    The ashtray is full & the
natives are listless, but
there is a swell love hang-
ing out on the corner where
they sell souvenirs to the
grenadiers & girls from the

seaside. I have bought me
a pink culotte & a racy
sort of vest to wear with
those remarkable earrings
you gave me. How are
you & that boy who's a
man whom you did
that to on the day after
Valentine's Day? The
weather here is good for
taking the wrinkles out
of clothes (rainy)
                    Love,
                        May

                 *

                Feb. 18

Dear Reginald,
    I still love your body
most aberrantly being con-
sumed with hatred of your
loathesome soul which
refuses to lend me your
body for a single violet
evening of your stay at
our picturesque little
resort which is all that
we have here except for
too briefly you—I keep
your lost or castoff cig-

arette holder the ivory one
with me always but
you are mean, mean,
mean! Jesus & Buddha
are made nervous &
sad by your cruelty to
humanity, me—

                    Love,
                              Congetta

                    *

                    Feb. 19

Dear Fuckface,
        Everyone thinks you're
the Goddess of Compassion
but I know you also have
piles & a scarcely controlled
urge to sing for a living.
So much for you. Here
everything is stupid as I
have a dwindling flu
which necessitates my
finally paying attention to
my dwindling pocketbook.
How about some bucks,
Goddess Baby? any amount
above five I'd appreciate &
continue to light at your
altar the incense I steal
from the neo-Rocky Mountain

healthfood store. I
still like you either way,
            Love,
                  Bubbles

        *

        Feb. 25

Dear Nutso,
    Wal, it's pretty blank
around here. The cat
is hungry, & Hubby hasta
get up early (those two
paired are not a sig-
nificance for your cheap
little mindlessness to ponder).
How could I ever
miss you? everytime I
do I slap myself on my
cheek & read a chapter of
The New Hairdresser's Manual.
If you should
ever get normally sentient
enough to notice the
weather, you might drop
a line to your,
           XXX
              Margie

        *

March 6

Dear Francis,
    I miss you very much
although you are always
here too—there I go, in
trouble in a sentence, dis-
tracted by the weather, so
silky-aired like Hawaii,
which (weather) is reminding me
of you while I am being
distracted from you,
from writing to you. I
guess you *are* the weather
practically, & today I
like the weather so much;
& also I can be *in it*
without thinking, & on
rainy days blame you
for acting like I have to
grow up, like a hollyhock
or something, so I'm
going for a walk—
                    Alice

[1982]

WHITE EVENING PRIMROSE

To make a priceless
thing for anyone
that can't be stolen
     Who wants it?
I'm not good enough,
          am I?
               A pose for your eyes
               & I look dumpy—
                    Glad of it, glad
                              of it, too.

[1982]

MEMORIAL DAY

All the beloveds are
doormen forever
under the dry earth.
Light mountains hold
the largesse of these ones—
in their red suits
beneath olive trees, holding
open the crucial doors—
remembering you, you

rememberers:
those lovers of yours
now your doormen to forever.

[1982]

MARGARET AND DUSTY

Margaret wrote a letter
sealed it with her finger
put it in her pocket
for the Dusty Baker

Dusty was his bat
Dusty was his moustache
Dusty was Margaret's pocket
They both got all dusty

If I had a flower
If I had a trinket of gold
     & silver & lapis
If I had a medal & a trophy
     & a fullup sticker album
I'd rather be all dusty
Like those two friends of mine.

[1982]

LA MORT

The cuckoo can't sing
& tell us no lies

Can't wander as
I was wont where

so, where? And no Lombard
for me, anywhere

Except remains in my mother's
suitcase. She brings

us the tidings
& tells us no lies.

June, 1982

CONGRATULATING WEDGE

All things belie me, I think, but I
look at them though. Well boys, at
least you're not dead, right? What's
the date today? Until something. What?
Of the lady of the whitening blow.
I'm ashamed to keep on babbling

as if I've always been oneself,
diamond flow through. Humble
flannel skeleton. Grin, laugh unbecoming
Living at the bottom of the water may
have been obvious all the time. But
I forget. What's my plot? Hand
of a child, paw of an animal. Paint
it red & make a pawprint in the psalter.
Protect her & give her back her hat
Entangle her dreams in demotic and
Warm her feet; cheat the judge
& protect the tree from which he was carved.

*

And now that I've explained the situation
Jesus my frame hurts, you say.
Fucking pain. Hey come & empty my ashtray
once more & don't get so excited. A
gentle heart was broken. Whose? No one's
It's a figure like a frame among
medlars & briars. Hand me that piece of
that, just that, yeah. I don't mean it,
I've never meant anything because that's
not what I do, in the mountains I call home
How can I tell you of my wound? it's
round & silver & headstrong, it's
nothing more than temperament born
of a custom involving a circuitous journey
This is all wrong. It rains today, my
son's singing love songs of this
country, already being ten.

*

And if to withstand this nocturnal pollution of the tiny
wanton stars with bent hook clauses of misprision
I'm supposed to sing the melody of an unexpecting part . . .
Hey a pretty honey come a listen to me
while I evening, darling, your messages,
what would you think then? But I
wouldn't do that. Light surrounded oranges
towels clouds. You don't think you're my you.
Not here not you. You still think you're he. she.
Because I wouldn't "you" you, would I? I only
"you" some other he. she. I
who write poems. When she writes them,
it's different . . . A world of words, right?
It's only my version of *The Entertainer*
Nothing truly personal, I'm way above that.
I've learned about it for a lot of days. I've
been to see the doctor & you have to have shots
for it. 17 balls of yarn & a sewing machine.

*

No I wouldn't know why anyone would
want to write like that. I should never
have had to do it. We were used to this
other thing we always know like when we're
here. And you have this clear head & you're
seeing things & there they are. You don't
notice they're spelled. That's how you
know you're alive. I never saw you

looking like a dictionary definition & if I
did I wouldn't tell *nobody*. People
aren't like that. They say, Hey
asshole motherfucker turn that radio
off! *But the sun's playing on it!* But
it ain't real, you dumb package!
I recognize every package the way it
comes. Now I'm mixed up. But I
always wanted to be a package, person
thinks. Do they? Or, I gotta de-
fine this package, me. Or, God if only
I was a package but I'm not.

*

Walking backwards makes me cry, tiny
roses die. Oooh! I would like to prove
not only that do I? I do not, have a mind, but
I am vigorous. Instead you want some
instructions. Okay, and this is serious:
take good care of your skin. It's like
leather; wash it, oil it. Especially
watch your neck—even at your age,
in the city, your neck is dirty a lot. Taking
good care of your skin is like
sweeping the floor, no worse no
better. Some of these monks should learn it.
Not just vitamins & diet either. You have to
rub stuff on you all over yourself.
It's part of a philosophy I won't
go into yet, 'cause I gotta get
back to my other kind of talking or the

vessel will sink. I mean, you
gotta brush your hair, too
toss it & play with it too. Everything
must be cared for. The problem of
America is my body.

*

How can you love me & keep on singing?
You have to be saying something else, and
Hey light years don't (scratched) (torn)
        illeg.
windowbox.
            Not on a star loom so tired
territory braid's all frazzled, chairs among
the branches of my little fatigue trees
hold up violet amber crystal kids, mine
The only spinning vacancy is I, where I'm
going. The outright mystery of . . . I
forget. Here's a photo of the actual path
of least resistance. Sun shine on
broke mass. We will be intense tomorrow
when the omens are vivacious like . . . ?

*

Polemic divine. I was insensibly led into it
that room. Together, touch, at high speed
until the molesters were killed. Then we
were free ship, whistling & swimming and being
our own furnish a place to hide. Take on a

smoky look on rock wall or tie of spider silk
It's all a look? Which bright with orange
The first thirty pages are a little wet.
I'll never get in any human interest again
because I'm no longer a dolphin.
It's so lovely out I'm nostalgic for
Indiana & the Inn there. Some-
where in room where face-dancing I had to
say something stupid in order to live,
like . . . I can't think right now
of anything stupid to say.

*

She ceaselessly changes for thine such chains as these
name of your country & why you are in chains
the gift I have made for you, my love & praise or
          blame I must receive
playful waters into tawny feathers
love affair to light breeze —
the smallest constituents of matter are
tiny tiny snowflake affairs each different from
          every other
they're always changing, each, but why? for
          their own amusement . . .
Hey Daddy, after this should I put on some country?
grief, were musical from place to place
I found aspirin & change for Mommy. One
penny. When my senses were restored I
was all the lines to the song "Blue Skies"
& my older son was singing me incessantly
Even though I was a song I still washed

all his shirts & made his dinner
Later I was freed to become "Blue Eyes
       Crying in the Rain"
& Later was finally freed to become
The cat jumped up & grabbed my foot!

May–June 1983

THE TEN BEST ISSUES OF COMIC BOOKS

1. X-Men #141 & 142

2. Defenders #125

3. Phoenix: The Untold Story

4. What if . . . ? #31

5. New Mutants #1

6. New Mutants #2

7. Micronauts #58

8. Marvel Universe #5

9. New Mutants #14

10. Secret Wars #1

1/14/84

SO MUCH

so much
going on. A head next
to an herb pillow
its poems of styles
changes
that I will make
& the saga of the
dreams every night
as I shift utterly
journeying through
this year of a
death
in a city come harder
to love or maybe
only to
define—

so unspecific I'm—

Alice, whose husband
has died
is a poet, whose
heart may not
change, though she
must.

12/5/83

POEM

Why do I want to tell it
it was the afternoon of November
15th last fall and I was waiting
for it whatever it would be like

it was afternoon & raining but it
was late afternoon so dark outside my
apartment and I was special in that
I saw everything through a heightened

tear, things seemed dewy, shiny
and so I knew there was a cave
it was more or less nearby as in my
apartment it was blue inside it

dark blue like an azure twilight and the
gods lived in the cave they who
care for you take care of at death and
they had cared for Ted and were there for me
too and in life even now

4/5/84

LOVE,

I can't think of that
Let me help and one
Green is for always then
Let me lay my head upon
I will not fasten it
Will not hold you to me

You to it I'll be one
Will that be better then
That I may not think upon
Love is taken through it
One is a rose and me
A lover still loves for that

July 28, 1984

IT WOULD

it would be that
but only if I knew how
again
        Could something like
that get lost? no only
a little a little lost

but if only I remember
how I mean she or I
    oh a freight train goes by
& they always do & did
        do
            I mean a real one too
    that I'm not on & am it
        very seriously

    in this serious love world
    that one
    where something oddly music
        will pass through your
    night
            and it will be me
        sweet me

                            Aug. 3, 1984

WEEKEND WEATHER

Whether in the course of
and in my arms when that was
the childish happiness of
a mirror when that was
was that of course happiness but now

Or now when all is course
course of what we know now that

life the new stranger embraced
until dawn and familial and
the new mirror ages

Still I, I and know of
its veiled still I in the
course of you and that all
that courses through the
mirror that opens to song
as always as my love's cradled thought

Aug. 27, 1984

AT NIGHT THE STATES

At night the states
I forget them or I wish I was there
        in that one under the
Stars. It smells like June in this night
        so sweet like air.
I may have decided that the
        States are not that tired
Or I have thought so. I have
        thought that.

At night the states
And the world not that tired
        of everyone
Maybe. Honey, I think that to

say is in
light. Or whoever. We will
            never
replace you. We will never re-
            place You. But
in like a dream the floor is no
            longer discursive
To me it doesn't please me by
            being the vistas out my
window, do you know what
            Of course (not) I mean?
I have no dreams of wake-
            fulness. In
wakefulness. And so to begin.
            (my love.)

At night the states
talk. My initial continuing contra-
            diction
my love for you & that for me
deep down in the Purple Plant the oldest
            dust
of it is sweetest but sates no longer
            how I
would feel. Shirt
that shirt has been in your arms
            And I have
that shirt is how I feel

At night the states
will you continue in this as-
            sociation of
matters, my Dearest? down

the street from
where the public plaque reminds
that of private
loving the consequential chain
trail is
matters

At night the states
that it doesn't matter that I don't
say them, remember
them at the end of this claustro-
phobic the
dance, I wish I could see I wish
I could
dance her. At this night the states
say them
out there. That I am, am them
indefinitely so and
so wishful passive historic fated
and matter-
simple, matter-simple, an
eyeful. I wish
but I don't and little melody.
Sorry that these
little things don't happen any
more. The states
have drained their magicks
for I have not
seen them. Best not to tell. But
you
you would always remain, I
trust, as I will
always be alone.

At night the states
whistle. Anyone can live. I
        can. I am not doing any-
        thing doing this. I
discover I love as I figure. Wed-
        nesday
I wanted to say something in
        particular. I have been
where. I have seen it. The God
        can. The people
do some more.

At night the states
I let go of, have let, don't
        let
Some, and some, in Florida, doing.
        What takes you so
long? I am still with you in that
        part of the
park, and vice will continue, but
        I'll have
a cleaning Maine. Who loses
        these names
loses. I can't bring it up yet,
        keeping my
opinions to herself. Everybody in
        any room is a
smuggler. I walked fiery and
        talked in the
stars of the automatic weapons
        and partly for you
Which you. You know.

At night the states
have told it already. Have
        told it. I
know it. But more that they
        don't know, I
know it too.

At night the states
whom I do stand before in
        judgment, I
think that they will find
        me fair, not
that they care in fact nor do
        I, right now
though indeed I am they and
        we say
that not that I've
        erred nor
lost my way though perhaps
        they did (did
they) and now he is dead
        but you
you are not. Yet I am this
        one, lost
again? lost & found by one-
        self
Who are you to dare sing to me?

At night the states
accompany me while I sit here
        or drums
there are always drums what for
        so I

won't lose my way the name of
    a
personality, say, not California
    I am not
sad for you though I could be
    I remember
climbing up a hill under tall
    trees
getting home. I guess we
    got home. I was
going to say that the air was
    fair (I was
always saying something *like*
    that) but
that's not it now, and that
    that's not it
isn't it either

At night the states
dare sing to me they who seem
    tawdry
any more I've not thought I
    loved them, only
you it's you whom I love
the states are not good to me as
    I am to them
though perhaps I am not
when I think of your being
    so beautiful
but is that your beauty
    or could it be
theirs I'm having such a
    hard time remembering

any of their names
your being beautiful belongs
        to nothing
I don't believe they should
        praise you
but I seem to believe they
        should
somehow let you go

At night the states
and when you go down to
        Washington
witness how perfectly anything
        in particular
sheets of thoughts what a waste
        of sheets at
night. I remember something
        about an
up-to-date theory of time. I
        have my
own white rose for I have
        done
something well but I'm not
        clear
what it is. Weathered, perhaps
        but that's
never done. What's done is
        perfection.

At night the states
ride the train to Baltimore
we will try to acknowledge what was
but that's not the real mirror

                    is it? nor
is it empty, or only my eyes
                    are
Ride the car home from Washington
              no
they are not. Ride the subway
              home from
Pennsylvania Station. The states
              are blind eyes
stony smooth shut in moon-
              light. My
French is the shape of this
              book
that means I.

At night the states
the 14 pieces. I couldn't just
walk on by. Why
aren't they beautiful enough
in a way that does not
              beg to wring
something from a dry (wet)
              something
Call my name

At night the states
making life, not explaining anything
but all the popular songs say call
              my name
oh call my name, and if I call
              it out myself to
you, call mine out instead as our
              poets do

will you still walk on by? I
            have
loved you for so long. You
            died
and on the wind they sang
            your name to me
but you said nothing. Yet you
            said once before
and there it is, there, but it is
            so still.
Oh being alone I call out my
            name
and once you did and do still in
            a way
you do call out your name
to these states whose way is to walk
on by that's why I write too much

At night the states
whoever you love that's who you
            love
the difference between chaos and
            star I believe and
in that difference they believed
            in some
funny way but that wasn't
            what I
I believed that out of this
            fatigue would be
born a light, what is fatigue
there is a man whose face
            changes continually
but I will never, something

I will
never with regard to it or
        never regard
I will regard yours tomorrow
I will wear purple will I
and call my name

At night the states
you who are alive, you who are dead
when I love you alone all night and
        that is what I do
until I could never write from your
        being enough
I don't want that trick of making
        it be coaxed from
the words not tonight I want it
        coaxed from
myself but being not that. But I'd
        feel more
comfortable about it being words
        if it
were if that's what it were for these
        are the
States where what words are true
        are words
Not myself. Montana. Illinois.
        Escondido.

6/28/85

FROM **PARTS OF A WEDDING**

"CORPUS SAGRADA"

Out there they're whistling
they don't know what color my
blanket is of browns & blacks
but you who are utterly
elsewhere know that, not,
probably, thinking about it
unless daydreaming
of times, of ours

Under his feeling he loves me
Love isn't an emotion (what is?

     leaves brilliant in the Park
     a globe on which I
       stand called St. Mark's Place
     a photograph of an older
       city I look at constantly
Above it, most ancient of
faces—her mouth

it wouldn't be cool
(not) to put up with this girl
she built this amazing

where you've been

_____

she is sitting here be seated
the world is blue pink yellow black & white, green & red
and also gold, and also purple
seen from so high above it

Love is not an emotion it is
the basic that it conquers death
at the point of dying because it
goes out towards so strongly

that's not the why of
but was it first
                    it is
what there is

Anne, Charley's wife shouts as talks

I wish I didn't ever say Gently along dark lines

"IN THIS PARADISE"

in this Paradise

they know

what I'll say

girl in red

girl w/ down coat,

pink

last night we were

almost permitted

I am enlarging until

enlarging until

I can audience

myself

and the I can

vanish

Window C

in this waiting

room of tiles

dirty green, & brown

pillars

where everyone lives

let's see I had

these ideas

              ideas

I didn't find you

    for forever

& you weren't for

    someone else

each plastic chair

    was itself

telephone?   you wanna

    go make telephone

call?   no interest in

    angels

Because of one's own

Legs & light jeans

She has a

    medicaid card

Let's see, the Hopis

Or someone like that

In their ancient

    superior, or you

with your,   marriage

& your work

"my work"

The people dream in

    tandem in some

funny where I

    meant to say

funny way

& what they dream

    is this room

the Photo ID Food

    Stamp Room

you are denying

that you dream of

as you read this

But you have

    dreamed me

in all my

      exigencies & my

sacristy of

plying.   am not

dying   Much too

warm in this

    watch

in this watch I

am only inside

      not going

around I'm too

    smug

I'm too dumb

I'm crying. She's

wearing

petals, of silk on her

jacket

left my I because

I'm my

hand & eye

No one can get

a food stamp

unless you sign

the thing itself

Sally Ponson

Window B

Alfredo

Casanova Window D

Am I

missing you,

here,

though? No this

    funny view

no one will let us

everything wills us

All the windows

fly us in & out

    them

finding you every-

    where

as usual   But

Being not I not I

Being my name

    instead

I will now be

    my name

I THE PEOPLE

I the people
to the things that are were &
    come to be.
We were once what we know
    when we
make love   When we go away
    from each other because
we have been created
    at 10th & A, in winter &
of trees & of the history of houses
    we hope we are
notes of the musical scale of
    heaven—I the
people so repetitious, & my
    vision of
to hold the neighbors loose-
    ly here in
light of gel, my gel, my vision
    come out of
my eyes to hold you sur-
    round you in
gold & you don't know it
    ever. Everyone
we the people having our
    visions of
gold & silver & silken liquid
    light flowed
from our eyes & caressing
    all around all the
walls. I am a late Pre-
    in this dawn of

We the people
to the things that are & were
    & come to be
Once what we knew was only
    and numbers became
It is numbers & gold & at 10th
    & A you don't
have to know it ever. Opening
    words that show
Opening words that show that we
    were once
the first to recognize
    the immortality of numbered
bodies. And we are the masters
    of hearing & saying
at the double edge of body &
    breath
We the lovers & the eyes
All over, inside her
    when the wedding
is over, & the Park "lies cold &
    lifeless"
I the people, whatever is said
    by the first
one along, Angel-Agate. I wear
    your colors
I hear what we say & what
    we say . . . (and I
the people am still parted in
    two & would cry)

"IN THE DARK I"

"in the dark I

pretend that

I hold you.

This sort of obsession

is a political correction

to

for the

lover *will* find him, and

the people *are* you.

"MORE IMPORTANT THAN HAVING BEEN BORN IS YOUR CITY"

More important than having
been born is your city
the scale upon which your
heart when you die will
be weighed

[1986]

Beginning with a stain, as the Universe did perhaps
I need to tell you about for myself this stain
A stain of old blood on a bedspread (white)
—how can I set a pace?—I'm
afraid to speak, not of being indiscreet, but of
touching myself too near, too near to
my heart bed—the bedspread
was white & thin
I slept on her bed with my lover
and thus was never
sure whose stain hers or mine? And when I washed it, or
rather, he did, it remained. And then

And then she died unexpectedly, as they say
became away forever
except in the air, and somewhere near
my heart bed—But
the bedspread
became of her ashes a mingled part.
The stain, my stain, or hers, but mine
My love stain is part of her ashes, & I rejoice in that, whether
she & her lover, or I & my lover
were the ones who originally lay there, staining the bed
Our stain has gone with her, you see,
This is the stain that

invents the world, holds it together in color of
color of, color. Color of love.
This is the love they spend in order to be.

And she was quite young, & I am much older (her step-mother)
But our stain was the same one
There is no double. And she is endlessly
clear, & good. Surround my heart bed
with my others at night
speak with me of the stain, that is our love, that
invents the world, that is
our purest one. Help me to stain, I say, my words with all us

(I love you I know you are there)
the song of one breath.
Outside where cars & cycles
I'm not afraid to begin again, with & from you.

$\sim$

I will never not make a sound not have made a sound
I will ride this voice as I change, as always am
galley slaves of the slow black ship, are the one, you are the
      one
I have always dreamed of for example
(will never not make a sound, and as well you will never
      not have made a
sound, riding our voices as you change, to have longer arms for
      example
having longer longer arms and riding the slow black ship Greek
      ship, in
which we brought our selves to the mouth of a poet—don't—don't
      mention a . . .
I will never not ride this voice by way of
a way, by way of keeping going deaths, for example, more nouns & adjectives
(don't—don't mention a—) more vivification,

        hope, rhythm
mild sweet dooms & longer & longer arms & then slowly a black
        & then suddenly
black & having longer & longer arms, until their arms (the arms of
        the dead) reach round
I mean reach all around the globe (which I am as well that)
        this is
a rhapsody of the sound of any dear starting-point, dear
        starting-point that is
I, any I, who will never not make a sound and we have
        taken a ship
come to meet us in the calm, out of our dreams, a calling forth
        of commerce for
dear starting-points, dear stars from which issue bright stain dark
        stain & then suddenly
dead dear starting-points, hope, rhythm, mild sweet doomed globes
        the arms of the
other dead reach around, clear around them, hope rhythm, more who will
have longer & longer arms, You are the one I dreamed of if
        that dream
emitter of shafts of lives who love intelligence, reaching towards
each dear starting-point, each dear not there dear starting-point a
        second a death a
stain a shaft of effect,

                                ~

Some people refuse to remember, & I
never sure if what I remember is true (doesn't
matter), today I remember
a picture of a story. The Cheyenne
are traveling on foot & on horseback, in snow

It blows white, & shadow blue, they are darker, they
are dying. Others
are enmeshing that death into the
snow, air, wind, the very air
surround contains a death carelessly willed
by thought barely thought, or by no-thought, or fear or
Now if you say greed you must qualify, it is a
will or an animal or even a song, an air of
to have. To deny those other ones their own
to deny them a theirs, is not what is generally thought of or sung—
You might be doing this now—

Wanting to tell a story, this
the one that comes, keeps coming to
mind—
Some of them did go home; and there was
one romance; one friendship's death; something like a
loss of hope, but not of instinct to keep moving,
in a way true to the thousands-of-years-old self—this
with reference to the Cheyenne—you
may *not* identify with them, this time,
or you will not learn. Your thousands-of-years-old self
isn't recognizably in your possession; you
don't know who you are. This *is* the story, now—
city of October warmth, our
myth is that we don't have one—

I love the dead so much, talking to me
through my masks. Are the live really the
dead ones, in their, our desire
to be wheels, keyboards, screens?
I love the dead so much, but I only love
you. The red flower I always mention, the

tough-looking rose that, she said, looks like a
cabbage. 'I got six of them right now, that's where I
really stand.' I love the dead so much; and
October doesn't know who you are. (the part of
the mind that wears no mask; and *you*)

~

Against all agony a bunch of flowers in the chest
petals desert spines or small old seashells
no they are dead-white rose petals are blank white are
mind flame are continually
lit & belonging to all who are, ever were, belonging to an anyone
or what has the sleeping person, face fair in the good moonlight
Descent into bitter remnants of, confinement to, tortured memory
descent to the possibility
of more deaths perhaps an utter crippling by sorrow:
at the point of breaking, comes as a voice
belongs to no one, having no longing
assumes the continuance of its kind,
because born in beauty, & dark that bed, & all dread, & the loss of
          loved one
is not the light of that one; & much else is, & it is (but also the
          untender dark red chrysanthemums, the
curling wind, the black boots that walk you away

~

born in beauty born a loved one, before history
          born before your time
Anyone was born

before the beginning, before an era, or now
Loved by the sky, & loved by your name, the sky (all there is
       space for) drops
closer staining blue your bed—'I fall & reach the sky,
       humbly die'

born in beauty born a loved one
before history I was one
who loved you for your name
As your name was beginning to be your face, equal to
       herself
at the beginning, before history, when the sky was gold with its
heartfelt abiding, its need of you

in my dream you were a child
you woke up on a bed near a window
in my dream you were a man
whose body was no longer of any comfort
We kiss your name & take care of it
Born in beauty, before history, I am one who
       loves you

~

They say something ruinous & tragic happened soon after
or close to the earliest expanse of us, I mean that time that
stretches even backwards from the first time in it the "creation."
And I think there must have been these several stains, light,
       blood, & paint, the
initial one being the first stain of light against that lovely
underworld-colored midnight blue or black that night is
All creation is a staining, a change in purity

out of a consciousness that intends to make something slightly
different from what gets made, or unknown, cannot predict
        that cruder ... beauty
that orange stain apposite to that suddenly-created
        blue.

Where were the gods? perhaps they suddenly had faces
Visibility acquires a future & a past—This is how the gods
        became the first people, walking on
water that lightens to the color we think of heaven as, for
        heaven has always been here
& the afterlife is another material carefully watching our
        kissing & crying,
as we endlessly reinvent our own fragility, & deny our kin-
        ship to the gods:
But I will take all that sorrow, which did not really impoverish me
& make it an expression of warmth for you. I know the gods became
        human to be
seen & loved. But the first bloodstain wrenched the survivors
        away from heaven

in that that heart of loss was almost too broken to care about any
        heaven, heaven receded
not because it was offended, but because it was found ir-
        relevant, to that first
despair. Though heaven stretches backwards from your first time in it,
        & forwards from
your grief, & you *can* bring it back down by calling to it,
        for a time, & then, finally,
it was always already here. But that first loss,
        was like no other.

~

"Speaking firstly forever"
"speaking firstly forever, who might we be?"
"We are mattress," "nearly invisible membranous tissue"
"not any longer disordered" "wings" "what
   the first feeling was . . ." "we must will its movement" "Praise
   is for precision, nothing else, as in, 'the hero did precisely
   what she was supposed to.'" "These are the yellow lines characterized
   by having the honor to be uttered" "They are yellow but only a
   color" ("I love you") ("Shut up")

"Bridges" "bridges, again" "Looking down I saw many of them
   at night, many bridges, an intersection of them, black
   but lit with lights? or, no, but" "as if" "as if the
   first stuff, web of light of color, lifted up from the first water,
   fluids & nerves & arterials" "& it became bridges" "But
   in the dance before there were bridges," "there were the stars of a
   willingness, yellow, red, turquoise, and this, these geometric whorls,
   thumbprint, not firmament" "not yet quite straight lines & angles."

"Do you remember the" "oysters by water" "that was much later,
   and heather a cloud of, purple, dust-green" "in the
   beginning, before a verse" "shimmering web pre-teleo" "I'm
   saying this pre-apparatus, I'm" "saying I, though, I, as if"
   "before there were bones there were flashes of colored light;
   and in your bones that messenger lives, it is solo in any
   animal, any boneless flower" "darker than that
   we are back in."

"In that dark before a messenger was released" "&
   do we return there?" "in that dark" "but, and dreams" "I
   have never drea . . ." "in our dreams we catch up with the story, and
   the darkens-back-to-the-first dream, the fragrant" "it wasn't
   fragrant," "in this dream of the first dark, I" "it wasn't dark"

"dark as water silk dark quiet no-limbs dark, no-skin dark, it's
so dark, but, not foreboding or heavy" "it isn't
dark" "what is it?" "it's slightly lighter than dark"
"that's later, but first, first it's so dark, no eyes, but dreams, dreams"

"knowing that it was even that moment, center of a death-like word"
"in the tank of darkness, what was evident, an even older"
"universe had died and" "unpleasant grand sound (I'd listened)"
"unchartered life underwater, merge the old distinctions"
"side, the side of chaos for awhile" "is good" "good for the" "The
golden world to come" "The 'And Then,'" "And then"
"now absolutely cobwebs, & leaking grass, beneath, green as a" "baby,
baby of a hyacinth, dual-colored, in pinks" "the water
has gone, flown beyond into" "evaporated into thousands" "true
angels, the first insects, the first ghosts of old are breeze of
intoxicate, new intoxicate, I" "standing toward the center of the
earth," "no one, as usual" "purely form of a," "filled with"
("filled with")

"what was made, & is, what was broken, & is, and" "I am hungry."
"eddying tangled & densely the white & pink with yellow, with
palest blue & against the black, the" "they are also something like
bricks, bricks of winged" "winged windows" "human caves"
"caves are windows, windows are children" "over the
bitter depths of" "fish to be perfect still after many, & at
my feet the antique new river of so newly invisibled and the"
"dissolved in perfect voices, anemones, starving"
"light-filled starveling" "after the break of and" "for
when the light broke"

"messenger has crossed the bridge now" "precious flames" "flames"
"the bridges forged in her crossing"
"the messenger" "a hero?" "she" "all we became of eyes ears & mouth"

"to perceive & join in a gold-lit . . ." "the messenger of you that"
"stay on earth, wants to be, in the golden deeps of the bones the"
"listen, listen" "what precisely happened" "only the sun to the
   window" "the messenger opened curtain & lifted window"
"thin pink rustled ruffled garment-like" "green lace was"
"shaft of light pierced the glass & in its gold the millions
   the infinity of the angelic motes" "revealed to the eye (heart)"
"the structure of souls, of wild animals, of energies, of drumbeats, of
   embryos" "steps wind two not silent today"

"precious flames, lacrimations of joy, warmth on the tongue that which"
"the lightest of, the densest of" "antler,
   river, thought" "Thought is my dream of more world or my dream is
   my thought of it" "in the color blue I have found,
   & in the color red, awakedness, & the abstraction itself of a love"
"& in that turquoise, or in that lavender,"
"& we are phosphoric" "we are tunes" "snakes & bone statuettes,"
"we are now praise & precision"

FOR DOUG OLIVER & KATE BERRIGAN

[1987]

You haven't saved me any time, but
I want some. I want some more.
So put it somewhere, take it & put it
in my jeans pockets please.
He was going to put it in my purse.
The music spilled all over everything.
Time was hidden in the handmirror & the
whiteout, but somewhere, she knew,
inside of her head or in her fingertips.
Catch it please so I don't have to
use it all up working. Time was an
important exhibit, to very many
it *was* the museum. It *was*, almost,
the house. The scholar waited
till the poet was dead & then took all her
time & reused it. She even changed it.
The "work" stayed "timeless." I
went to a museum. Great. I'm
glad you're doing something valuable
with your time. She's so old she's
almost dead. What took so long? Where
are they all, those, you know, con-
figurations? All those women,
waiting for thousands of years, because they
couldn't vote & so on & so I
guess they didn't really live, all those
million unemancipated years of wasted
lives? Who, then, of them was ever happy?
those women those mothers
Someone obviously wasted all of history.

[1988]

What does she think? flowers of
privacy? green & yellow, don't try
Oh there is my medieval gown.
I think the stars go flat & then
deep if I blink my eyes & make my
brain go mentally clink. I think
some of my babies. And those which
didn't, didn't live, one of
those, I squeeze up, red furze,
purple gorse. Pretend something
faster. Close eyes & click. Bodiless
& being pre-body pre-sex where
it seems that everything is
black, at night when you don't have to
work, when you sleep & nothing
ever happened, when you dream &
no one ever died, no one was ever
hurt by you, never a fool & even
you don't die yourself because
everything is instantaneously
change, moment to moment of
you dream, you dream it, out of
your own deepest own—aren't there
sexes? will there be history?
There are many things the woman
has never 'cared about.' 'It
doesn't really make any difference.'
Can't remember some more, close
my eyes. She should leave him alone
for awhile, & take a little walk. He wants
to imprison matter, every single bit of

the world, in his understanding. She
on the other hand keeps it in
her eyeball. He gets the museum,
he deserves it. They're both so fucking tired.
Something about the pain of
numerous children, their going awry,
founding races, waging wars
The parents' loins very tiring
that the present world comes out of
He gets the fucking museum, he deserves it
Gets the Sistine Chapel too,
& fucking-ass Divine Comedy, & Iliad all
that stuff, all the leatherbounds with gilt on
etc etc. Shelf of all the containers,
there it all is the
cosmos, the dead men's cosmos imprisoned for-
ever for your very own pleasure, madam;
thank you, thanks so much. You were
geniuses. You were.
Let's have a *new* kind of baby.

[1988]

HOMER'S ART

Homer's *Art* is to tell a public story, in a measure that makes that possible—that the
story unfold with quickness, clarity, & also the pleasure bound up with the music
itself—a pleasure in the music as the truth of the telling, in its vigor & precision,

& in the fullness of its sounding. This is very hard to say. Or it's that, as the story is told in this measure it becomes really true—the measure draws from the poet depths of thought & feeling, as well as memory. This line, this dactylic hexameter of Greek, is simple & grand, and gets deeply into the system. The story is told by a teller not a book.

Both of Homer's public stories—as everybody knows—are generated by a war & are male-centered—stories for men about a male world. They are two of the oldest stories our culture has, & we are still reading them, telling them, using them, handing on Homer's world. The epic poem is taught in universities as the epitome of achievement in Western poetry—a large long story, full of "cultural materials," usually involving a war either centrally or peripherally, the grand events of men. Men who have written them since Homer have tended, or tried, to be near the center of the politics of their time, court or capitol. Thus, how could a woman write an epic? How could she now if she were to decide the times called for one?

Meanwhile we ourselves have experienced a rather strange faraway but shattering war. Say someone you know dies many years after the Vietnam War, as a consequence of it. To tell that story, which is both personal & very public, you might distance it from yourself, somehow, & find a sound for it—as the Greeks did—that makes your telling of it listenable to & true. One might invent devices, invent a line, make a consistent & appropriate sound for the story—anyone *might* be able to, any poet. But a woman who is affected by or even badly damaged by events in Vietnam will probably not know what it was like to be there, had no role in the shaping of policy with regard to that war or any war, has no real access to the story or even a story: what she experienced contained very few events. If she wants to write a poem about it, she is likely to write something lyrical (/elegiac) or polemical, rather than epic or near-epic (in these times, a man would be likely to make that choice as well).

One way for a woman poet to hook into the world (& thus the scale) of Homer has been for her to identify with one of his female characters & extrapolate. At this point, perhaps, it is tired for anyone to hook into Homer to write a poem; but for a woman it is an especially peculiar undertaking. But what if one were, say, trying to write a poem having to do with the Vietnam War, mightn't points of comparison between the two wars be of value? Might not Helen be an idea of something to fight for, something to bring back from a war? But Helen couldn't be a *person*, not a real person now, no. No woman is like Helen, no matter what the male poets say, or like Andromache (or Penelope). Only men are like them, in the sense that they invented them—they are pieces of male mind. Besides, those women & those men are all royalty & aristocrats—people who are sacrificing the countless unnamed, as well as themselves, to this stupidest of wars. The greatest point of comparison between the two wars, Trojan & Vietnam, lies in their stupidity—which is where tragedy begins & where a story must be told.

The pleasures of a poem engaged in telling a long story are considerable at this point in this century. The 20th century poet engages language, basically, uses language to generate more language. Poets variously suppose they are describing something or freeing language from something like description: both camps are simply playing around with words. The Homeric epic is a whole other kind of poetry, one in which language hurries to keep up. It is not language, it is a poem; though it is also something like a novel. What a service to poetry it might be to steal story away from the novel & give it back to rhythm & sound, give it back to the line. Another service would be to write a long poem, a story poem, with a female narrator/hero. Perhaps this time she wouldn't call herself something like Helen; perhaps instead there might be recovered some sense of what mind was like before Homer, before the world went haywire & women were denied participation in the design & making of it. Perhaps someone might discover that original mind inside herself now, in these times. Anyone might.

[1988]

MOTHER MASK

Mother Mask has twigs in her hair
she is all eye that sometimes closes shut
stars on her eyelids, open are oceans

open are history movies, closed are
blue skies, open are sorrow pain iris clarity events
I forget if closed & open make any difference
one or the other, one is the other, Mother
Mask has a woman's face, she always looks
in the mirror—she has brown blue eyes, & has
thin thick eyebrows, a straight round nose, it's a flat
pointy nose, & a red pink full-lipped
rosebud mouth straight crooked teeth
she has white black brown green skin
she has a wooden face painted by men
sunken eyes protruding mouth & raffia
hair red green white black & birds
birds all around her face & in her hair
& into her the wings & she flies the
whole mask flies away with the woman
Put on mother mask & fly right now
A man can fly in mother mask
so can I, Mother Mask
take me to here, beginning ending
Mother Mask seep into my self & meet my
self & both of you change the goddesshead godhead
Change the very self godhead which must be
the world, Mother Mask, you must
change us, by speaking our old new selves
Mother Mask open your set wooden mouth
Please open your carved wooden protruding
live dead mouth & let your green
bronze dark light skin shimmer with
life death, close open your eyes & close open
your mouth & be dumb speak to us
be still sing to us, tell us an old old new one
an old new story truth lie of our own life deaths

our peace wars, tell us our own old story we don't
know it any more, haven't had a
Mother, a Mask Mother, a wood real
mother for forever

[1988]

WHITE PHOSPHORUS

"Whose heart" "might be lost" "Whose mask is this?" "Who has a mask,
  & a heart?" "Has your money" "been published, been shown?" "Who can &
  can't breathe?" "Who went" "to Vietnam?" ("We know who died *there*")
"This was then" "Is now." "Whose heart?" "All our heart" "the national
  heart" "Whose mask?" "has its own heart?" "A mother's" "mask"
"Whose money" "do we mean?" "A woman's money" "Woman's money" "Who

  went" "to Vietnam" "& just died of it?" "A son" "Evolved"
"a man" "evolved" "a woman" "into America" "into the" "just before now"
"It was just before now . . ." "When men made the forms" "& women made the
  Air" ("& now no one does that, & who can breathe now?") "Who cares, in the
  Air?" ("All *our* poems, women's were there," "there, too invisible" "and
  now" "become male" "acceptable") "Accepted." "And they're welcoming us"

"among" "their forms" "among their forms only" ("what forms might we
  have made?" "which ones did" "we make?") "Whose heart is lost?" "oh not
  mine, & not my darling's" "Or only our whole heart?" "not mine, & not my
  warrior's" ("has your money" "been accepted?") "And this is what happened,"
"he went to a war" "old style, he went" "to that war" "No one cared"
"that he went there" "as no one cared" "what was lost" "with our air"

"no magnanimity" "to an enemy" "no feeling for what" "is invisible" "for
    magnanimity" "for what's lost" "to air, in air" "As if nothing
    replaced chivalry, not something" "invisible" "but nothing." "No one
    cared" "what was lost" "with our air" ("All the forms were already"
"men") ("politics, a man" "philosophy, a man; a building a" "painting a
    poem, a man" "science, a man") ("Now, we can all" "be men") "This

is what happened." "She is a mother." "This is what happened."
"Or she could be a lover" "or a sister" "This happened" "Find green air
    green breath" "Later, he tries to become" ("did he become") "air,
    air, as again" "This is what happened. And she's trying" "to breathe"
    ("the mother") "And she's trying to wash" "to wash off" "America"
"from herself" "But what" "is a mother" "now?" "In America,

everyone is else" ("else" "aside" "aside from their" "whole heart
    has crumbled") ("take your own small heart, own heart & go")
    ("& breathe" "try to breathe") "Who is she? and who" "is he?"
"Whose mask is this?" "Whose heart might be lost to the" "bigger heart"
    ("not his nor hers but") "whole country of heart" "might be lost"
"to the bigger heart" "biggest heart" "heart of the universe" "heart that

might not give it back" ("we maimed" "another, a native land, we"
"helped maim another") "Please" "give it back" "Give us our heart,
    whose" "heart might be lost."

                                    *

"Air" "What that's real" "happens in air?" ("She wasn't pure dream")
"Air, full of us, full" "of live soul, live" "of the dead & the
    living" "Thinking & talk" "Play, dream & merging" ("She's active,
    & working") "What's real" "is war" "they say" "some say" "some say,
war is" "the only" "reality" "The warriors mistake war for" "reality,
    the reality" "Because they pierce" "the centers" "the physical centers"

"of each other" "Addicted to this?" "Addicted" "& our government
of men" "organizes" "this addiction" "in the guise of, protecting us all"
"All of us part of it" "part of" "this addiction" "protector, protected"

"And when he came back" "from Nam" "at first" "he wanted" "to go back"
"back there, was it where" "he belonged now? war?" "He wanted"
"to go back" "into the bush" "'where I belonged'" "And then later"
"that's exactly" "where he was, in his head" "years later, he was back there"
"in his head" "where everything" "everything" "had happened." "He had
a family" "but he'd" "fought families" "He had a family" "he'd been
made to" "fight families" "How can we" "compete" "with that?" "Pierced
their physical" "centers" "pierced" "Is that" "the only" "reality?"
"How can we compete with" "that?" "How can we" "have him" "back?"

"Can't he come back?" "Fifteen years later" "Can't he come back?"
"Years after" "he'd left" "Vietnam" "Can't ever come back" "Can't ever"
"His soul" "soul" "He couldn't believe" "that had been he?" "he
couldn't have" "lived through that," "done that, in Nam?" "And in his
soul" "he hadn't done that" "no" "And in his soul" "he hadn't"
"And his memory self" "went back there, went back" "constantly in dreams"
"How can we" "compete with" "that?" "They finger our souls"
"for their addictions" "we let them, we comply" "After 15" "years,"
"he said he'd been used" "We were talking, talking, in green & blue air"

"He was very" "nearly back" "nearly back" "We were (four of us)" "sitting
on grass" "This moment will last" "last forever" "lying down" "I was
lying" "beneath" "tall trees" ("like Nam, he'd said," "without elephant
grass") ("he said it was where he" "needed to be" "Outside, in the
trees" "behind the rehab") "we & he" "very nearly home." "But
he was dying, already" "dying" "nearly home" "dying of dying of" "what"
"will answer the call of" "I think it is something like, gravity:"
"will die, of the Furies" "but will die" "of a pull" "from the center"
"of the earth" "& from the sky" "Or will die" ("most honorably") "of

something like power" "Power, become his, & so powerful" "Something
I've felt before" "flooding & pulling" "Can't you feel it? I've felt it"
"He's dying" "of his power" "Go" "He came home & died" "Go" "Power
of, power of" "forgiving" "forgiving himself for so much" "It took too
much power & he died" "He died of that, power of that."

*

"Who is the one who's" "behind the mask?" "mother," "first one"
"Who is that nature of ours?" "What have we done" "Bring her home" "she
should be freed" "by us" "bring her home" "He is covered in white,
fresh flowers" "at home" "He's innocent, now" "& now, we won't"
"let *her* come home," "let someone be her" "won't let one be that"
("who is she") "first mother, & only" "& one who lives" "a spreading
life, not a" "job, not" "doing what no one needs" "doing it for
the unseen," "Who is she?" "& Not just music (& not" "just poetry")
"The last of what" "has no currency."

"It takes so long to free him" "no light loves are left" "freeing a
soldier from guilt" ("frees himself") "But she can't be free, exactly"
"No place for a mother, no" "place for a full-time" "person is left"
"*Everyone's* just like a soldier" "everyone fights, everyone works"
"For the army of money we guess" "Slave to a faceless" "our country is
unthinking soldier" "money the" "uniform government texture of air,
army of money" "Everyone says it, don't they" "& So" "& so there's no pity"
"& only, mathematics" "a mother's no currency" "grief is what filters"
"filtering out my light loves" "my tolerance for" "Money is numbers
dead bodies are numbers" "dead veterans are numbers like

hours we've worked" "country of numbers" "mother of numbers"
"your child will be numbers" "mother of numbers" "your lover is
numbers, walking the numbers" "to numbers of hours worked, for salary

of numbers" "working for" "Father of numbers." "& She"
"Mother Nature" "Without Father Nature" "Father Nature mostly dead"
"thousands of years" "Mother Nature will become" "Mother of Numbers:" "says, I
sent you my" "sent you" "my self" "I sent you my self" "you said,
'there's no self'" "my love & you called me too selfless" "I
sent you my self & you asked for a form you could recognize" "a
dollar a number—or painting or book" "by a man-like

woman" ("as good as a man") "But my one
my soldier is dead, my" "one who was numbered" "I sent you my self
was it he" "he was part" "The body counts" "remember" "remember them"
"they" "wouldn't let him" "they wouldn't count" "ones he killed not
in uniform" "& you, you don't count the" "ones not in uniform" "the
child the mother" "& you don't count me" "what I do; for I" "send you
my self" "all I have" "I will" "put on this mask" "put back on my mask"
"Streaked with dirt" "I have made my own mask" "faint pieces of money"
"faint numbers & words" "And I have a mask" "to wear" "for you"
"I wear this mask, but"

"leaks" "skin of the planet" "leaks" "leaks" "white phosphorus"

*

"Flowery mantle." "Homeric sacrifice?" "noise of darkness" "fear of
 darkness" "now mantle of innocence" "King of his death now" "Home"
"I've come home" "He said, 'I've come home'" "They were sacrificed for
 nothing, for distant" "instants of thought" "All for your thinking"
"He said, 'I've come home; I've finally come home' then he died" "flowers"
"Magnolias & lilies" "innocent now" "I've come home. Who's there?
 at home? all the dead?" "To come home from the war" "years after" "To die" "To

wear mantle light honey" "mantle dead white" "in sunlight, in late"
"Homeric?" "he said it was hideous" "all of it" "hideous" "every
instant in Nam" "theatre of worsts" "now mantle of
white" "phosphorus & lilies?" "trees now lean down" "over our faces"
"Tell details of battle?" "As" "in an epic?" "As" "in lies?"
"We don't want that now" "We want only our mother of
dirt" "our mantle of white" "want each other of soul; and"

"we want" "our mother of spirit" ("rich sweet in dirt") "we want"
"our father" "of leaves" "We want our fate fragmented to air for
our children to breathe;" "light on water for widows to think near"
"moonlight on water to ease you" "we want no poet, we want our
homes in the earth" "that's all we can have" "want no place in
history or poetry" "want our wanderings our sorrows, after the war,
not remembered," "we want not

to pain her" "we want our love mingled" "with yours" "no place in
history" "only in love" "remove us from history," "All of us sacri-
ficed" "all for a thought" "They played with our souls." "Used our
souls to fight, be their willfulness" "willfulness" "we were made their
willfulness," "nothing but that—" "And you too, you yielded, one
way or another" "to their will." "They" "who are
the subject" "of all history" "& of poems" "as if"

"we have ever, in all ways" "yielded to them" "by speaking of" "always
speaking of" "Kings" "presidents" "the Great Men" "their mistresses"
"Generals" "Communist Kings" "Leaders" "Warriors" "West Point of Greeks"
"West Point of Greeks against" "West Point of Trojans" "Isn't it more
beautiful, under the Earth?" "Or to be sunlight, not history?"
"Now I can love, & only" "now" "Remove us from history but
not from your air" "History is willfulness" "is" "precious parts"

"History's for those" "who ask not" "to be forgiven"
"We ask to be forgiven" "& loved" "No, we ask" "to be absolved"
"And to be" "elemental" "ask leaves & wind"
"Ask leaves bending down towards our faces" "Ask light & dirt" "we ask"
"our children" "we ask our wives" "Ask that they live" "We ask
  to be" "with the ones that we killed" "To history" "saying nothing"
"being that" ("nothing") "& to history" "having been" "nothing."

                              *

"In this moment" "before" "anyone, ever" "died" "before we were born?"
"in this moment forever before" "before we went to a war"
"Before we died" "In this moment, now" "In this moment before, it is
  not before" "In this very moment" "where is it" "where we
  haven't died" "or died inside" "In this moment we haven't" "in this
  moment, no one" "in this moment, no one has ever, died" ("But I have
  been born") "in this moment" "where, where is it" "in moment" "who's here"
"Catch it catch it" "moment where we are" "merely as it is autonomous,"

"autonomous moment" "Without a war" "without a guilt,"
"Can we exist" "Outside of what was?" "in the air of our thoughtless,
  female, moment" "the air of our moment" "not grievous not iron"
"moment, not air" "but air of our moment" ("woman-made?") "faithful,
  faithful & boundless" "reticent & light" "fond, & kindly" "not reticent
  but shiny," "morning-starry, not bloody" "not bloody, in the morning"
"in the star" "it is a star" "it is autonomous" "star & it's mild" "Is
  it a little" "of us" "from before" "we were born?" ("that was

  never") ("I know") "It is now" "autonomous" "moment of white,"
"white flowers, stars & white flowers," "not before we were born, in
  this moment our childhood" "have we our childhood" "in
  this moment he has his childhood, I think, it is center of"

"moment, of childhood" "center of, moment" "wings of his pigeons" "white
& grey wings" "moment a feathery" "center of senses" "center of
sensation, is this moment" "Center, as sensation falls away"
"He has his love" "this moment" "forever" "center of brown eyes"

"seen through his eyes" "Only through" "the eyes" "the real eyes"
"of the dead" "this moment" "through his eyes" "as child, as
childhood" "Only through" "the personality" "can this be" "of the
dead" "the lovely person" "holding" "this moment" "this moment in
place" "this moment forever" "center of sensation" "Soldiers,
we are center" "of the morning" "we are moment" "we are dearest"
"we are heart" "Soldiers," "we are pleasing" "we are center"
"we are moment" "are not soldiers" "never soldiers" "never were."

*

"Mask now" "is complies" "complies" "with the forms (too much of everything,
everywhere") "All of this is" "the mask" "my mother's mask" "& mine"
"wronglike forms, too many of" "Complying, to live here" "always, more
complying" "Too many things" "machines" "too many" "too many clothes"
"cheap roses" "kleenexes" "membranous" "bags, of plastic" "Too many
ideas" "vocabularies no color" "too many paintings" "too many songs"
"too many Tarot decks" "& poems" "& books" "Too many" "things to eat"
"too many" "machines" "magic machines" "too much magic" "much too much of it"
"Stupor" "distress" "& abandoning of others" "too much news" "news"
"everything" "made the same" "too many names" "too much knowledge"

("knowledge, so endless" "is nothing") "A war" "more news, more
to know about, to know" "Excuse for anger" "indignation" "you can still
keep your money" "know the terms of news" "terms" "& Not be nature"
"don't be nature" "mute" "not knowing the" "terms" "Know what news knows"
"What words know" "Do words know?" "No they don't, only flesh knows only

soul knows" "in the words" "A mask is rigid" "on warm flesh on
dreaming mind" "on fleshly mind" "rigid" "But my brother now is
nature, pure nature" "however that be" "Or I have dreamed so" "Owl,
not an albatross" "He's an owl," "not an albatross" "I have twice"
"dreamed that Al" "is an owl" "intricate with" "feathers" "texture of

thousands of feathers" ("I've seen" "an owl" "only in" "a museum") "Owl,
I didn't know him, I searched" "the owl's face for its" "identity"
("Al died later" "that day") "grey owl great grey owl" "wisdom, & war"
"Master of nights (Al's terrible" "nightmares") "He rose up, finally
as an owl" "Is he owl?" "Where is owl now" "I've never seen one" "I
later" "dreamed after" "I'd realized" "Owl was Al" "that he was a" "snowy owl"
"white, with black spots" "A man said," "he's not an albatross"
"Owl, not an albatross" "Al" "whom I have seen" "also seen in a
small" "waking vision" "standing, in his living room" "wearing
a white mantle, flower mantle a" "mantle" "of fresh, white flowers"

"petals, like feathers" "white petals" "white feathers" "a cloak
of nature of" "purity" "of purification" "wilder, milder, he is
nature" "he is better mind" "My brother" "is owl" "Athena-like" "wise"
"I know things only" "this way" "My brother" "is Owl."

[1988]

FROM *THE DESCENT OF ALETTE*

from BOOK ONE

"One day, I awoke" "& found myself on" "a subway, endlessly"
"I didn't know" "how I'd arrived there or" "who I was" "exactly"
"But I knew the train" "knew riding it" "knew the look of"
"those about me" "I gradually became aware—" "though it seemed

as that happened" "that I'd always" "know it too—" "that there was"
"a tyrant" "a man in charge of" "the fact" "that we were"
"below the ground" "endlessly riding" "our trains, never surfacing"
"A man who" "would make you pay" "so much" "to leave the subway"

"that you don't" "ever ask" "how much it is" "It is, in effect,"
"all of you, & more" "Most of which you already" "pay to
live below" "But he would literally" "take your soul" "Which is
what you are" "below the ground" "Your soul" "your soul rides"

"this subway" "I saw" "on the subway a" "world of souls"

~

"There was a woman" "in a station" "with a guitar &"
"amplifier" "who sang" "sang a song" "that said this:"

"'As the old man lies dying" "in his bishop's robe & gown"
"surrounded" "by museum cases full of jewels" "& gold"
"shards of Venuses" "oldest potteries" "He" "is on exhibit"
"too" "as he is dying" "As we watch him," "the women,"

"we receive our" "emerald rings" "They grow"
"begin to grow" "around our fingers," "as we watch him"
"Because" "we're his loyal" "secretaries" "as we
watch him" "on exhibit" "always governing" "always ruling

as he lies dying" "He" "could die forever" "On exhibit"
"in his mansion" "in his Vatican" "in his Parthenon" "in his"
"admini-" "strative offices" "See" "in the emeralds"
("which can get murkier" "uglier") "an endless" "endless male

will" "But the tyrant" "is a mild man" "Look in our emeralds"
"& see shadows" "We are those" "against the green" "green
lush light" "We are weightless" "Left with rings,"
"we will be old &" "left with rings" "By the time the

"lakes thaw the" "green lakes" "of the great cities"
"of the North" "We will be dead" "With emerald rings"
"Green stones upon our" "fingerbones" "That is our love"
"Must be our love" "that we" "will be dead &" "he"

"will live forever," "on exhibit" "in his museum'"

~

"We couldn't find" "our fathers—" "there were several" "of us"
"We were walking through subway cars" "looking" "for our fathers" "Endless
train" "It seemed the longest" "train there is" "as if it circled"
"the world—" "& we walked it, we were searching" "for our fathers,"

"when we entered" "a car of" "suited . . . animals—" "men, actually,"
"in business suits," "clean shirts" "Charcoal suits, &" "navy-blue"
"ties (crimson stripes")" "—beautiful suits—" "And the men all" "had
animal" "heads" "It was a dimly" "lit car" "the lights" "on occasion"

"would go completely:" "Darkness" "Silent" "Animal" "Faces" "Shaggy"
"or Sleek:" "He is a falcon, a gyrfalcon" "his head cocked towards his"
"business-suited" "wing-arm" "His eyes," "clear-dark-round," "stare"
"Or he's a lemur" "a reddish lemur" "reddish eyes" "fur, tipped in orange,

 glows orange" "above his gray suit" "He's a panther, black sleek hair"
"You want to touch" "above his nose" "feel his short hair plush face,"
"black velvet" "He's an owl" "His face is feathers, it is ruffed,"
"his eyes are critical, a" "gray owl:" "Were these our fathers?" "And

 if so, which" "was which," "who" "was my father" "your father?"
 ("And the men" "couldn't speak to us" "made no sound" "made no sign")
"Can you" "find your father?" "Mine is probably" "an owl" "He stared"
"He stared at me" "But owls stare" "And then he looked away"

                              ~

"A mother" "& child" "were both on fire, continuously"
"The fire" "was contained in them" "sealed them off
 from others" "But you could see the flame" "halo
 of short flame all about the" "conjoined bodies, who

 sat" "they sat apart" "on a seat for two" "at end of car" "The
 ghost" "of the father" "sat in flames" "beside them"
"paler flames" "sat straight ahead" "looking
 straight ahead, not" "moving." "A woman"

"another woman" "in a uniform" "from above the ground"
"entered" "the train" "She was fireproof" "She was gloves, & she"
"took" "the baby" "took the baby" "away from the"
"mother" "Extracted" "the burning baby" "from the fire" "they

made together" "But the baby" "still burned"
("But not yours" "It didn't happen" "to you")
"'We don't know yet'" "if it will" "stop burning,'"
"said the uniformed" "woman" "The burning woman" "was crying"

"she made a form" "in her mind" "an imaginary" "form" "to
settle" "in her arms where" "the baby" "had been" "We saw
her fiery arms" "cradle air" "She cradled air" ("They take your
children" "away" "if you're on fire")

"In the air that" "she cradled" "it seemed to us there" "floated"
"a flower-like" "a red flower" "its petals" "curling flames"
"She cradled" "seemed to cradle" "the burning flower of" "herself gone"
"her life" ("She saw" "whatever she saw, but what we saw" "was that flower")

~

"'When I was born,'" "I was born now" "fully grown," "on heroin" "When I
was born" "fully grown" "in the universe" "of no change" "nothing" "grows
up from'" ("Who sings this, whose voice?" "This person" "is in a shadow"
"down at the end of" "the platform" "I can't see him" "at all" "He continues

his song:") "'When I was born,'" "I was now" "When I was born" "I'm not
allowed" "to remember when I was" "the little baby" "in a darkness, joy of
darkness" "Was I the cub" "for an instant?" "if so" "only an instant,"
"before I" "was a soldier" "before I" "was a soldier . . .'" ("Where is the

battlefield?" "At a station" "no longer" "in use" "Train goes right
past it" "But veterans" "know how" "to get in" "In that station" "is kept a
piece of" "a battlefield" "of the old war" "In that station" "grow white
flowers" "large blossoms" "that are faces," "with eyes closed" "lashes

closed white" "White skin white hair" "Soldiers go there" "Call to"
"the victim-flowers" "They don't answer but" "seem to grow" "The soldiers
water them" "water the flowers" "which were" "their own victims:"
"'When I was born,'" "I was born now" "When I was born,'" "I'm not allowed"

"to remember if I was" "the little baby" "the little boy" "Was I the cub"
"for an instant?" "Or was I" "already" "a soldier . . .'"

~

"'I once" "found an exit" "from the subway" ("the woman told me")
"I once" "found a staircase" "that led to" "an exit" "temporarily
unlocked" "I opened the door to—" "It was an" "Antarctic"
"light, up there" "As if dawn or dusk, but" "neither" "Everyone

wore black" "black cashmere" "discreet diamonds" "had guarded,
dark eyes" "Was it" "the winter holidays?" "I saw" "crushed-red lights"
"reflected" "in snowy puddles" "White lights" "in naked trees"
"For me it" "was frozen time," "from past pain," "from a time"

"when I was young," "before I came beneath," "came down here—" "before
I'd willingly" "walked away from" "that upper world," "had left"
"a university—" "I then remembered from" "long before" ("as I stood"
"near the exit") " a library I'd entered" "in that partial light, in

Spring" "There was grass," "there were blossoms" "Huge windows"
"looking out on grass" "And shelves" "of books" "all the books there
were:" "The books were decayed matter," "black & moldy" "Came apart"
"in my hands" "All the books were" "black rot" "Were like mummies"

"More body of" "the tyrant" "It is all his body" "The world is" "his
mummy" "Up there, up there" "Down here it is" "a more desperate"

"decay," "as if" "rich emotion," "pain," "could still transform us"
"despite him" "despite his power, &" "tyrannical" " . . . ignorance,"

"passing as" "knowledge—" "And so of course I" "re-entered" "re-
   entered" "the subway—" "I can't leave it" "ever" "unless"
"we all leave—'"

~

"A car" "awash with blood" "Blood at our feet" "& I
   & others" "have small springs" "of blood from our"
"feet & knees" "There is an inch or two" "of blood"
"all over" "the car floor" "Replenished" "periodically"

"by our body springs" "of blood" "And trickling out"
"the door" "when it opens" "at stations." "The
   tyrant" "sends a hologram" "a life-sized hologram" "of
   himself" "into our car" "He stands mid-car" "& says:"

"'The blood at our" "feet" "has cost me" "so much"
"The blood" "at our feet" "has cost us so" "much"
"To clean" "the blood" "is difficult" "to clean the
   car.'" "There is a litter" "of things" "in the

wash of blood" "I see sanitary" "pads," "kleenex,"
"black-blood encrusted" "old bandages" "An old black
   suitcase" "spills out" "torn men's clothes" "& frayed towels"
"The hologram tyrant" "says, 'Here" "are my tears'" "Holds

up his palm" "His tears are" "small drops of jade"
"Red" "& white jade" "His tears have turned to jade"

"They will be placed in" "a National" "Museum" "There is
  something in" "my ear" "I pull it out a" "white cord"

"a long" "silk cord" "I pull it out &" "hear our blood"
"It hums" "a unison one" "note loud a" "sheet of sound"
"It hangs there" "sad insect noise" "insect-like"
"Our blood."

~

"I stood again" "on the platform" "of the station" "where the snake
  sleeps" "Stood near" "the snake herself," "in the shadows there,"
"thinking" "I felt poised" "to be decisive" "be decisive in some way"
"But only knew" "the same decision" "Get on the next train" "or not"

"The snake" "the sad snake" "opened bleary dark" "gold-ringed eyes—"
"crusty sticky" "around their edges" "Opened eyes" "& opened mouth"
  ("I'd never seen her" "awake") "Extended" "a black tongue" "& said in"
"a woman's whisper:" "'When I was" "the train" "when I was" "the train,"

"flesh & blood" "flesh & blood" "took you to your" "destination"
"to your life" "to your life" "carried you through your life" "Flesh &
  blood were" "your life" "Flesh & blood were" "your time" "A soul"
"was not so naked" "so pained &" "denied" "abused &" "denied,"

"when I was" "the train . . .'" "'You're not big enough,'" "I said to her,"
"'not big enough to" "be a train'" "She ignored me" "& repeated" "over"
"& over," "'When I was" "the train" "When I was" "the train" "When
  I was" "the train . . .'" "until she" "finally" "fell asleep again"

from **BOOK THREE**

"'It's time to go,' he said" "'Go where?'" "'You'll see'" "He
    perched on" "my shoulder," "& directed" "me down" "the other side of
    the hill" "on top of which" "the camp lay" "I saw a lake below,"
"black & flat," "almost perfectly" "round" "We proceeded to" "a gazebo,"

"an old open" "wooden structure," "with a peaked roof," "at the
    water's edge" "'We will stand here,' he said" "'What is this lake?'
    I asked him" "'It is the center . . .' he began" "'I find it difficult"
"to define" "It is the center" "of the deep . . .'" "Of this underworld,

    I guess" "But you must" "look into it" "Look into" "the lake'"
"Though the trees" "around the lake" "contained among them many lights,"
"none shone directly" "on the lake:" "it was very" "very black"
"'How deep is it?' I asked" "'Infinitely" "deep,' he said" "'It

    connects with" "the great darkness," "connects with" "one's death—'"
"'Is it—" "can it be—" "really" "water, then?'" "'Put your hand
    in it'" "I did" "& felt nothing" "at all" "'There is nothing there,'
    I said,'" "'but it does" "look like water'" "'Look into it,' the owl

    repeated" "'Don't you see" "something there?'" "'I see eyes,"
"pairs of eyes . . .'" "darkness" "with fishlike" "pairs of eyes'"

~

"As I stared down" "into the black lake" "I saw more & more"
"pairs of eyes" "The eyes were" "flat yellow" "fish-body-shapes,"
"two-dimensional," "with irises suggested by" "drawn-on black lines"
"The eyes were bright," "seemed lit up" "They unpaired," "mixed

together," "swarmed like fish," "yellow fish" "I tried"
"to concentrate" "on the blackness between eyes—" "for hadn't"
"the owl just said" "that the darkness in the lake" "was the great
  darkness," "the essence" "of death?" "Wasn't it" "extinction,"

"my own end?" "But the yellow eyes" "multiplied," "became so numerous"
"that the blackness" "was covered over" "by them" "All was eyes,"
"lit eyes," "fish-bodied" "lantern eyes" " 'What do you see now?'
  said the owl" "& when I" "told him, said," " 'Keep trying" "to see

between them'" "And then I" "concentrated" "on a place" "between
  eyes," "a thread-thin black line" "As I frowned & stared" "a space
  widened" "The expanse of eyes" "was drawn back" "like curtains"
"revealing darkness" "On this darkness I saw" "a person appear"

"composed of more eyes," "composed of tiny eyes," "minute eyes"
"As if the smallest" "constituents" "of matter were" "somehow eyes"
"The person died—" "died then—" "She lay down on black air"
  ("as if there were" "a bed there") "Air now interspersed," "here &

there, with the" "minute eyes," "to show that air too" "is eyes—"
"Her head rolled" "to the side" "& she was still" "her face partook of"
"the stillness of" "the mouse that" "we'd eaten" "Then she"
"began to decompose" "She decomposed, she changed:" "all of the eyes"

"that had been her" "floated" "away in air" "Her mass of eyes"
"became dispersed eyes," "dispersed everywhere" " 'Is there nothing that"
"isn't eyes," "that isn't eyes?' I cried" " 'Was she—" "is she only"
"eyes," "all eyes?' "

~

"The horizontal" "black void" "where the woman" "had lain—"
"defined by dispersed eyes" "as corpse shape" "but empty
  black space—" "slowly" "became a play of" "new" "con-
figurations" "Haphazard-" "seeming lines" "of white light"

"began to fill it" "Many lines" "of several thicknesses"
"spread themselves" "throughout the woman's shape," "organizing
  themselves" "into an" "apparent system" "like veins" "or nerves—"
"And all the eyes," "all the eyes," "completely" "disappeared"

"All around" "the woman's form" "was even" "blackness now"
"'What does this mean?'" "I asked the owl" "'Who is" "she now?'"
"'She has entered" "the other world," "the simultaneous" "one"
"As when" "you dream" "But it is" "no one's dream" "It is the

other" "being," "free of the body's" "time, its heaviness,"
"the body's slowness compared to mind—" "It is" "as when you
dream," "nowhere" "& everywhere" "She has entered there" "Is
there now" "You must enter" "it too" "before you go back"

"to the tyrant's world" "You must enter that world'" "'How can I
do that?'" "'You will die" "a little death now—'" "He flew
up at me" "Talons thrust at" "my neck" "Pierced me" "And he
pulled me" "into the lake"

~

"Talons tore me," "tore my flesh," "as I was dragged" "into the
darkness" "The pain was fire in" "spreading pools," "quick-opening
flowers," "fiery blossoms" "with torn" "pecked centers" "Till
all I was was fire" "Fire &" "screaming" "But soon" "there was

no pain" "There was a numbness" "& an eating" "An eating of" "my
body" "Sometimes" "I was eaten" "Sometimes I watched" "I was
watching" "a woman pecked at by an owl" "Her face was eyeless,"
"pocked with red holes" "Sometimes while I" "was being eaten"

"I was inside" "the owl:" "he would swallow me" "I would float"
"into a warmth," "a dark warmth," "that was his body" "The noise of"
"the eating" "was mutedly" "deafening," "a low crunching" "gulping
noise," "that filled my senses," "myself," "now scattered," "chaotic,"

"dissipated" "into his body," "& also hovering" "outside of it,"
"outside of her" "Then finally" "I coalesced," "was unified" "again"
"somewhere outside in air" "I looked down at her," "my body" "She was
still," "a still lump" "Though strangely" "she was intact now"

"Not eaten," "not even pecked at" "But I was sure she" "was dead"
"I hovered over her quiet face" "tenderly," "recognizing" "this &
that" "idiosyncrasy" "of brow & nose," "of hairline," "of earlobe"
"The owl had vanished," "we were alone" "And then I fell into"

"unconsciousness"

~

"When I awoke I" "was in darkness" "& could see nothing" "at all"
"I was surrounded" "by voices:" "'She's come to'" "'She's ready'"
"'Please stand up,' one said gently" "I moved" "as if standing up"
"But I seemed to have no form," "seemed to move nothing" "as I made

motions" "'Very good,'" "the voice said" "'Have I stood up?'" "'Yes,'
it said" "'I can't see anything:" "am I blind?' I asked" "'There is

nothing here" "to see,'" "one of the voices" "answered" "'But also"
"you have no senses here—" "you are hearing us" "without ears'"

"'You don't have" "bodies either?'" "One voice laughed" "a low laugh—"
"I couldn't" "identify" "any voice by sex—" "& said, 'Walk this way'"
"I thought of where" "my legs should be" "& tried to move that," "move
them" "'Good, good,'" "the voice said" "'What am I walking on?' I asked"

"'On nothing,'" "another voice replied" "'Stop her now" "Someone is
joining us'" "A voice near us," "somewhat more" "authoritative-
sounding," "saying, 'What" "do you wish here?" "You are not really one"
"of the dead'" "The voice was" "before me now" "'I must,' I said,"

"probe being's depth . . .'" "Before I try to" "change its surface—"
"But how can I" "not be wholly dead?" "An owl tore me" "apart & ate me'"
"'That is only" "what you perceived" "The owl is" "very powerful'"
"The voice fell silent" "a moment," "then continued:" "'Some of your

body parts—" "your *death* body parts—" "parts of your insubstantial
body—" "have been" "replaced" "The owl replaced them" "They will stay
functional" "within your so-called" "real body'" "'Which parts are
different?'" "'Your sex is now bone'" "'My sex?'" "'Your vagina is

white bone" "& your eyes," "your eyes," "are now like" "an owl's eyes"
"Though they seem more like" "two black flowers—" "two black hollyhock"
"flowers" "They are black flowery" "craters" "You are now equipped"
"to experience" "what you need'"

~

"'We will be silent" "& wait,'" "the voice said" "Then we were
truly quiet" "& being that," "were nothing" "Really nothing" "but
the darkness" "This moment was very long," "very long &" "very wide"
"It had a" "vast diameter" "I felt as if" "I could be" "falling

asleep forever" "Then I saw it" "coming towards me—" "so stately,"
"so stately—" "a light," "a white light" "A radiant" "small sphere,
I guessed" "Diameter" "of but a few feet" "It was seeking" "me out,"
"this light so" "unexpected" "'What is this light I see?'" "I asked the

voices" "'You are blind,'" "the voices whispered" "'You are blind'"
"'You do not *see* it'" "'You have no senses'" "'You are effectively"
"dead'" "'I see it,' I said" "'It is a small light—" "It lights up
nothing" "There is obviously" "nothing here" "But it is beautiful"

"Beautiful'" "'It is not a light,'" "the voices said" "'It is yourself'"
"'It is something like" "yourself'" "Then the authoritative" "voice said,"
"'We are going to" "leave you now'"

~

"I looked into the light" "directly" "with what I knew to be black eyes"
"Light streamed down through" "my eyes" "into myself" "And"
"as if inside me" "were only mirrors" "which faced each other" "I
felt myself" "light up within," "entirely," "the length of me"

"I was sight," "pure sight" "Was being," "was seeing," "with no object"
"whatsoever" "Nothing to see," "nothing to be:" "There was" "an other
though—" "the light which lit me" "& I loved it" "most purely"
"though I" "was also it" "'Is this" "the deepest darkness?'" "I

asked it" "'It is,'" "it said," "in no voice at all" "'It's what you've
always" "suspected" "It's nothing but" "what you've always known,"
"always been" "For you've always" "been being" "It's simple" "Simple'"
"'This light,' I said," "our light," "is the same as the" "surrounding

darkness'" "'Of course,'" "said the light" "'Both" "are being"
"There is no darkness" "or light, here" "But when I leave you" "you
will be lit—" "even if the light" "does diminish'" "We were silent"
"awhile;" "then I spoke again:" "'I'm at peace with" "being" "In

this moment" "I've become" "all that" "I am" "I'm ready" "to
go back'"

[1990]

FROM ***CLOSE TO ME & CLOSER . . .***

(THE LANGUAGE OF HEAVEN)

I have to . . . talk to you. I have to tell you . . . some things I know now, I mean now
that . . . I'm dead. See I see this . . . <u>world deal</u>, where you are, clear—or clearer . . .
I see what . . . It's like, I see, a world where . . . it's going to, not blow, but just . . . It's
already, a <u>machine</u>. I <u>sold</u> parts—it's all <u>auto</u> parts . . . gaskets & fan belts . . . batteries
. . . & gas. It's like <u>that</u>. That's all it's going to . . . be. No one knows . . . what they call
an <u>essence</u>—no one <u>has</u> that. Think of yourselves, as <u>cards</u>: king, queen, jack . . .
Taro<u>t</u> . . . if you're a card, if you think you're, the Queen of Hearts, the Jack of Dia-
monds—or one of the Taro<u>t</u>, those <u>people</u>—I mean—I mean people think about
themselves as . . . <u>types</u>, or even, that word . . . <u>archetypes</u>. King . . . queen . . . youth.
And so on. Why now it's like . . . cards that have no paint, or color. Like the lines on
them, are dim. 'Cause they look like cards, from here—people do; but we see them
. . . the colors're <u>bled</u> <u>away</u>. You need a new thing, another way to <u>think</u>, but . . . what
if, the world . . . Well, anyway, I thought I'd try to tell you—since you're a poet—
about <u>here</u>. A little about how we <u>think</u> here. It's not with . . . we don't think in
words—or pictures—necessarily. Not the way you're, translating <u>me</u> on your page.
Translating me into <u>you</u>, which . . . but sounding like me since, you're my <u>daughter</u>.
But thinking . . . is a fluid here—a . . . connection—or <u>light</u>. If you thought like <u>that</u>,
why the essence could be as much <u>between</u> . . . between you, as what you <u>are</u>. Not
such a struggle, trying to <u>be</u> something . . . especially something that doesn't . . .
really work. Instead you can . . . float <u>between</u>. <u>Around</u>. <u>We</u> do. We are . . . <u>that</u>.

~

I sit mute Nothing mutely
—Flowerlike—
I sit being nothing of petals
be nothing And then of petals

This new is new shape Any new thing
is a flower A mute flower
flowing color Are you

Come closer & watch me cry for
Watch me cry for new air

What story are you showing me, Daddy
The story you must write of being me

~

They gave me, it seemed to me, an Initiation, into . . . how they think here. When I
was initiated into the <u>Masons</u>, we were keeping it a secret . . . forget why . . . because
always had, Masons always had, but . . . that was <u>fun</u>. They are having fun <u>here</u> . . .
these, this . . . they, us . . . it's hard to call it. Being dead is like <u>one fun</u> . . . that's a
Chinese joke . . . if. Like that there's no time, or it's all one time—you know, Eter-
nity—it's no different from living, in a way, except you don't know it on schedule.
I'm <u>telling you</u> these things, so you can live. And not . . . air, not live in air. Because
here isn't really, either—But it isn't air—I can't <u>explain</u> it good. In the Initiation, all
they did, someone with a white arm, sleeve, put a cup—maybe a <u>seashell</u>—against
my ear. Because what thinking is, is <u>hearing</u>. Hearing yourself think. Even if it right
away becomes something . . . you <u>do</u> then. If you can listen, you can think, in the
<u>true</u> way. Then the thought comes from nowhere. Where's nowhere? Is that where
<u>I</u> am? Maybe. Anyway that's how to think, alive or dead. Even when . . . god thinks,
the thought comes from nowhere, which seems to be <u>inside god</u>. To make a thing—
you hear the thought, to do . . . whatever, <u>next</u>, as you make it. That's how the uni-
verse . . . got made, & that's how I'm telling you, these things. Well actually—we're
<u>both</u> listening. The truth <u>comes</u>. Reality . . . comes. You don't, tinker with it till it <u>is</u>,
what you want.

I asked someone, could there, have not been, anything ... a universe, or earth, or god ... They said, that's words that's still, the old thinking, like you did on earth. The idea of, nothing, that's like, that there are <u>opposites</u>. There aren't opposites, something/nothing ... Everyone laughed. <u>Nothing</u> isn't ... it's mostly, an <u>idea</u>. God <u>fills</u> everything. "Everything" ... though, doesn't <u>mean</u> anything either, as a word. When you become ... a dot, listening to, the one thought, <u>that's</u> "everything."

~

Why do we make
ourselves aliens
We must invent ourselves
mustn't we To be here to make
a sea of difference
For humans are
nothing Unlike apes
& birds & fishes
Who understand themselves And
in their natures are
perfectly obvious Do what's ob-
vious Aren't we
aliens Our shapes
suggest not Our star-shaped
hands Our shell-like ears
And flower genitals
But we *are* aliens
fretting to belong here
Inventing words & frets
Inventing folksongs In-
venting rich & poor And
the song of that
Sing back Sing

[from *Close to Me & Closer ... (The Language of Heaven)*]   **215**

back into
Origin tongue
Poetry The
tongue to
touch the
beginning
It's all we have
Poetry
It is the Human difference
Though we've forgotten
But we are poets
We must not forget That we are poets
Ever again

~

What I say to you—I, almost, transfer a shape. When I told you, about the Initia-
tion—that wasn't strictly true, it was almost corny: the way people are, & I am. Cer-
tainly. It isn't ever corny here. Because it has to cover . . . rocks plants animals—as
well as people & they aren't corny. I told you something, that was sort of like the way
it is. I transferred . . . But there aren't . . . And there wasn't a shell. That was dumb.
I'm probably not going to take back, anything else. I show you now . . . a sort of body
shape. It's something bagged—as if it were covered by—a long dark sweatshirt
cloth—all bagged up. It's dark or dark blue. It's got a head—a round, like, ball—& a
long . . . torso, a sausage, no arms & legs. Now what is it. It's already a human, isn't it.
It's all of you. It's anyone. Without anything. It might be dead you . . . or sort of, you
not born yet. Or you like . . . someone who doesn't know you, thinks about you. If
they have to. Or that is . . . shape, you know, the idea of there being shapes. We don't
exactly have shapes here—we go too fast in mind for them. But I have told you now,
fast, if I hadn't had to explain, this shape. You see all I've said—flash, instant. In an
instant. You have . . . some word uh dust, word dust, in your head, sort of blowing
around, the body. But you get it. We are in Get It, here. It isn't . . . far from you. I'm
not so far. You're not so far from me.

It stands up—the bagged body now. It walks on . . . stubs, inside the bag, you can't see. But. What can it do like this? Any, body bag, does what? How can it . . . change? What's inside it? Whatever <u>something</u> is. Whatever anything is. Where did that come from? That's just a question. I think <u>you're</u> the bagged body. I'm going to help you.

~

In eternity There is no story
For in the simultaneity
of everything compressed
To one round mosaiced
Bead on a bracelet The story flattens
out And sinks back To its origin
Glints of what? Lost in color Lost
In a room's flow In a street's flow
of luminosity Flecked with gesture
With sayings cries And twinges
'I am trying to I am trying to
Become the heroine Of my story'
But there is no such
Shape to life There are flowers
Growing up from earth There are
rocks In damp grey day of snow
This day passes Leaves no mark that lasts
Unless you cling to it Humans cling to
it To days To shapes To patterns
To say 'I won't cling again' It-
self makes a dramatizing
Marking of oneself A clinging a
story-making 'I won't cling on Oh
I won't cling on Let it snow on me
Forever And cover up The outlines
Of what I do and feel Let it

Snow between and over My thoughts and
feelings For they are nothing
And all there is is snow All there
really is Is snow'

~

I'm . . . interested in, what of me there is . . . here. Then, I might be able to tell you . . .
what to bother about, where <u>you</u> are. Because — this is hard — they are the <u>same</u>. I am
almost, being <u>there</u> <u>now</u>, where you are. I am almost in, myself there — because I am —
the <u>main</u> thing I was — That's the same. And it <u>isn't</u> . . . you don't . . . my personality . . .
you . . . respond to them, <u>the way you are</u> . . . is that personality? It's that, some . . . tone?
. . . feel to that, is here. With me. I'm that. In a plant, well, can I do plants? I don't
know enough — yet — In an <u>animal</u>, each is a same . . . they have <u>the same thing</u> . . . of
essence. Each human, has same & different. Because the nature of, the species, is that
each be, a little different. A duck can be different . . . around people — but with ducks,
a duck is, the same — People <u>make it up</u>. What people are like. They keep making it
up. As that <u>bagged body</u> (It looks like a schmoo, in L'il Abner) is . . . part that. They've,
you've bagged you <u>all up</u>, all around. You . . . I mean you not anyone — don't <u>want</u> to —
cry when they say to . . . or laugh . . . do what they say to all day. And you want . . . to
be here, some, where I am — and <u>know it</u>. If the bag <u>breaks</u>, the <u>real you</u>, comes out.
But. You'll still. You'll still cry when, humans cry. I don't cry here. What happened
. . . to me was — so tiny — but you <u>must</u> cry, even break apart. Then you see . . . the
bag breaks. But then gets . . . sewn back up. But it breaks <u>because</u> . . . you can't stand
<u>human-made-humanness</u> any more. You can't stand love — if someone dies. Here . . .
there's no death. Or <u>love</u>, actually. It's <u>like</u> it, but it's different. I tell you, See? so you
can . . . well, love <u>better</u>. When the bag bursts — and stays burst. But what about your
<u>shape</u>? If that is you . . . that bagged body . . . 'bagged body blue' . . . before you — were
born? Is it always . . . before you were born — till now — Like me. I think I'm born.

~

[from *Close to Me & Closer . . . (The Language of Heaven)*]

I'm going to tell you . . . a story. There was a man, who had a little girl, when he was
alive. His biggest wish was . . . not to be poor. Dirt-poor. But he didn't care about . . .
a lot of money. Another thing he wanted . . . was to belong to people. These were
hard for him . . . reasons I won't go into . . . when he was a kid. He got those things
in life, The End. Except he also got some troubles. And had a . . . flaw I guess you'd
call it. That's all what people are like—or a life is. Now from here, that's <u>several</u> things.
That's an ess-shape . . . in a circle. See? <u>I'm</u> the circle, I mean he is—the story line is
the ess. It bends when he . . . starts to make more money. See, look. The circle isn't
flat, I mean the line is but not inside of it. The ess is flat. But . . . winds blow . . . cold
& warm . . . between the ess & the circle. What was the <u>point of</u> everything he did?
Does he . . . remember when he's <u>dead</u>? Where does it . . . go? Memories seem loose
and . . . outside of him. They blow by, like insects—Here, I mean. The point is, noth-
ing had to have been, the way it was. That's the whole point. What they call . . . pre-
ordained—<u>humans</u> keep pre-ordaining. So they can be . . . secure . . . like animals . . .
So they can know what they're <u>like</u>. God <u>doesn't</u> do that. Or, nature. God is in charge
without being in charge. But that . . . doesn't matter. Not in the life of . . . once there
was a man who had a daughter. And now, what about the daughter? It goes on . . .
Any point along that man's ess-curve, can light up, & if you entered . . . that point . . .
it would be a moment. Any moment the man was . . . is still here . . . in god's eye.
Any moment . . . <u>participates</u>. A . . . damped-down moment . . . A wicked moment . . .
(What kind of poem . . . comes next?)

~

I don't have to
  Because
To be contrary
inexplicable
Is the light burst that
  will change
    us
  To go against the

way of things
Right Now
Break the rhythm   If you Break it
        Keep doing
That
    No one
Dominates you   No <u>past</u> can
    Don't walk straight
Don't think
    straight   Don't dance
except to
    a sound in
        your own "ear"
This is a time for Eccentricity
    Break the
patterns of
the Universe   Itself if   you can
    (God
        doesn't mind)
Change your Breath
Change your heart beat
But
above all   Change your mind
Change the
    paths of   The planets
        But above all
        Change your think-
ing
Change melody
    Change anything
    continuous
This is dangerous   Of
course

The stars are tinny with
small alarms
Don't cry
   when you're
   supposed to
Don't react
    Don't re-anything Or
   play right
Don't
do
right
Don't do Wrong Don't do
   right
Break all the un-
   written laws
Destroy
   the song

[1991]

FROM *DÉSAMÈRE*

from AMÈRE AND DESNOS

'I dream,' says dead desert Desnos,
'When Kennedy sends the first Green Berets
Into Vietnam, 'sixty-two,
White moon stains a lake, watery flower
You're young, Amère, you say
"This view is corny"'
'It's the sixties,' Amère says, 'I want a city
Soon it's the eighties, the city's ruined
Which person am I, am I ruined?
The rents so high, animals sleeping
Outside at night, drugged and dirty'
'In the sixties, behind the war
A building grows larger,' says Desnos
'The war's a transparent movie, the building's
Windowless, a double-black domino'
'Can't humans escape each other's
Exigencies?' asks Amère
'Who doesn't serve the building? It
Makes weapons, cars, appliances, jobs
In the sixties Reagan's its ad-man
While the young try to block entrance to it
Human products are more powerful than humans are
But I'm not really like a decade'
'So you say,' says Desnos, 'but anyone
Smokes when the others smoke'
A voice from the dark says,

'The sky's full of smoke, everyone smokes'
'Nineteen eighty-four,' says Desnos,
'Oh isn't a woman smoking?
Black woman in a log cabin, fashionable
Blue dress, gold earrings and bracelet
Smoking, furious, cigarette, cigarette
Black men parade past the open door
They tell her they're headed for
Twenty thirty thousand dollar jobs
She sucks a cigarette, shouts,
'What's a salary, without a future?
Our heroisms, agonies, gains in social justice
Nothing without a planet
Reagan spends it
Squanders it sitting at desk
Like everyone else'
'Am I ruined?' Amère repeats
'If it's ruined is each person ruined?
Is there something that can't ever be ruined?'
'In a zoo,' says Desnos, 'in the nineties,
I see Przewalski's horse—
They live mostly in zoos now you know
I dream you're one, bare your teeth, try to speak
You want to say something about ruin: It's not that
Soul won't outlive you unless species does
Soul is what there is, swallows ruin
And yet, you strain to say,
I am ruined if species is ruined'
'I have such a sadness,' Amère says
'As when a husband dies, magnified
Till it replaces all that we were
There may never be anything more
Than this feeling, and then nothing'

~

'See this piece of amber?' Amère says to Brother
I give it to you for Christmas,
In nineteen eighty-three
So you can be buried with it five years later'
'It outlasts my body,' Brother says
'Outlasts the Human Era,' Desnos says,
'Civilization of rocks is what there might be'
'Yellow amber from the Baltic Sea—
This is when I'm *La Veuve*, the Widow,
Like a Tarot card,' Amère says
'I replay these times for their
Perverse richness—painful and lit with mystery
Before them I was part
Technological person
Pills but never cars, destroy own
Body, but not the world's
Are pills and cars really the same?'
Desnos says, 'The dream's of earth
Pills glide over it producing smoke
The pills eat black pills, earth's black beauties'
'Take a pill and talk to us,' Amère says to Brother
He just turns away
'*La Veuve*,' Desnos says, 'I see the label
Outside the animal cage, mute and
Sable-furred mammalian female'
'My cage was haunted,' Amère says,
'A man's voice would tell me, "Leave this room"
How leave a cage? The whole world's a cage
All that's left of the old world are beautiful voices
Voice on cage fire-escape sings a

Song that goes, "Ain't a body happy?"
Or another song, "From
The past to nowhere's where I go" '
'That's the human song,' says Desnos,
'From the past to nowhere, not even
Leaving amber, because of course
Amber leaves itself behind'
'The voice in my cage,' says Amère, 'says
'Blindness can come from nowhere and be
Accompanied by temporary insanity'"
Desnos says, 'You're condemned to *see*'
'Brother,' says Amère, 'Why are you and I
Like this . . . soldier, widow,
Why aren't we cars?'
'Because you grieve like animals,' Desnos says,
'Behaving as your species would
If it hadn't turned into cars
You're still the animals'

~

Desnos says, 'I dream I don't die
Have somehow become a soldier, after
My death—I know I've died before—
While the French cling on in Indochina
The year is nineteen fifty-four
I'm supposed to be as patriotic
As when the Germans threatened my own *quartier*
In my Nam I lift in two hands
Water to drink, but it's bloody
I find I have the capacity
To divine things through the patterns

Blood makes in water, the swirls and currents
And layers of its spreading:
France's bloody reign in Vietnam,
Its one hundred years there become
A red tide of algae in the future
Multiplying on excess carbon dioxide
What's the connection? It's in the absurd
Ductility of human response
To phantom realities, colonial empires,
Communist and technological ones
But I, Desnos, have only ever
Responded to the empire of the spiritual
Why am I here in this grief, as if
My nationality, French or human,
Has dominion over me after death?'
'What do you do next?' Amère asks
Desnos says, 'I die at Dien Bien Phu, and my
First pure death is erased
I'm condemned to return in future deserts
Dreaming the truth for others, until
A more human future is won for us'
'Is this dream the truth?' asks Amère
'Only partly,' Desnos answers, 'for
I am dead, and I am happy
I'm not French now, or an animal
With the lucidity of a jewel I trap thought
Change phantoms into figures so
You can see how they manipulate you—
I see now that saints are needed,
In the old way, to counteract leaders
To sit still, withstand
The onslaught of the phantoms

Burn to purity, turn to soul . . .
I dream someone walks towards
A flower which bears
A mane like the sun's rays
And searing dark center, a mouth
To enter, be eaten by
In which there's no Frenchness, Americanness
Human or beetle or rock
One finds a future in that mouth
By admitting that nothing is something, and
That all our contrivances are nothing . . .
The oldest truth of all'

from DESERT POEMS

I

Sphinx with a ghost-head, circle of sun lions . . .
Sphinx
White koala black turtle . . . Now push past the curtain of fibers
White biting snake long snake who is in fact the Milky Way
Push past and past, dead, no dead is different
Past and past, asleep awake, creature-face is still the
       darkness . . . a forehead hides behind a slab of light as
       if reading creation's newspaper . . . I must not be broken
       enough yet, still the white snake there too mischievous-
       faced
Something touched a corner of me, there really is an other

Fierce bird hawk or eagle all guard it are more it than I
       am, elegant dark dove turned away quiet, receding white
       barn owl eyes quite closed in the owl way
Something that is only eyes there, what has touched me?
       You who are all its corps of angels pieces of the universe's
       way of being itself, something did touch me before,
       a square black-faced window is reflective, an eye floats
       by itself in whiteness
Naked try to stand naked—there's a greenish plane of light
       upright, there's a valley amid snaking curves, I see a
       human or a guppy swimming small dark in light gel
Choirs let me in, a wall of light holds out its arms
Anyone's better than I am, please let me in
Jewel winged jewel you have a death's head
A long-legged insect covers my page hides it from me
Transparent swelling a lump in my chest I am streaming tears of
       crystalline abstraction, tears of work, the transparent
       pearl a gland or a source
My black featureless face turns, towards the left . . .
Nothing I'd known, nothing like that, overwhelming, nothing seen.
       world cracks, it isn't like that that, I don't know, the black
       sun in the web of fiery veins my human filigree, inside
       touch me into countersphere, chest cracking, spherical
       wings are there . . . that there were wings at all . . . ever . . .
       pointed ears, pterodactyls . . . please touch though the place
       in the chest . . . there's no chest . . . no, I know . . . I don't know . . .
A hole in darkness, light streams through it
Necklace of fires
Primitive saint
Something swimming underwater bumps me bumps me
Four lines of light target the dark thing

II

The sun is sinking but its black penumbra doesn't accompany it
Eye that faces right is framed by pincers not eyelashes
A man looks through a long box attached to his face
A fist is again a face a turtle-like face with aggressive nose

Turn away from them, there's my face featureless and shapeless
      like dark moss, planes of green light join me on either
      side

Streak of light encircles my forehead quickly and stays

I see black bands filling with light from the green planes, I
      see the tiniest fetus, some sort of eye in jelly, what
      does it see? Sees *my* face which is darkness spreading,
      from under peaked whiteness a snake lifts its head
      up towards up towards, we're all asking together for
      the favor of infinity, worms dance slightly, upright
      and begging, mountain opens its round mouth to ask
For an instant we're facets of a jewel angles of light but
      unconstructed merging intersecting heartless thoughtless
Something spins dances toward me a naked filament or tendril
      or stamen light-drenched with just the trace of a head
      a mere swelling at the top of its slenderness the first
      cerebrality? A flower in motion leaves a wake of lines
      behind it icicles of non-thought
Dark face of mine but face changed to white face with
      only lips
River flows towards me size of everything claws of foam in
      its advance
How big is everything . . . has suction cups on tentacles the
      length of, or I have, has a bracelet of suns on an arm

the length of . . . as length ceases as an idea the
        lizard's eye closes voice becomes a dot casting a long
        long shadow
"Dies and it's over with" snake vertebrae hovers, still
            searching for the true touch, hidden in the next fold of
            darkness? One has never been so happy, searching, waiting
Four channels meet at a basin cup of light
The bird is astonished as its wings grow longer
And around the next curve is the tree of light with its lazy
        old serpent
And around the next curve the core of us sleeps
The inside of my eyelids in shreds
There's a crystal palace a jewel covered with tissue of flesh
        or vegetable
Ghostly floats half of an apple delicate seeds and curves,
        my sex
Is the . . . center asleep or awake? Neither, non-existent as
        I am, the universe dissolves into tiny clouds lumps
        spirits or pieces of matter, the world is over, it
        never existed that way, the world is a shining bird
        flying bearing the dark sun on its neck, the world is
        half-mask animal eyes, the pearl born in no time

III

More purely, what flower speaks? Two hands hold a long stick
        contemplating enlarged words on page . . . an individual
        skull or a sphere above them
Lateral lines in air everywhere, come from the mouth of the
        flower, and hills which pour down into a tortured
        canyoned river

A white eye arises from words to look at me, I'm now a seahorse
      I see myself delicately armored and scaled stiff-eyed
      knowledgeless, swimming into central depth
A figure that might be a body, or might be geometry as you
      wish, as sphere floating near a triangular mass, looms
      ahead in a darkness—power's figure for convenience
      if seahorse is mine, I swim through it—A skate
      rises up in front of me in ecstasy
Fish all eyes four surround a circular patch
The skate is closer gauze-like overwhelming
To be sucked into the cervical rose
Sweet seahorse I'm suspended
The relation of knowing to this vast is non-existent, the
      nerves snap—floating floating, light—
      Skate has black hole for face my angel but topples
      not being the core of this ignorance—cross drifts
      casually by—a piece of a brother drifts spherical
      bubble
The images of creation ghosts drift by
We don't come from here to go back we are here
So large to be nothing in, floating pearl scum, along such a
      current through universes
Like a ghost in the world harboring world one will move through
      it, person this desert's in, flowermouth speaking in riches

[1992]

FROM *MYSTERIES OF SMALL HOUSES*

WOULD WANT TO BE IN MY WILDLIFE

hold pen improperly against 4th finger not 3rd like when I was six why won't I hold it right

if I'm even younger four I walk more solemnly walking's relatively new but talking's even more natural and I can see you really while we talk

if words are a sense in motion the universe has always had it

I'm not sounding young

though holding the pen wrong

I don't have to sound young but I couldn't say "oil well" right

erase all that it's not right. You have to erase whatever it is and erase before that and before that to be perfect

no   perfect's here from ever all along and if it doesn't say it right it's right and I am it from then now Alley House I am

and get scared till I *am* I

scareder and scareder

then calm and enter where oil of I does flow

oleanders ah touch and steps up aha oleanders oleanders and touched they make me be here in the strange scented present

up and if I enter I have truly to enter

stars weren't alive before me anyone's from the most ancient wildness

that part's blue floor that part's pink floor kitchen washroom bathroom backporch all small

it doesn't matter what happens here what matters is not to lose judiciousness which wildness has from before its befores human wildness does it isn't self-deceiving like cruelty but's unbrokenup into the parts of the bad

that's why the house is so small and I am so simple because one thing seeing and being's the one thing there is though each one's it and though each one's different both at least from the beginning socialization's what makes us the same in the made-up way.

ONE OF THE LONGEST TIMES

My brother's always in the gully
Too ugly for me down there
But in the vacant lot next to the house
I pile towels on a creosote bush in the corner
We all go in and sit
Does it smell like creosote oil and have flowers like stars

Albert Margaret and me, holding sacred things here
Sticks and rocks
Small black-scored rock is
The quantum life-story object, take it
Life's beginning and over compact in your dirty palm

We're huddled in here don't need anyone we're
Star-sent-out light that's still alive
We're still here sending out us
As stars from the first world melt
Why aren't we the same as each other
Rocks look the same I'll never be you

This rock's me from before the flood and after the fire
This rock's you and what happens to you it adds up to
This rock this time and
This time in this bush is long, long
Becky's our baby our sister and this one
Is hers from before the flood
And after the fire that comes
I am a rock in these shadows who
Am I speaking to who am I speaking

I got this me. This one's you. What's the point
It would be better if
We all died together
We put and put rocks; I have life coming (life's
Nothing but THIS minute
Something for you a brown stick for you)

This is the longest one of the longest times
It lasts after we're dead and after all people
Are dead; how do you know
Because thoughts have lasted since the first thought
'Cause I think that we're in the first thoughts still
Lasting and we last
And we last, making real selves

AS GOOD AS ANYTHING

I don't see the point of
remembering you; you're too boring,
Iowa City, Iowa,
much duller topologically than
Needles, California. I'm here
in the Rebel Motel, with
my grape-colored sweater
and maté tea, whose smoky odor's
bound up with first rooms and foods here
sex and snow. I
write about Needles
Herman and rocks, the story's called

"As Good as Anything," and in it
daft Herman—true local
of Needles—says
"Rocks is as good as anything."
I figured that out summer after
first love affair in New York:
hung out, home, at a rock shop
inspecting geodes and thunder eggs
Arsenic samples and petrified
dinosaur dung.
What can I say about Iowa City
everyone's an academic poetry
groupie, I haven't yet written a poem,
there's a bar where for 25 cents a
meal of boiled egg and tiny beer.
Really I don't know what kind of poetry—
what's the name of the make they
use here—or what kinds of
poetry live people write in the world.
Is there a right and wrong poetry, one might
still ask as I patronize,
retrospectively, the Iowa style,
characterized, as I remember,
by the assumption of desperation
boredom behind two-story houses
divorce, incomes, fields, pigs,
getting into pants, well not really
in poems, well no "well"s and all
in the costive mode
of men who—and the suicidal women—
want to be culpable for something,
settle for being mean to their wives
and writing dour stanzas. God this is bitchy

I modeled for art classes
that's rather interesting
the hypocrisy: nobody *needs*
to paint nude women
they just like to. So here I am
naked for art, which is a lot of
dumb fucks I already know,
same with poetry.
Written and judged by. Those befoibled guys
who think—you know—
the poetic moment's a pocket in
pool; where can I publish it; what can
I do to my second or third wife now.
Nothing happens in Iowa, so
can I myself change here? Yes
I can start to become contemptuous
is that good or bad, probably bad.
In New York I'd developed a philosophy
of sympathy and spiritual equality:
out the window, easily, upon
my first meeting real assholes.
"A rock's as good as anything"
there are no rocks in Iowa
shit-black soil, a tree or two,
no mountain or tall edifice,
University drabs, peeping Toms, anti-war
riots, visiting poets
treated like royalty, especially if
they fuck the locals or have a record
of fighting colorfully with their wives.
You can go to the movies once a week,
like in Needles. You can fuck
a visiting poet; you can be paraded before

a visiting poet as fuckable but not fuck.
You can write your first poems
thinking you might as well
since the most stupid people in the universe
are writing their five hundredth here.
I'm doing that now. What
difference does it make.
I like my poems. They're
as good as rocks.

CHOOSING STYLES — 1972

I thought of words breaking open in the mouth but
also as jewels
of old sexless poets, of the dead dessicated
except for those emeralds or topazes
I still get a thrill when I say, emeralds and topazes.
Who wants to say "freightage," what is the charge for that word
who wants to say "distress" and wear the black chiffon
scarf inside it
who wants to write in old long lines clearly and not be
slightly more inscrutable
askance in freakier
lines, in brilliance
outflame
blaze; flash —
Chose sometimes more for beauty or for clarity
or for some arbitrary reason — no reason I know go
against word order: firstling you

by dint of me, clean, sings up in the clerestory
of the donned doom show. Worthless filmy daughterous
contagion in the durable shell
take the horse nearest the door—
maybe that's what I really did, chose, and the other side's
hissing,
hissing.
There are these sides I'm tired of it
Float in air liaison with illicit spirit
Who cares how I write?
Okay. Pained and similar plants, now don't I have to
give? The poem will tell you its secret light-of-hand
that everyone will die before
any knows which way to write right
mouthmouthed I mean foulmouthed motherfucking turds you are
shit in the wind, frail shit blown back, because I
am onstage. Ah, frag you John. Glisten and twisted fingers
into unmouthed ruby of glum blood we'll go,
doing what with our digits—counting the gloaming light
in anyone's glass legend coursing through them
one glob two globs rounded mass of wishful self is in
these tiny red boxing glove particles, these
ultimate pieces of identity, which permeate
any poor matter's glee and grief. I forgot: My style is to
forget whence we came; the origins of
my style. I'm gnarling at you.
Moon and underworld, queen and cunt where the molten
metal flows. My style comes from death.
A jinni, a power, I don't have to care
how I write, in what manner—up-to-date *are you
kidding*? You're dead!
Menstruation covered with sand, garnets and amber.

"You're accusing me of something in these poems."
"No Ted, I'm not accusing you—can't catch your voice though."
"Through dead curtains," he says. Gives me the disgusted
   Berrigan moue, casts match aside lighting cigarette
"So what are you doing?" he says. I say, "As the giant lasagne
   on Star Trek—remember, Spock mindmelds with her
   and screams, Pain." "So this is pain?" he says.
"I suppose it is. Was. But not from you," I say.
"We don't say pain we say fucked-up," he says, "Or
   Kill the motherraper. Inside yourself . . ." (he fades)
"I can't catch your voice . . ." (I say)
". . . there's a place inside you," he says, "a poetry self, made by
                  pain but not
   violated—oh I don't say violated,
    you're not getting my dialogue right, you can't remember
                  my style."
"Would you say touched, instead?" I say.
"There's this place in us," he says, "the so-called pain can't
                  get to
   like a shelter behind those spices—coffee and sugar, spices,
   matches, cockroach doodoo on the kitchen shelf.
   But I was exhausted from being good without pills—
   went off them on Diversey you'll remember—and you were
   wearing me out. Well just a little. I took pills to
   keep from thinking, myself. Do something else don't think
   you're a poet write a poem for chrissakes, you're not
                  your thoughts;
   but I was afraid . . . you were mad at me deep down then."
"I don't think so," I say . . ."Men were a problem—I
                  see that better

in the future, but you, sometimes you were 'men'
usually not." "Then were men men?" he says, "I mean—"
"No, I'll interrupt," I say, "Someone was being those times
  why else was I unhappy." "Do you want to know," he says,
"if I loved you in 1970?" "No," I say, "I don't."
"Anything later than Chicago? But I've just got
  a minute," he says. "No that's either your business
  or something I already know," I say, "I really enjoyed the late 70's
          in New York, you know."
"You haven't wanted to talk to me since I died," he says.
"That's true," I say, "Too dangerous. But I want to say there's no
          blame here. I see your
goodness, plainly. I want to be
clear; I'm a detachment"—"As I am obviously," he says,
his voice getting fainter.

THE TROUBLE WITH YOU GIRLS

In the chair covered with shawls
I'm wearing my favorite red shirt
Maybe it's November near my birthday, sun
On my shoulder and coffee too in what cup chipped;
So, happy, open a blackbound notebook.
Ted pulls on one of his colored tee-shirts,
 "The trouble with Jackoff is . . . no the trouble with *you* is"
 (Because I'm not listening) "you're stuck in that chair"
 It's true. I sit, wait for the greatest
 Poem I'll write . . . "Just want

To drink things and write rocks off." What else?
I don't know what I'm for. To praise, he might say.
I don't think so. "You have no philosophy," he says,
"That's the one thing you need to be great."
I'd fight back, but the buzzer rings, Marion
She comes over daily, before everyone else
In her halterneck denim jumpsuit, anemic, what's
A person for. Answer me late 70's. I think it's
Partly to be with a plant, that potted begonia
What's *it* for, I try to hold it alone in my mind
Without a thought *of* it, just it, as red and green light.
Marion and I have coffee. Day's lovely before I'm
Too many thoughts, I've become content this year;
In October, without looking down I climbed out
On the fire-escape, cleaned my window.
I see you through me now, not just me, I think.
"The trouble with you girls . . . you think it's all
Sunshine and coffee. It's money, lots of it
Everything's money. My ass is money, yours too
Even if your asses aren't as ugly as mine . . . Got any
Money for cigarettes, Marion?" Marion and I
Cleaned this apartment, when I first took it and
It was so small, before everyone came in.
"How about a little extra, for a pepsi, and the paper?
How about some doughnuts for us all?"

HEMATITE HEIRLOOM LIVES ON
(MAYBE DECEMBER 1980)

I saw him bleeding but I thought all blood was a dream.
Certainly I had none

I may be making erotic art near the red telephone
that connects Ted to his mother dying of cancer
I cut out photos of nude women and place them on food signs
Chicken Pot Pie. Why—because I want to save
the women in the photos, so make them humor-filled or
truly connected to the fountainhead of sex as I imagine it.
She holds the most amethyst grapes to her breasts
I've cut out her face it's off howling in space
sex is for god because it's a furious
violent brightness so I make a straw fetish
with a red tonguelike clitoris to protect me . . .
from literature and from my dear friends. The women don't
approve the men do I ignore them but this is minor I want
to be there to describe the harmony between the fact
that I make these collages and write "Waltzing Matilda"
that and the red phone to Peg. That and all the speeches
            which must be made
by Ted in the other room waiting for bad news for years.

Oh kids life is feelings like these it's the talk of it
            drawing
the others outside to our house: the news is throughout us
the mondial flames of hell, the funniness, we are
            unironized.

Yet I keep not being able to be there. From now it's because I'm
still hurt. As sweet as pain to a saint is the door

to the actuality of those events.
Will the door open. Not unless I
give up my fear of my anger. I'm just a girl from the desert
am I. I'm still so angry at people I know, I can't go in.
How many of you sexist feminists think I'm only part of him
           part of him?

You, I remember you then.
You said goodbye to me, outside on
the streetcorner, two years later, because I was "part of him"
and you were making war with him—though I
wasn't to take it personally. You were too much trouble anyway
you always had to be adored. You made me say
I love you; I lied; I've adored no person.
Love isn't your present, you can't ever have mine I
don't *own* a love; saying goodbye now, then

the pizza shop there (from where I once saw, in subzero
           weather
at night, a naked man barefoot streak by)
the tawdry bar's over there; I want to win this poem, don't I
a poem can't be won by a person, I can't come out of this one
clean I'm too mean; though there's
the cleaners there, and even the sneakers store, four
           corners crossroads

I'm telling the truth. I'm going to tell it
anyone's: that never being what anyone thought
I never cared what anyone thought
as long as I could go home, and resume my work—am I
back in the door? Oh Ted's here, kids asleep, dark window dreams
oh airshaft dark window I often mistake for
the panelike sails of a clipper ship taking us home.

MID-80'S

I'm not on a mission
I'm not local
I have never been so, though I'm
local to my condition of being a widow
Obviously I'm more serious than these times

Keep on being my times
Why am I wearing these women's clothes
Earrings with magic stones
to ward off the weight of my feelings
to adorn the vacancy of the times

I am a secret when everyone else seems
some sort of pastel whore
selling it blandly for not having sex
pussy and prick for no sex
offered up without a smell to an age of making it

I'm not my life now or yours
blackberries wears a blackberry dress
because I'm a widow wear a black lace mask
Is there a present? never
The 80's is the weakest, the least existent ever

Strike a spark off a pinhead
Trying to get lost in it being bigger than it
the so-called present one sings an
adulterous song   This music is pure, pure
But secret

The poor say that in their desperation
they invent a sensuous music
Those with money can take it away
Can take music and sex away?
By making it records and porn: suppress our insides

There's no self in the 80's don't you know
Say there is none and be selfish
Empty the glass of sexuality   Fill it with
Madonna's piss
analyze it thoroughly write a book

I behave badly, to capture sex
My love is to conceal myself
How much am I my life?
It feels as if others have stolen
my life, my old music, my culture—

even my alcohol's been stolen
In place of a life they have images
When a whole country a world becomes
moronic, that must be willful
It isn't that easy to be stupid, is it,

why *am* I wearing these clothes?
waiting to be colors, love, that glow
from the shock of physical contact
radical contact, a scarlet cloth torn
beneath a glass dome where it snows

Inside a time are its lies
There seems nothing else in the 80's
No one did anything but lie for years
Not just the pols, the artists the poets
concealing their bodies and voices —

there's hardly a prosody now
I was dead I was stupid that way
didn't see the advance of such organisms
They took over by denying everything as rich as
fucking or grieving or singing

Why don't I have a kinder voice
to send into the helpless past?
Because it's not helpless, it's still going wrong
the love there's concealed not concealing
Who took our lives and gave them

to industry of every kind of image
make and wear them, see and listen
teach and learn them — they're us
pieces of appropriated authority
legitimize my crumb so I can sell

I've always wanted the whole love that is,
a poetry not in pieces:
love conceal nothing, and hate?
Though I loved in it I hate that age
I don't want to engage in more politesse with it

I'm not on a mission, I'm not local
Poetry's global, everyone
participates in the same poem
Into it we project our demons
ourselves torn out of us in dangerous clothes—

make an age like the 80's worldwide
I'm still watching, in '94
the men of careers proliferate, though
in the 80's I'm in shadow
fascinated by the shadow's silkiness

by the secrecy of my mutation
I feel as if I'm becoming something I
already should have been
eroticized, spiritualized
by tragedy, surviving in darkness

Most people's currency is such survival
Tragedy's the name of some dirt
it's rich, it purges and redeems
but some people never change and they're always
in charge of suppressions and lies

SEPT 17/AUG 29, '88

We get out of the car and I think
I see him, he waves, coming from a woods.
Looks like our dad, shape of head and current
slenderness, moustache; is wearing dark glasses.
Hugs. There's only going to be gladness
at seeing each other. We go into
lobby of rehab, Margaret and I get
visitors' tags, girl asks if we're twins.
Al has to give up our birthday presents for him.
He says he can't stand to be inside; we climb a hill
and sit down on a bench. Occasional
interchanges with other patients who
walk or jog past. Mostly we talk about
Vietnam, some about our family.
In the afternoon (we've left and come back
with Fred) we sit in a meadow, same
subject matter, some of the same stories. I'll
fuse them. In the morning he was
shaky but not in the afternoon.

"I come back up here all the time. They know where
to find me. (Even if I'm not supposed
to be here, so it's okay.) It's just like Nam
but we'd hear crickets all night there, I hated them.
The nights were terrible. Every night.
I never wanted it to be night just day."
The tank story. He's in Quang Tri. Usually
he's the gunner but today for an unremembered reason
the driver. There's something called "white
phosphorus" which he's so scared of that
he always fires it off first to get rid of it.

248   [from *Mysteries of Small Houses*]

Today's gunner doesn't. What happens is
a shell drops into the small top opening
of the compartment where the gunners are.
Albert hears their screams and knows
everyone is frying from white phosphorus;
he goes for the escape hatch on the bottom, but
it won't open, for long long seconds.
Finally he gets out, everyone else is dead of
course. This is the subject of his most long-
standing nightmare, and first point of guilt,
this escape. "I thought I'd be safe in a tank,
but after that I didn't want to get in one again."
We ask him how he became a sniper. "They
came around asking for volunteers. They said
you're a volunteer and *you're* a volunteer,
I was a good shot, good with guns, they thought
I was good. I wanted to be outside. So they sent us
down to sniper school." The snipers would go in
ahead, take a village, then others would follow.
Snipers had to kill civilians and "it started
to seem like murder. I must have killed 49
or 50 civilians. You see a mamasan with a baby,
you shoot first and ask questions later, she
might be carrying explosives. But they wouldn't
count the civilians in their body count.
They only wanted the NVA. They'd ask if
you got any but wouldn't write it down."
Al witnessed executions by the Phoenix Program.
"They'd come in after we took a village. They had
a list of people to kill. They'd pull up their
hair and shoot them in the head. They'd put down
say, the mayor of a village that was sympathetic to
the Communists, but you could also bribe them
to kill someone in your business you disliked."

The Phoenix Program was CIA-affiliated. (Later
in Needles Dicky Roten confirms that Albert was
in the LRR and a lot of what he did was top secret:
he has a double record, one with blanks.)
Al thinks that at a certain point he was supposed
to die because he knew too much, about the killing of
civilians, Operation Phoenix, and so on.
Members of his sniper unit stopped ever coming back
from missions—everything everyone was sent on
was incredibly dangerous. "Then we went into Laos.
The fighting *never* stopped. The Vietnamese Army
was supposed to show up, but they never did.
I got left back with 150 men. If you were left back
it was pretty much assumed you would die. Finally,
everyone was dead except for me and this other guy.
We decided there wasn't any sense in staying
since everyone else was dead. We went back to Quang Tri."
It took about seven days. Around 30 miles walking involved.
They caught fish and ate them raw. He didn't
know the guy he was with and never saw him again.
"When I got back they were getting ready to send out
an MIA to Mom and Dad. They sent me *instantly*
into North Vietnam. Then I *knew* they wanted to
be rid of me." I think this is when
Albert Trujillo was killed. Albert Trujillo was
Albert's best friend in Vietnam, he was from New Mexico.
He and Albert had sworn to keep each other alive.
N.B. Our Dad, also named Albert Notley, had had
a best friend named Albert Trujillo, in Prescott, when
he was Albert's age. But Al's friend Albert was killed
because their sergeant was too slow and scared to cover him.
He let it happen out of fear. Albert held a gun then
to the sergeant's head and told him, if you say one word.
Albert brought the body bag back. The last thing

he remembers from North Vietnam is shooting in a circle
all around himself. He got picked up by a chopper,
went back to Quang Tri but it had fallen. Makes his way
down to the South and is eventually shipped home.

I love my brother so much this visiting day, but wonder
if he doesn't know too much to live. He's been
remembering and remembering—the therapists want him
to remember even more, but he doesn't want to, he wants
to go home and see his kids. I wonder how he can
have a future. I want to be able to sit around some
kitchen table with him but can't picture that.
I wonder if he could be the way he was—happier and
lighter—before he started remembering, but
I don't think so. He emanates too much knowledge, power;
his self is huge, bigger than any I've ever witnessed.
His boundaries are too painful and too small:
they keep him where he remembers, they keep his
knowledge concentrated, personal. He must get free of
this self now, but I don't know how he will;
yet escape's fated, written already (we all know it and
don't know it).

1992

It's dark down the rue Caulaincourt
where I don't want to be in a red silk shirt
when we first ate at Au Pierre de la Butte
five years ago this wasn't my city

it was us not unmoored I'm walking with you
it's raining we're wet down the hill down some steps

towards the bridge over Montmartre Cemetery
over history dead great men unlike me
I've always wanted to be a
dead great man though not exactly dead but
I'll never make it
partly because not a man
partly because this is no world for greats
anyone's buried under dross of so many
made prominent by technology's pomp
of produce its certifying empire
I have a dream of staying at that Hotel Ibis
I want to lie in its sterile Americanized arms

what was I, fear to be no one here
you aren't you and I'm not I
but that's why I came here to see how I'd change—
implies that "I" sees and registers the change, unchanged—
haven't youth now, with which to conquer a few
have only a tradition in poetry
bound up in me which who wants in a world
where all art's patently successful
ratified by treaty packaged by conglomerate celebrated
by comment and dropped to consider real business:

prizes, photos, advances, GATT Business English the MLA
the Booker Prize Oxford Cambridge the New York Publishing
Houses Pulitzer MacArthur the Dorothea Tanning Award
administered by the Academy of American Poets the Penguin
Poets the Bloodaxe Poets the New Direction Poets NAFTA the new
CIA the Market the Stock Exchange

empty
as I am except for my self who observes me
both lovingly and detachedly, and my tradition:
I'll make a poem for you which holds locked up a living voice—
the key's on your own tongue—
I'll teach you some things about Berrigan Padgett
Kyger Thomas Oliver Riley or how to
win a poetry prize given out by yourself
but that's not the ending it's walking
in a wet Parisian dark that's
utilizable, every inch, even used up

LADY POVERTY

Sings in the gullies
To all you go without is added more as the years
Youth's face health certain friends then more and
so to get poorer
life's arrow—tapers thinner sharper

She always sang there to purify
not the desert always pure
but me of my corrupt furor
So losing more further along in this dream of
firstrate firmament fireworks—
consigned to roam above brown dirt occasional
maxilla, and be shaped badly—
twisted internally: join her truly

She's I

She should be

the shape of a life is impoverishment—what
can that mean
except that loss is both beauty and knowledge—
has no face no eyes for
seasons of future delivery—rake the dirt
like Mrs. Miller used to
down at the corner had a desert yard and raked her dirt.

Beginning in poverty as a baby there is nothing
for one but another's food and warmth
should there ever be more
than a sort of leaning against and trust a food for
another from out of one—that would be
poverty—we're taught not to count on
anyone, to be rich,
youthful, empowered
but now I seem to know that the name of a self is poverty
that the pronoun I means such and that starting so
poorly, I can live

[1995]

CIRCORPSE

there's really only one, but there's hardly any interest
if there aren't two or more:
That's why I keep on letting Hardwood detect me.

———————————

No one cares if the world is a big fat America
as long as we've got our windows windows windows.
(Change immediate past)

Suddenly everyone says
they care and they have been caring, that would be an example
of changing the past in order to go forward
"Well that wasn't what I did because I didn't have a motive yet.
I was waiting for disaster itself."
(Who's speaking?)

"I wanted to get lost inside I would die, going in through wind—
so imagined have I become
that I will never die
in fact have never been . . ."
(Who's speaking?)

———————————

Trying to find or be a dark woman. the soul I am.

Caves now enter along thin stream through cracked rock
a waterfall and flowers, smell of moist rock turn
down into caverns (like Mitchell's Caverns   lost secrets of
        the Chemahuevi)

a ranger/guide is with us . . .

"Many branches of the caves
  are beyond both dogooders and smartasses," he says,
"haunted therefore by Dante-like creeps.
  If you want to find a woman here she isn't 'good' either."

——————————————

Another bomb exploded in Paris a few days ago,
left in a trashcan at the Arc de Triomphe
eighteen people including some little kids injured.
This is probably a crime motivated by religion
The suspect group has especially targeted women, in Algeria . . .
as dispensible commodity prone to be filthy
dark as a dudgeon (I wrote that last word by accident.)

So there was a bomb scare yesterday at Métro Cadet
someone left a blank gray package on our train
we were ordered off panicking.
What does that have to do
with a big fat America?
Plenty.

——————————————

The entrance to the caves
is pinpointed by graph lines this morning
when I enter it's spooky dark.
The ranger's here again

Don't misunderstand good, he says,
You would, being disinterestedly good, transcend it.
Where's old Hardwood now, that stick . . .
See via such banality as a detective/actor? No
The figure Dante *could* absorb old Hardwood
But no you're not worthy of such an asshole as Dante
for your confidant or guide or foil,
people might get offended . . .
presumption, pre-emption.
Dante's gonna get lost. I know I'll choose
Hardwood/Mitch-ham.

———————————————

Priority to some creatures?
As I outfoxed some others

I'm sitting on the same old flower sheet
in my same old leopard-spotted lounge-dress;
having dreamed last night that Michael J. Fox
chose to wear his animal suit, in a musical theatrical production
on top of buildings in New York City
where many full bins were—I suppose they were my "beens."

———————————————

Am I seriously Soul?

When time goes away I don't care about
me (him or me)
The phone rang; we're meeting at 1:30.
What do I use my personality for? Humor was there from the beginning . . . And
the behavior of certain elementary particles seems rather humor-filled;
certainly unpredictable. There are equations that 'cover' this unpredictability.
The relation of I, soul, to particle: I think I am its field of familiar
the non-niggling corpus
playing, like a photon, myself: watch me I'll behave another way from usual.
Deeper, under the fox costume,
I'm more than I say in time
but time's less exact than I am.
Want to be with just about anyone who'll let me talk too.
Hardwood yaps at me
"How can you catch the bad guys if you like them?"
I say, "I only want to yell
at them."

————————————

I've found a dark woman, a chicana
she's just let another man enter
the ancient, former Needles Auto Supply
after attention, flirtation, on her part. She sees that I'm jealous—
of those attentions or of her?
Was he my man? this is complicated;
'We'll get you some,' she seems to say, and hugs me
and her friend, a small black girl braids sticking out, hugs me
then I'm placed on the belly of a fat sexless man
lying on his back on the ground, and bounced up and down.

————————————

She speaks but I know she is me:
mouths words—what are they—and smiles:
"Am I ready to be different now, in a world of bloody souls?"
Am I ready for the world of you, slippery
you whom I may never understand

HELP ME CORPUS SAGRADA

to be as tough as mean as Akhmatova
as durable as her last tooth.
In my dream, an old crone
she's finally gassed to death by a dentist
who wants to extract her one huge
tooth and analyze it.

———————————————

Last night a Martiniquaise, tall woman a "danseuse"
is barred from the Polly Magoo.
She's always paid her bills she says so she obviously hasn't
she never picks up men, for the past ten years has masturbated
that can't be true either
and she's exultant.

———————————————

Hardwood is dying to tell me his life story
says he's tough too.

———————————————

Enter the caves to find out what's suppressed
is that a specious project more E's.

This angel's wings are limp ribbons
her body floats circorpse, the surrounding natural love
'Gone to the grave door, you stupid dress
the grave door of the future.'
Spoken by her or Hardwood?

My insolent features, young, long suppressed
swim in the face of my future concern
for a fucked-up world: could only be a jerk when young.

Could I once have lived to be so wrong? Yes.

I must be pretending to be someone:
have you all been making me pretend
along my whole life of E   A-lice Elizabeth

Go to the grave door, dress
and pretend that the future will be more, more of this . . . procrastination
a woman walks to a gravestone covered
with E's. Evolution Forever, it says
she opens a door

and enter there's light down here
and more descent of course.

———————————

I don't want to be like.
My old hair floods you with cars in it lice,
kneel down and listen to the ground:

"We will be in the new deluge,
we the wake of the former flood.
And there is an island in Sumer
where the inhabitants are descended from people
from before the flood."

———————————

The sentence:

You will always be in others arms
                                        and
the horror of society
                        is its friendship, most certainly
In order to help or love you must be like.

Flies' asses. What's that French expression?
A fucker of flies up the ass: a stickler for detail.

———————————

Hardwood first saw the light
in a birth canal in the Southwest
flies swarmed
so he could grow up to be like details.

I still like him anyway
I have to

And Lady, I have to like you too.

———————————

Child-abandoning home-wrecker Anna A
Forgot about her along the way.

And so left holding the fishbowl?
that contains the tiny ones, the usual the men
gesticulating in the mid-night of de-struction.
Their vicious fleas bite my hand and cause blood to flow
purple and foamy
but I'm still glad to be alive
not dead like Anna,
though some of the dentist's gas almost reached me.

———————————————

These lacunae are most great, most restful.

Do I really want to fill them in with suppressions?

———————————————

The Choros of the future howls quietly.

———————————————

"I'd see her number if you'd see her really,"
Inspector Hardwood says
(is that the dark woman I am)

THE ISLANDERS REMEMBER THAT
THERE ARE NO WOMEN AND NO MEN

in the antediluvian island
in the primordial swamp
Hardwood was already my friend

The porcelain basin of memory is black
I spit down it brushing my feral tooth.

———————————

'A double? oh really badly'

I have a
double a self I can't stand

I was discovered by primordial Columbus
and became his land?
Cliché says Hardwood.

———————————

Wanting the real
and as a dream is a dream
I try to remember something:
the trees at Blythe
at night, going home
inside the steel cab of a pickup,
road lined with athol trees. salty, drab.
Home gone to feels empty
a little shakily and that's
more like a dream than a memory.

No I want real and dreamed to be fused into the real
rip off this shroud of division of my poem from my life.

I am a reflex an E for effort
(what I can't stand)—

equal to a shroudperson.

Eating eels near the Loire I learn to slither
not between poles but being the one pole the river.

Now that I've visited an *étang*
I always had visited one—
I knew these swamps when the stars.
An island of Sumer, no dead other
dark woman or enemy-maker.

Become
this:

I haven't known such
efflorescence   like the gold dust and red laughing tree
I was trying to remember before
what is exact here an E for example
or my tooth chattering, almost, with excitement

because first it happens
and then you make it your life,
                                        this,
that when we were at the swamp on Sunday
it wasn't the swamp till yesterday
so I go back sometime before the swamp
to make the swamp happen more exactly,
to a night of stars after eels were eaten
out of such a night, with the town stretched out
a flotilla with trees and above, the old castle
out of that modern and crumbling past
create something older and more original
and so in this one windy swamp (the next day)
become, and in company, saltier, tangier
a taste from the future of my union
when I'll have been here.

———————————

ugly Paris

———————————

Hardshroud I mean Hardwood
says of course the city is my shroud,
if you unwrap it Babylon ugly
Ninevah, Ur ugly
it's so ugly to be here
with salt on my tongue, of dying into
a worse future I'm leaving
that you can't change.

———————————

I've been there now a very sharp experience
on an island of Sumer where I had no impatience with Hardwood
that frog don't jump
don't jump away.

Our opposable thumbs will be opposable shrouds
and one will then pretend it's been made equal
to the other, the left to the right

This poem is a lefthand path

It's about me, exactly

I'm diminished by anyone's refusal to be equal.

So tied up and gagged, still, I'm a view of a body on the floor
feet first so you can see that I'm wearing jeans.

How will I know when I'm untied
(Déjà vu, saying that)

RED FISH

but I've changed something . . .

———————————————

What's changed,
I've cleaned some rooms. Ugh in one

dream a woman finds a large
banana-like turd with a slick skin.
As I flush it it speaks in a high-
pitched male voice, vindictively,
"You won't have no Momma!"

———————————————

In order for there to be   one fixed quality
another quality must   remain fluid
between its   two   possibilities
in these   electron box   experiments.

I am fixed though not a quality when nothing else is fixed.

———————————————

Caves. Going down to beautiful words descending to rosettes
I want to follow
a delightful path.
Inside this petalled swamp or Sumer
a lotus's wedge perforated
through which are emitted perfections of transient sensations . . .
scents, tastes, flourishes on warm temperatures—
everything I've ever wanted.

I show the red blossom to others
but after August the island of summer we change
we live in Europe where
all now work as hard as Americans.

———————————————

The French call
homelessness, unemployment *'l'exclusion.'*

———————————

Who do you exclude he says

and I was just thinking 'It's better to let her squirm first.'

Where are those heights?

Dante has turned
his familiar ass to me that peculiar sun

and yet I feel clean.

———————————

Oh yes some arts are much higher

At the top of my waterfall I calmly let go
pronounceable E torrent

I'll show you, Dante Hardone! . . .

and show you the more usual misery, of which you said nothing.

———————————

Dante and Hardon I mean Hardwood
are different except for occasionally,
randomly, in the hard and soft electron box
of these times' preoccupations.

―――――――――――

Inside this arcade of Parisian India
there is first a barefoot alcoholic
filth on feet, and the bottle, green I think.
People call us to eat here but, actually,
it's too expensive . . .
(not a dream). So many men with dirty feet
try to sleep on the métro, try to sleep through
              their own smell.
That scent that temperature, August
inside, that I can appreciate I think
if I can only be I. So much I wouldn't 'mind';
to mind such smells is to think in bonds.

―――――――――――

This story without bandages
will take place, my left hand
is unwrapped.

Hardwood wants to know
can a turd be a mother
Not if it's a man, I say.
That turd lied when he implied
he was my Momma.
The Turd Man, Hardwood says, not me or Dante
Of course not, I say, reassuringly.

―――――――――――

Down in the gentle caves
sit on sand a river's near and air from the outside.

Who is Hardwood has willed me this far,
sometimes he's soft because   I am now dark.

The lines on the river form words only the river can read
this is the I the Loire prehistoric
I let my arms get dark as I slept while I worked
carrying scum from tree-site to sandbar
depositing it in banks for inspection and approval.

I is for *ire* to go; remaining stable that way
so far,
soft, so far; Hardwood floats, happy scum

ENUMA ELISH

caves.
Is there a woman painted on the wall?
by a man his stylization . . .
'I can't like it'
let wind blow more words in, drift of a stone bed.

———————————

I saw *your* people, mine
seemed less well-defined
yours all dressed in the same rags
but no not mine.

———————————

Maybe even before the flood
in the backwards city   cubist
her dark face becomes blocks and chunks
she is being formed from a description
or possibility of human making.

———————————————

I saw Mitch-ham old and drunk, formed of his cubes for my eye.
When I wasn't supposed to be looking he
dissolved into a puddle of mirror mercury.

———————————————

The high sheriff of anyone is choice.
Will you choose cubes or not

I don't want a choice at all I want fundament

stop thinking
float script E's so pretty
enuma elish

riding the first flood itself, of bitter chaotic water
(and what a tangy aftertaste)

not the second flood god-sent but the first flood a god itself.

———————————————

It's always Mitch-ham himself
down in these caves.
A sort of light says the words,

'you are not   choice,' or is it
'chair.' The chair you sit in an
illusion that a person can matter.
No person matters
unless humans choose a mattering style
so we choose it in various ways all over creation . . .
but, before
I didn't
choose or *matter*, nothing was so *important*.
One wasn't so urgently ready
to excel or kill or write—
was one just bored?

Is this the same old origination shit myth and apple?
'I am origi' a voice says to me
in a real dream
'She saw a voice; she saved her; sea of faces.'

——————————————

Enuma elish la nabu shamamu . . .
the caesura comes after *elish*.
A-lice Elishabeth Caesar.
'When there was no heaven, no earth, no height, no depth, no name . . .'
wasn't I there partaking how lovely with you.

——————————————

Underground river is what
chaos, Tiamat, becomes.
I follow her stream through caves
sit down beside a pool.

My reflection is
'ashes' I want to say—why?
For I see I forthright and youthful.

––––––––––––––––––––

E's and A's skim across the water ashes
letters we've never needed?
spelling words like 'heart' and 'bear' (endure)—
or 'textual' 'intellect'—
Asking me to put up with it.
I must accept others' superpositions
Well I don't.

––––––––––––––––––––

face form feral familiar flush

––––––––––––––––––––

Mitch Hardapple, you who are my
will, take my hand . . .

letters and words circling in a wind

An E has fallen on my cheek like an insect.

––––––––––––––––––––

A you who isn't Mitch or "real."
You are watching me? Who are you?
This is that crystalline

substance or spirit—I mean I feel it substantially
within and without
is it an I or a You?
Overmore.

(The vowels are different in her or his
language, here
in France—
this substance the same.)

There is
what knows me
what is it

[*1996*]

AMID THESE WORDS I CAN KNOW

canyon and spirit mountains peaceful spring with springs; not paying attention to
glyphs. there are rabbits the springs are damp circles on the sand among greener
bushes sunlight a lovely tone what can i do with it one says. musnt. try to know
amid words which are deep and alive large as dolmens glyphs whose lines cut deeply
into the past which is not a gone thing linear but a depth and a returning power
also. know. in a clearing what i'm doing. not at all walking through my life as i often
thing think but standing in place where i am been will be not using words not making
them not being them but being among them as they are nature. past may be a gracious
door always open skylike but in place a, wind in place or as a massive invisible process
is both carven and calmly fluid the sky moves. i never move. chunk rock but not ice
will never weep, when i cry its to break open to. you will not know if you dont suffer,
why, a closed system cannot know but a knowing sky can be a mountain a knowing all
can be carved as well and the words, the words part of all are like these.

use me suddenly i might say, and the canyon of my youth goes mosaic, i'm in the
basilica by rights. walk towards that mosaic, as far as the spirit mountains,
flickering light, across the glass cubes of. precious stones have been used in places, the
mountains themselves are partly made of.
agate. jasper. quartz.

and you have disliked me last night in a dark hall. meaningless or not? if
i am a thing and you are, the forces between us those emotions are the small
winds of the universe lines or forces between things but undiagrammable and

being an aberration of the lines of like or a part of. no, you have disliked me disrupted
me last night in a dark hall, is abstract and whats real is, that i am not a thing and so

not dislikeable and cannot dislike on the real plane. where the glyphs are, and
the dolmens, left to tell, of what is permanent, messages of, from the enduring
"feelings," such as existence itself.

go on a little faster now in the wind the blank blue and theres a rabbit will he shoot it
so we can eat it tonight jack rabbit cotton tail eat cotton tail. all these rocks
pebbles in the mosaic from the past when i was a child one april in grapevine canyon.

lines of motion and emotion telepathies and paths all intertwined like
grapevines with leaves of and the purple globes of, the
telepathic the sending of all the messages all the thoughts ever and going on all in
those little lines scattered towards and blown away ever everywhere everything ever
thought at all blown about

in the canyon the glyphs
are paradise as preserved in the mind thats why theres the past.
i mean why theres no past

PARABLE OF CHRISTIAN

underground she killed her and a man named christian sang
the song 'let me tell you about my friends'. the dark which means
soulful, woman, stabbed and stabbed the seamstress
then stabbed into the wall of the cave
bits of blood and tissue
from her victims remains, let me tell you about my friends
musnt try to sew pieces together reconsis reconstitute us from this em mess or she will
cut you to bits again
i havent been broken enough perhaps died enough to find out what
is it me, are they both me

to break more in order to find whole go bits to the expanse in the largest room
what is a mind, my crafted repository is this craft let me tell you about my friends my
pieces, cant find the point of
fracture yet i broke yesterday didnt i
rip out from me the old wall and replace with, replace with what lights up, beggar
that is the wall of beggar for truth in rags like the head of the bird skull like the head with
tissue in tatters the outwardly
disgusting church of the sacrosanct regions of my, my own, break me
this isnt the body but just me is juster strict and straight light up
the future i am already broken into pieces stabbed by
let me tell you about my friends, sings the youth named christian
all those youths, my guide a woman now man has been tornt tortured and bound
well i think shes dead
oh tell me again my friend to accept my murderess because shes a friend too
and you do you always do what ethic is this is it christian, to stab another to bits so she
can forgive you and so and so
so nothing can be accomplished except forgiveness and compassion
stupid. you are killing me over the success of the cloth i've sewn will sew in the past
you have cut me to bits because i was reconstituting all of our pieces into a whole cloth
and you thought it would be my success not ours, let me tell you about
bits of blood and tissue by knifepoint into the earthen wall in an obscure somewhat
lower room of the church i'm in pieces again who am i i am thus everywhere pieces of
organic rejuvenation what and who though who can i be distributed seed and in this
worlds thought, destroyed
destroying the body surely destroys, to raze the body is to raze the church
of the mind, you can   get   me   anyone could   surely
seam stress seam stress   which lettuces will you buy, small or large surely only
large ones count surely only the large large anything counts count the money youve been
paid for this assassination
ethics no ethic do you have a have a snakely mixed with
old skin old murders and deaths of old friends
breaking again, the only poetry is live snakes snakes who might bite you
who will get the poetry prize for the poem called crown of gold, no snakelike

all the pieces of me a panel of that mosaic stylized tatters garnet and jet the pieces
ask you pie so, pie goes with bloody and what will come of but nothing does. asks me
to enter her story again wont stab me if i enter her story, wont destroy me if i enter
your story, all, tell me about my, thats what a story is
too susceptible to, that covers everything that goes wrong
i keep being me looking at you, was too susceptible too open
she is speaking in my dreams again smugness
oh not now do you know what youre no and bestride wind in pieces and ride lake and
float upon ocean. whistle in marshes nothing
chthonic cells seeping down, blood fertilizing, but where am i
who am i,
smeared anniversary drunk then your friends will accept, they love the drunk one
they always did thats society for you, not the truth o plotin and only you unacceptable
understand understand is it me
her wholeness is here and not here, face blown, on the wind of no speech only
thought, torn in pieces to keep change away keep radical change and the charge of the
light and the good from us
come receiving affection from drunks and also people with wallets, receive
accomodation from titles, receive rings receive estates descriptions of grandeur as if
they were you, all these are yours, if you will accept to be pieces pieces if not we will
hack you to bits
eat eat this bloated aniam animal jointed its yours too, and play with whatever among
the myriad images here they are certainly yours, you are the friend so eat with us eat
us, come to work for the rain and the wind which scatteres the worlds goods
everywhere this is not real to look to reconstitute what never was why you were
never whole
i couldnt find my dreams last night they sank into black water again and maybe i
dont need them anymore theyre just here all around my walls my head myself and
there is no con or unconscious in here because that would be pieces but i must
reconstit how
do you sew them no i no, i must see them whole
wipe my airy blood on my airy cheek from the mess, let me tell you about
your friends,

ever asking me to accept the other the broken the holding back wing

where is my check this and must you and say saying this reconstituted objects will

attack i remember her drunken ethic and sex is so is so mine. i will love you if you say

that its all mine, i'll give you worl my love if you give you to me give praise to me i'll

give and give if youll just give me you, if youll say its me, say its all me

these are my pieces, and their faces stretched distorted melting and coming closer and

closer asking for praise such a drug praise has no essence who did i love

then the parts they tore out of me probably the bits of me you took you took them you

are using me for your purposes which have no essence

threw away your essence gone on the wind there when you stabbed and had no

essence but that of a drunk an ever bloated and criticizing while drinking from it again

critted its wars and drank its products ever prey ah who the black and unessential b

wind is for you it makes your words sound everywhere in nonessence you are

winning within the stale realm of that wind within the boxworld of that air oh you win

you win

coming to call i'm calling sew me back together instantly i'm calling put me back

together and sew my jeweled and past my jeweled bits back insert them in the wall not

stabbed jaggedly but in deliberate design to catch the light

she stabbed my bits into the wall to make a grisly mosaic, hated me because

hated because i could sew, hated me because, i had been praised and loved s needed it

more than i did had had less and needed it more they always say that that i have more

just being mysel and not not so in the real the essential there is no such but

she stabbed and stabbed to make this story, because i could sew but now i can never

sew myself together can never thought because i thought i could do all myself would

do to me what i could never, who will gather up my pieces

lost the church in all these so piece blood and loo loss i cant see its structure anymo

is there but loss first in fear in fear and loss in acceptance and in convivi v

conviviality and all yours, loss in group wish a los in love if you love them youll

lose you not als always well it isnt always well to love there is a

calling me up to ask if i loved her so must say yes but thats just saying thats just a lie a

stabbed me because i

and the piecemeal of society little stores and actions dont you lov it no i dont i dont

and asked and asked me to be eaten, and asked for effacement selfeffacement, so she

could gorge who is she a double a hawk a bad wing a torn self a troub and asked more
and more and always ask more for and for the good our society

you must act as if all this is nothing do you understan

how many pieces can i be i wonder how many am i tonight am i all of the raining
down for example or the plastic in the trees how many am i that make you happy
how many do you want me to be

the wings are both torn its so still the win who won then you won on this wall how
could i win against all this is the real war the war of ever the war of compulsory
everything i see it everywher

scattered how can i how can i say this why is this is it true what are you why saying
this this the you part of me cries out why is it lies why so lies and why and why accuse
let me tell you and who are you let me tell you and we who love you let me tell you
and love and love

lov tender night ma ma open the fac remains that she stabbed stabs the seamstress
repeatedly

MOSES AND THE BURNING BUSH

youve got to serve and so but is it really cause and effect is it really guilt we are in the
flames of the icons of mt sinai st catherine is it really gold or flames mose or old
workman ship walking down the rue st dominique its really russia everythings on
russian orthodox fire but not of the burning bush its pages in a store and the next store
commercial wall street catches thats how fast paper catches on fire so pass through the
hotel blocking the street too stylized flames are everywhere i open doors and hurry

through and out of the conflagration tell the journalists thats real smoke its not an
epiphany its danger its cause and effect the hotels on a hie height

catch a another kind of fire take off your shoes its holy ground gilt is it cause and the
bush is a desert tree not lush on a bole thin enough for the icon which swells from the

wall and moses is not he its me i'm on fire of not talking to god its another kind just being here and managing to know it do you know theres no cause theres no effect inside this flame i'm which is another kind of thing where it didnt happen nothings happening and no ones doing though they think they are but inside these flames all

their actions are burnt burnt up

did someone die again child almost but burning as usual walk up the staircase to the fantastic height of the hotel and others try to pull you down in cartoonlike motives invented to explain invention our invention of human cause and effect we are causing each other to be more enchained in the infantry infirmary the all of people hugely numbered together making a hell to carry on money in of fire apple garden steps the hotel the conflagration everything cach catches when its star when it starts

then so soon everything and everyone you know is on fire with desire or more or most of our definitions

so dont but so gold its so dont but its gold we're making it everywhere someone old and young has died in the flames of why so what so click cliche youre on its your turn your death your guilt your golden apple of effect through large room with flames of st catherines in the desert of monks theres no cause and no effect just gold of no memory i cant remember go round and go on beauty stable what do people have or have to do you have to i mean i do and staple it all together so theyll know i did that

and pay me some flame and no stand here on fire its enough inside the flames there are no demons that was our lengthy of thousands of time frames millions of time frame that we have invented a joke its a joke all this pain flame and guilt near the

skinny trunk tree with small leaves on fire on the mountain not a hotel its a mountain

take off your sandals and stand here in the quivery flame of this molten sea sear to shiver of flame but how long for a moment just tell come for me bring me message

what do i do in this timelessness there must be something some him her ring me
with nonevent of a kind i'm familiar with doesnt happen hap nothings happening
but flames gold or ghastly it can be pain or ecstase can be the worse worst or nothing
sheer nothing here of fire of thin flame of a stylized whats true go through with it

with time or not go consciously or not is a consciousness necessarily in time ti who
cares for us our ownness who can care for you in the flame red the fruit of this tree is a
red on fire a red plum a currant a red fig a red a flaming ripe fruit of your actions or of

of what or of of cause and effect but no there is no cause and effect no guilt there is no
own no go on

i dont want to be alive if defined i only want to be right here in where others not i die
and hurt me so for it a cause and effe dont want the grievous air of our heart and to be
and to summon more courage for time why do so that in your air of pain shiver the
progress of vanity is a hearsay the heresy of belonging is flaming gold of host i am it
the flame and the host the tree the feet the no death the no time spelling away the
pain of dont die on me dont i die dont die dont die how do you go on by being in this

icon on the walls of the inside right here so go on and dont die and dont die as you die
again this time but dont die in this gold not in this gold hes on fire and beautiful we
are burning here as aptly as we should in this gold and dont die dont ever die

so dont worry or think in any figures of flames or gold dont think and dont theyll
survive you real its so real here of what it and walking along on rue st dominique rue
st catherine rue st afrique on fire with on fire and the with isnt there though youre
with me but dont die talk to me and dont die talk here talk to me and you be god talk
to me here say you never realized a self of world it was a flame and you were always in
the gold and so your crippled development didnt count except in eyes of no flames we

are burning through all of this timelessness could be hurt more do you other know
how much hurt how much you can be hurt just open up every pore and find out you
can find out from this icon how much you can be hurt are open to the hurt here of the

gold flame are burning with the hurt of time and of the cause and effect of the creation of it which never was it never happened but one thing i can tell you and in a million years of flames into the future it never happened

what helps what hope where and what helps it what hope and where i'm hurt too hope and where for what might hurt me again so you cant go so real so god int he flames just a person you were just that and god in the flames never anything else like cause and effect but we're right here dont go you will always be here and not going we'll never go and we'll never go from each other the pain of it couldnt be born so it doesnt exist i conjure from flame the requirement of another way of seeing i destroy

the cause and effect of this world and its making inside these flames i will do that by facing the hurt of you the hurt of our creation and burning and burning i destroy it the cause and the effect burn it up you are gold and we're burning up our world

JONE JONAH

fangs at will near the best western in airport city where is emerald city, we are filthy industrial cars and oval busstops at night i'm looking for a. i'm looking for my. i'm look- ing. looking a out, doe, to find the forms maybe, find some saints to talk to. in airport city, wheres my dad theres a german lady here hostesses to restaurants of tasteless foo, i've left my suitcase back there and cant remember where back and back before i even entered the byzantine era of forgetfulness of ugly before i even thought of the city of crystal (they say theres a city of) goodby though boo goodbye its an airport city and so one says goobye over an over and is forever in transition waits to go waits for the sched- uled moment waits here a whole life. inside my theres unexpected the suns out inside my and the mosaics are out too the verge is on the wall her dots are luvleigh. looovely lof, please pleasant inside and and outside the hectic search my father isnt anywhere around i know that what can you expect or dead friends their voices dont like to come here even if its in telepathy (what isnt) euro city aeroport. he says hes in rehab for the second time and i was too stupid to tell, loops in his letter let you know these things we're all detectives here in the smoke of smo smoke bountiful particles of worldmade folk things folk particles and the new lore the cheap shoddy story told everywhere walking through and talking talking trash thats in telepathy too you know shoddy story the paranoid number it idiot so many idiots extraterrestria the national murder jury the divine face of whore on the ceiling some broad another girly makeup face you musnt be sexist about or a boyface who makes more mon than said slut and they fill all telepathy with cliche little short phrases of telepathy they fill all its a form of cosmic television every where or you can read the penguin novel the most intelligent vers verg not vierge version of the idiot nonstory everyone feels in thats in in a back era city never quite up to you assholes never quite here. i wont let the man i hate get stabbed by. a lot of purply blood in telepathy aint there int everyone do you agree voted for the movie version didnta ya, wanted this very culture and got it got what you get what you want, you all do and have always get what you but i don hag it and fly off byzantine wingly mysl the hieratic aspects of what early times conserved in this heaven on the top of my head and if i could only get your mental garbage out your polluted telepathy. yours when i first visited i the second world in the dream i had for my friend the dead man no one told me the second worlds air might be pol- luted by the firsts so is it is it really or is it me only is it my mind get your filthy out of it get out of my mind (they will never get out) everywhere you walk beneath what wintered tree they fill filth they fill it the mind and its yours with. in origin i acquire radiation, in humanmadde time humanmad or made i acquire pollution i want to be clean free reasonabl lady justice that is only just in your in your dots your glassy cubes there your deep green your swath of purple isnt it. she has a fierce eye as the previous story from book not telepathy descry my situation everywhere its yours with know or not has justice ever been a virgin of the code of assurances everywh says, her fierce eye is true and sees but her power is not called on as you know but in the wrong way there is no justice these days its done by telepathy television vision viso hectic main- stream torrent of abuse free lady. at the meeting of the who reads books publishing co a pampered author of whats calle fiction wants to have a real i real rose in the white box edition of her book thats influenced by fi rilke and she says she wants a live snake in the box the rep says it might hurt someone and i think that was my idea as usu but it doesnt matter my editor leaves the room there will be no book no book yet there is a book and it is exactly a live snake slith went past again when you tripped and feel fell its also a poisonous snake, a ghost explains we're all in danger but thats danger of not being published not danger of my poisonous snake its the kind of thing no one believe but if you've come this far with me you're satisfactorily bitten you are poison you'll not be the same again in mainstream torrent we must unpollute telepathy i think and this may be the only way byt by jamming all its frequency freqencies with these too many words mispelled and fuzzed out sentences for clogging all the airways do you get it now? a clean old poe wont go you can too easily read and drop without changing emotion at least i might piss you off. dogshit mind you're smeared with it and your mind wears clothes and glasses you ugly bastid eatting the slop of your doubles far from the rosy quartz path what fucking er emerald of newage horse faeces smeared faces all of telepathy is shit smeared faces isnt it sucker, uhuru coffee uhuru coffee is really tea colonialist and comes in a can so well sealed you cant ever ever open it no wake up coffee in tele pathy. looks familiar says she'll call the lipstick in the wind lower broadway woman well everyones calling and calling throughout this air because they all WANT. we enter florence at k night which is an immense industrial city everyones fille thrilled cunts, i must be still stuck some jonah inside a grey meat ceilinged whale and o i am can walk through his immense but cute ribcage no air in here a smear of plasma and blood in the vast meaty system of real there is no pollution but there is no air, spit me out spit me out again. knight comes in and stands at the do door to help, i suppose i'll have to. something and oh somethin something has been thrilling an explanation by a woman of how life has and does torture her how they and how they. stick it. im looking for my it. remember remember the birth and before it can you and if you remember. i just dont know what to, press more aggression against my my heart whats that no aggressing my reason and sense of justi again, lady justice still standing there through the unclean motes of the air in byzantine green and says fiercely clean it all up clean it up. well yeah but how, call calling jonah comes somethin does remember and stands at my birth from the whale which may be the may have been the fo giant roy rosy quartz formation that big egg may be a whale wall no pollution in rock no misspellings there no untidy sentences no unjust sentences no mental fecal material dont spit me out into, but i havent yet used the dead mans medicine bundle a ruby an emerald a sapphire a garnet what can i do wi remember remember the last birth and the one before and the one. no remember the birth of this universe if you can and why not take those the four and hold them and remember. one of these is the first dot the first piece, the fi first thing it stands for that, these were the first four colors the first four senses that heaven had reason justice tenderness and so then pain, perhaps an explosion or perhaps nothing you may imagine but so painful to all who have since been and death was conceived you might say as a sense but why is birth fraught with amnesia as if we force the forgetfulness on i will remember this one this one keeps on. holding me in arms, and he was there too in his most positive outlook but that was before the air of the world, so how can i be born again be born properly i mean justly, now. am not then but am am here in ever birth and ever anguish at not birth but smutty senses all around me. what have you done to your mind

LEAVES

the blonde dropped by, changed into brunette whose name means beginning
everything keeps meaning that but daily, arent i always in middle
i was in middle when she visited, didnt know how
to accommodate. something else, that the stars were star were try to but i cant
remember the other lim glimpse i had into the present or future what else is a drea
coming down on me like cottonwood leaves leaving town no wasnt we were
harvesting leaves from immense trees near the cemetery,
also mowing the grass. he said i had to wait til tomorrow to harvest more the leaves
remind one of tesserae. i'd been thinking about my young face surrounded by
brunette hair and i understood that i wrote to make the present of the past happen
then back in the past. because when i was eight i fell in love and my face changed
as if it acquired a slightly satanic more brunette more shadowed look and now i wrote
about that time or transition in order to have made it happen
it happened but didnt happen until i wrote it write it. but now its there

remember harvesting tesserae in order to but what do we do with these leaves
count and study what. falling from trees in the desert or france out on the east side of
town, heading into arizona forbidding mountains
would be behind them the walls are empty what walls the present is it happening and

all because i fell in love fell into the sin of life when i was eight

thats why the present back in the past when i didnt understand in the sun there
suffering meanings but these arent meanings theyre tesserae of world and worldliness
arent they what am i looking for among these canopic jars full of body parts
nearly burst out a star or light from my forehead yesterday wasnt a body i wasnt a body
forgetting the names of the parts acquired that time
mowing the grass because. privileged and not counterbalancing
have you kept faith with, what
would all thats suffering write something long to be recited inest instead of a spy or a
crime, love. they cant figure out what the crime is
so they dont know who committed it. so they read about any old madeup crime
the walls are thus empty or flickering only with phantomic from my forehead not
essential like, like st bak say glittering with starlike bits of wholeness
go back to my changes make them real. didnt fall in love the right way whats the right
way i dont know didnt do it it wasn whole then whole
it was part of the crime, instead
the crime of going towards a single forgetting the future thats been
catching you round on the play ground. i was only eight says the dream the wind the
cool february one invests these meanings into the pasts present was it a stranger a

passing older man with a leer sort of thing
made me believe that. there was something else
consort with something sharp for what purpose but what anyway for what purpose

do. still do. blue and part blue not part blue dress of reason up there a woman, this
mans eye denies it. why and tries to tell you something tries to make you think so he
can make you think what he wants. they kept thinking they knew.

now we have to harvest all of these leaves. myself and the driver of the truck, its my job but hes my driver. wait till tomorrow i dont want to. scooping them up for what theyre bugged for sound have to make the right sound. have to make the right sound under surveillance or i'll be ignored once more. grew up to be ignored like most everyone. you do what you do in isolation from
and preaching tomorrow like a jacket. fax it fax your jacket to the office and look

this was when i changed because i fell in love. now by thinking about them, the others who've done so. winged amor, stands above the city right above the crystal where the heavens, open above those towers thats where he might hover am i

interested its a current a rushing towards a physics a liquid account. i have no recollection of who i was in love with.

all of my poems will be long

making it come into the park or cemetery the byzantine truck the harvester of leaves the car. my rubys purring, lets get it done r tonight, cant ever tonight. gee the entire is sinking or slipping again, as always seeping into the earthbound earth the manufactory of, body of not what we say the spiritual coherence of the earth has been violated why didnt i care when i was eight. the spirit of our interr, but and star flash from forehead again, isnt a body need another say. body of, body of, not to go forward but to gather in place the more and more crop of the and eight hats of spain say voice for no rea or anything it wants to why no and more rotation of crop int he spring field when the weather is more marvelous with us is an ache from the past made into something else these consequences we ignorant stand against, as if they were a blank wall not an illustrated one. opposite you i'm not hat the pasts present will my poem always be long, thinking if theres an outside of earth but the second worlds here both here and in death the weathers reprehensible, we're trying to be in love on earth but we think thats only human. not between us and the weather animals stars. river. frightening mountains are part of it. i'd always wanted to, nothing. what did i want when i was eight. i'm eight though i'm eight. no such thing as anything. make it part of roses theyre tere there arent any in town. forgotten but nothing forgot or you want we'll ignore it, if what we call love tells us to.

the consequences of all your actions would were never apparent until now. can you change the pas

i'm sick with it, the changes i have to separate.

GRAVE OF LIGHT

how is this wing different perhaps it isnt if half of a unity the. the tail tall grass the grass not so tall grew around the cement slab which was littered and said to myself ill probably have to clean up here clean it up house in the mountains this is my house in the mountains my wing my loaf of bread. up in and up in a crevice in a causse we are eatting bread and cheese see berries black gloss last summer this is where near i live in last nights and so and so inside. up in or down in may be the same. as much is the same folded leaves a bud i was suddenly in a damp cave and could smell the damp and could hear the water dripping dark and gray black and blue and gray there is the cave of light ahead it is round and full of gold golden light try to see whats in the midst of midst of the light no youre trying to see a thing again but there may be no thing no thing at all except for that light and in fact i saw no thing because if you try to see a thing youll see it but then theres always another thing after that because in see seeing things you i am then involved in the chain of things the light glows but then the caves vanish and i am back back up here we will try to keep it clean please see that my grave is kept. in the concept of two dennis and denise one has a tailfeather stuck on which one its so hard to find the cats eye and in the concept of two black gloss or gold light is the wings call to be all one and forget bread the light is stolen always is it midst of midst is that stolen ideas how to live in the here and now is stolen from all the others in stolen light of grew up around the grave. grew up around the grave of

the original person and littered it why do this a second time why enter a church mind a second ti im being led on led on and by what is leading me on in such trials of theres the cave of gold again as if but not as if it were an altar or a central cave cavity calling home in the chain of thin things to find the thing. thing might be what these shape are its all about a door oh rood spell backwards recent supersti interstices and superstices amid the lattices invis unseeable of the crystal and its own strange chain of

what allows light through in the cave in such w a cave where the crystal giants were found. immense structures amethyst actually werent they or was one rosy at the hall of gems and minerals the mountain the mountain queen in vaginal rock sac world in situ in in situ the lattice lines of the dragonflys crystal wings show black faint as chain of things high above the water of her thoughts the virgin of dragonfly the great insect mother mom the ma these wings are for enfolding the slave to the heart who is a slave crossing the river of death into the mountain with the symbol of death outside above who is the slave amid lattices of world and notworld and which is whic. i am the slave parker near the velvet dam why velvet tri twigs and the soft spring soft as an anus or the skin shrivelled near in the thing chain and the chains exist because named but the slave is not named so the ma the river the slave and the river winds like chains around the mountains but not like and in the mountains in the mountains is the great giant light good death gold no not like that. enter it and you enter thing. there is this all thing and outside there are all the things many of which are forbidden often unless you have money the concrete worlds all thing like the concrete slab of the probable grave and thats like. please see that my grave is kept clean but why. the grave of the grave of the chain of things. all night wander the airport world for no. and do things all day for no did things for no a slave shriveling the slaves partied all

grave of

light

night can of confit of preserve leaves of s preserved springs and long preserved temptations near the grave of the original person which i thought i had long ago exhumed. keeps not happening so i am shrill all day. keeps happening as well but gets buried buried again, happens not happens he met me near my first house and told me i had no right to the death song the dying song because no one was dying as if he knew and i didnt they do this for a long time and together they behave badly if thats a thing in order to in order yes its a thing if youre trying to live in and readjust the chains the chains on the sla chain of things. i remember that she is trying to poison me that is mentally because she couldnt bear either my talent or my where or when i was pure and these events have marked me but the marks are superficial i think because i excavate the cave not excavate but because you cant dig up a cavity of cavity of golden light the thing not the chain of things. keep on my go there was a man with a gun and a grid a grid of red no blue and green there was hunting hunting on the grid for never the golden light but for thing in the chain they were all in chain a necklace for a time because a time was thought precious but there is no and so the time is still now. the time is still now that i speak of above the buried and i am still trying to get to the gulf states and the great gulf ive been trying and trying to find two wings to fly to the gulf. past the hunting of wild duck on the grid and past the poison past the old

litter of newspapers in the cold wind on second avenue because i have no coat against

it except for black past its a black past to get past and they want to poison me. that was the spring they used poison. down here hear the drop of water cave the buzz of insect and theres and theres the golden glow of the cavity of the excavation the exhumation of nature stand in it stand its the veritable door of stand. to be that ever hawk the trees stand with wild flutter in the tangle. and in the after but there is no after no shift. explain explan it was an explan not a now putting on a coat and leaves burning softly

no one sees. we could do this every day in the crystal city the light strikes us from the usual outer source but the source in the buried might be functional in world the boundaries multiply lattices how big how big do we live in burns up venality. grave not afrai excavating structu what toehold in gold there how to explai ever black down golden the tangle where the path around the block where he denies me leaving cheyenne is implicated in the exhumation of the original and that house is lit up back there i enter. he is trying to trying to tie the string too tight to cut off circulation of the light. and this blood cant be poisoned and she cant poison the wing of it and cant poison dragonfly make the poison flow in those lattices flow but wont in crystal you cant poison rock or fly wing they cant and could never have me enter walk up the few steps and walk in the door door keep doing this keep doing th nothing special that is of a species. breaking break me but cant poison i have broken myself on thing like grief but they could never break me only such a large bounty as fri as grief was broke me open and exhumed the gold cavern they cant come here and though they havent yet succeeded in using me i have used them over and over to be in this story in order to get to get to the rock the grave the cave the church the wing the place that is marked by the double or cross that x is the door rood the oo the exhumed air itself breathy light tinged faintly with blood red.

WHERE LEFTOVER MISERY GOES

if its a spiritual offense does it as wrongdoing take place more in more in the second
leftover
as a leftover and is the significance of the double now that i might be might the one who offends in other circumstan or that it takes two to make an offense but how was i used and why were the others not usable was it because they were always too selfinvolved to be exploited. oh keep this mostly masked as always these events are of the sort are replayed shadow in the second world or perhaps in the overlap the border was it a spiritual offense and did it take place more in the mind than in any outside it surely does now. it only takes place in my and keep this masked keep it low shes awaiting attention acceptance as exceptional her face corroded i have to avoid her like poison but i have to keep remembering shes poison there is a machine that allows memory to be memories to taken into the futur i have to remember shes pois and that isnt a known a universally accepted fact that shes poison to me wants to poison me and make me hers of her emotional her emotional camp make me live of the camp of she thinks but she is poison shes acting like she isnt and i can barely remember the last time i was poisoned and now in the now in the second world there

is no linear time no many years past and i dont know when they last said in the first world accept her poison bu because its only you dont bother us on the cold wintry avenue in your coat lined with papers another wild looking night darker than the last one which was purple this ones deep navy with slivver moon behind a raggy cloud in this wind the buildings are dangerously high and here and there a gold lights tossed i didnt see the two strangers my former fr is that possible strangers until i suddenly did staring at me but the real point is that i'm not them nor her i'm not the double and i want to be hard about this i am only the double as i must straddle two worlds but i am th not the double who did wrong to me i am not thee there is no key for the brilliant red lake in the top of the rectangle map of me which seems to be a sort of early area is desperation a pleasure i'm so thirsty and i'm suppose in joy but do i believe remem desperation joy or guilt approach me from a side street trying to make me talk to them i'm singing a song and the he double says not enough facts in that song though theres a lot of poetry one word has become coeur of me what word it must be poet coeur de coeur no longer no longer a word we have driven up high to this mountain town where the gypsies live but must leave live but must leave he asks me to talk to him but i wont now an she all fuzzed up in the head wants to give me an entire shelf of old books as a bribe to poison knowledge of her mind but i'm resolutely in black fur burning into a snowbank a dream a tall snowbank that is taller than i am and its hard to walk hard to walk here in the death you are helping i am being assimilated and wear a long dress and shawl watch me make love as a prostitute so i can be your friend because youve only ever wanted to see my body what you think of me the villagers want to circumcise me sunday so i can be everyones theyre gypsies in the mountains on luna something street i used to live there but i have since cut up the sidewalk and carry it with me carry luna something street with me wherever i go and lay it down so i can walk towards or away what away from what i must walk away from them again board the ship my other sister life will go to the camp where the actress a second a
second
demonic womans face must be kept out of the movie you cant know about her you cant know in the first world and in the second thus there are these dreams which play out shadows on the street useless kindness curiously useless until the play the playing out is over in the head of what you did used me to stay you and so i'm a gypsy again wait for the camp to break up in the mountains encased in crystal you used me but

said you were use in the first world on the street on the street of poison words b was it only words no there was the deathhole that was burned into the snow it was supposedly another who died not die because i was never the one was i never the focus was other so how could you ever affect me when you were trying to ki fight another and only poison me lightly who died not die but there was the deathhole burned into the snow here in the second world as i play it out play it out in the crystal a lighter story now where i never die have only died to that world. no one believes in poison thats why we cant breathe. someone has left me a book highlighted in black always do that leave a book and the letters hop and try to transform but tha they cant nor can the shelf of old book of esoterica change the nature of poison which goes towards because only because only thinks of self thinks story so the poison flows outwards in the bad air in winter tinged with yellow and corroded face bookstore bookstore ever if the double lives in a book. others support her because i have never needed story and the letters hop and try to transform they are snow the letters try again i dont know how to tell you this letters i dont care about your transitional stages i dont care why you used pois i dont care whose real name or person i dont have to be tain tained certain of the action of self without salt keep doing this keep doing this so old. because it happened once in the first world and in the second doesnt quite go away the actions in the first and the real story as dream as dream in the seconds milder haunt where who died not i but died to the first and died to that camp and died to that bookstore and died to that oh keep this mostly masked dont feel a thing or be pois get poisoned theyre still all waiting for that i dreamed i lived them they wore black robes and lived in a cluster of wooden houses in a clearing but there may have been woods and i was being assimilated i wore a long black dress and shawl the narrator cut in to say that i was prostitute and my boyfriend john watched me make love with the village men there seem to be many and tenderfaced what does prostitution symbolize half of the villagers are leaving and then i will be circumcised because he dies or somethi take part in the rite of becoming a woman can withstand of pain of that she tries to poison again wants me to be on a side and not in i wake up for a few minutes fall back asleep many years ago they are gypsies this movie will star us and the stars are familiar in the part where i'm taken away on a ship with other prisoners but am no one just movie stars just parts and theres no point in falling in love with the commandant hes just a star and i'll die anyway theres no point in and when she says

love theres no love. this is a spell to get out of here how long will it take the border is
endless. wants me to be on another side she wants t wants me to be on her side of the
border and i stay on the side of the second world always but am still in the border the
border where the nightmare sucks me into its feeling want to say her keep saying

saying

about her because no has believed it and so say it and say and so remain in the border
will the circumcised women feel after death will the real w will the real e include
sensation that cant be manipulated by ones feel fellowcreatures on the street denying
me to the point of point because i think they like and if you maintain sides you are
always near the border and never in the snows come again and the purple sinister sky
so i can die and read the books they leave me always alive the letters and the letters

letters

hop about and try to change but never do because no one wants them to change.

[1998]

FROM **BENEDICTION**

CITY

we move back into a damaged city   figure of love and i   near the
entrance from the hole of images, that old theater.   they were about to throw out
a box of presents i left here when i moved   still wrapped in silver foil   i
choose some and scoop them up   and one of them is perfume, and heres an old
checkbook   the same old checks. old checks   when you move back
into the damaged city the old apt doorless with ripped out floorboards   a rat
and a cat to chase it   a skinny cat with a patch of   blue coloration a reasonable

cat, the mice are pissed off at it chasing it   next in the store, going to the store
          oh i never wanted to do this again buy pasta and a pasta pan   listen to the
ignorant young women prattle in hero worship   of a heroine poet, amid sauces,
while the proprietors wife   it was supposed to be her all her in an apron she
got stuck here lost and now im looking for drinks that i dont want to   drink,
i want to be in the crystal city crystal city   i dont want to live in the damaged city
amid the same   stop off at a different apartment   to get cared for

No not me.   this tall herb this light colored grass   protects you from
AIDS   a couple says   i am walking out the door now, going home where is
that   in the wrong city no i am walking out the door now going back to the
ghoulish dead of the damaged of the city of worldwide   spread of the damage of
the damage No. im going home to the crystal   where you are glints in the
pearl   your eyes are light glints there

light glints there.

will the secretary of state ever take you home to such a place, she is trying to shake me as we walk together from the drugstore on front street towards broadway but i wont leave.

you are using me again you dead men, that's why i shatter   all your empty bottles with a hatchet.

all of this anger was given to me for use   where did it come from   it first appeared i believe when there were different rules for male spiritness. then there were always different rules for that and for his hat, his political ideas he would always be the expert   no now im in the crys im going there ive broken all the bottles and ive followed albright to the all bright city where

she has disappeared, because she has no distinction here, as my prizes dissolve and your expertise. here, there is no. you and you have no charm here, and your loud voice cant prevail because a voice isnt a voice its a mind you might say and all minds are working all the time so no one mind can prevail. im listening to the whole mix speaking colors and shapes dissolvable tendencies no bell rings how can i find you not walking exactly because my function as use for as use for a previous definition of the animal kingdom is defunct.

tony has shown up
at the conference at the womens college   he   shows up everywhere, though he looks lost.   he has stayed young, around twenty.

back and forth i go   between the two cities
pain of the damage down here, in me, because all the facets are joined. down here, up there,
tony doesnt know what to do at the conference at the womens college
they arent going to discuss how he was used, made into a soldier and killed, before he finished college   because the bottles are kept separate
and the facets and the facets
are only realized consciously in the. so you see

me, breaking and breaking with an axe all the bottles you have emptied
destroy use it is sinking

                           because all the facets are joined. cant keep him away
        is hispanic minority   no he is tony twenty   no he is tony
whom i have known   since we were six.   he stopped having an age
at about twenty-two now im fifty-three   he is tony whom ive known since we

were six
hes here, looking lost   at the avant-garde conference at the womens college.

every night i plead i ask the veritable air   for a vision of the crystal city   and i
get another dream of   people i know and have known, of course   they are
the city.   Last night the crystal city was down in the métro down among staircases
where you catch the Balard-Créteil line to Invalides   the city was young male
lovers who say, why dont we use a sap or a knife or other object in sex? because this is
love   we dont because its love   And that is   an answer, o philosopher-
scientist, that   the skin of the body that the flesh and muscle of the soul   are

love   its your procedures are foreign knives and clubs   in the holes to the
soul   the crystal facets which open   in skin   In the lower depths
a hassled thieving life   of an unmoneyed sort   is transpiring here mirror of
the corporate, but with love just a little more love   spills out in sloppiness of cheap
alcohol vieux papes the mentally defective   transient we used to see around
is back climbing a staircase Up   i guess hes supposed to be me because   the
others say theyll find him anywhere, writing a poem   and there, a

waif   is   old friend whose name is now   carol nadir   Yes
this is the crystal   city   i know it well have always known it thus

i must enter city right now wings of dew and hawk eyes i must fly right in through the
blazing clear light of your voices vi the strong we pouring forth in individual
consciousnesses talk talk like li stream of the ignorant man laughing at him hes there
but hes still susc unconsciousness he'll never unfortunately because he decided we
were a weave a habit a concatenation   of evolutionary scientific trick so now
hes here but not not really hes about   as here as milosevic who is, is here but will
be mute soul for eon. too bad you   splend in the night and that dead man
was there i was talking to him next to where the train come in a slab of pr pork a slab
of cold prk station next to the métro métro to the tall the building where im huste
hutl hustled in so someones old wife wont see me, oh you who care. i enter
into the middle of it the building of facet for tricks beyond wives and habits beyond all
trick of con of scientific   conning. but wouldnt you like to be conscious? but
all those whims of yours   pretending they explain this thi blaze blinding voice and
you cant even expal explai the liquidity of the voice that is conscious or uncon
because   explain   is   a con a con ah riv

you are as here as the dazed dead is

        I saw them all as equals
        in that moment it made me feel as if I were standing
        up very straight   everything else was wiped away.   to see
        everyone as equal to one
        and all accomplishment erased   is the most mystic of experience.
        destroys science there is no fittest

and all your wives and husbands are there   and all your rapists and your victims
        and every bit of difference from you   what you werent born and didnt become
are there is there   being addressed by you now   truly now murderer
in its or your state of splendor or mutedness Thats our description?   Isnt it? Wah
what is important then nothing nothing at all Thats why I like   this is the ethic of

what matters   the exact blazing nothing you can be   caring to be but not
caring about thing at all   caring for but not caring about   to careful like
a hawk, an apple and not a hat

                                              i saw her throughout last night
young and alive and i saw the old ill dead man the night before. slab of pork
slabs of pork either they or the métro platform   and she was at the college and she
was there all night city of women   but we are the city of no one. drop of a hat

the fish in the foyer are overfed he says i can smell it when i take off the top of the
aquarium. let them out to cry from scum from the underside of the riverbank let us
out so we can eat scum   let us out so we can learn to be the nothing necessary
to survive in full consciousness in the crystal city we want to eat scum and be scum
let out of cage and be as good as scum   be as good as algae if you dare   have
as much soul   as a bacteria if you dare know as much of crystal if you know how

i dreamed i was that small in the black black ocean of all   swimming towards the
awful shore that we had created   out of our manly arrogance. in the city of crystal i
am all of the crystal   all and one   one facet   all of it and i

i have to have the key to the himalayas by tonight. i have to get out of here
i have created a diagram or picture   that allows the woman me in the picture to

rise up riding a skeleton-butterfly   butterfly with skeleton body blue winged
with gold light bars on the blue   riding a skeleton-butterfly to the very top of

the himalayas   the picture is of an indian   woman other   nationality oh
what difference does that make?   none of that matters, you   and via the

agency of this picture   i have the key to the himalayas   red dinosaur
laughing   red dinosaur soul smiling at me.   there is the iron rose

and there is the petrified vaginal hole   of images skeletons, there are all the nines of
competition and rating   im flying up above them riding an

image   an image riding an image   in a diagram   of how to get there

no i have to go back to school first he says. hes a hard man a middleclass middleaged
school administration man says i have to go back to that same womens college theres a
darkness to my right in this room, this room which is at the same time the outside campus
and grounds of the school as well as a piece of paper hes showing to me, telling me id
previously achieved a score high enough to get in go back to school for further education.
this paper says. i wonder whats in that darkness that school wont ever tell me because of
the bottles and of him, i know the city is in that darkness the city i am in keep entering
and leaving keep describing but not and thats because. the door of reason. thats because,
is in that darkness the city and not the college tony the highest of mountains a darkness to
my right in this room. there is my anger given to me for use but hard to control where i
have unwrapped it from its silver foil what do i do with all these things these perfumes
and further dreams? i have a new blue book of reason in which to write down more
dreams. the crystal city's towers never shatter are they a learning denied will not be tried
by you i wont be in keep ive shattered male bottles we're entering the city through the
darkness the crystal roads and streets not walking at all not used by definition or
evolution breaking the heart tony and i. are entering the crystal city bright blue sky
throughout the body we are of reason not of use we will not be of use. and if there is no
use here what will you do. that is for me to find out that is the new knowledge youve
never thought before.

the poem says 'we have finally found our house' and is presented interlinearly in a
different colored ink with the accompanying letter, viz there is a line of letter followed by
a line of poem then a line of the letter followed by a line of the poem, and so on. the
poem and the letter clearly different but can not be easily separated. as each beings two
lives cant be. the figure of love and i are standing reading the letter across from the park

which is two parks in two cities. green trees it is spring. then we will enter the pharmacy
while i am young as young as long hair. as young and long as the long skirt im wearing
here that i once wore. this is the drugstore of my youth drink a cherry phosphate red like
a thin silk blouse with short sleeves a soul red blouse.

ive forgotten that man is dead he isnt always dead

this is the song you sing when youre dancing with a ghost i dont mind, this all this is
the whole song you sing   when   youre not being used

who invented use and all the schemes to justify it that book gets published endlessly,
we're not being used now, not being used here

LOVE

        tall woman shortish pony tail high on head in smalltown theater not as movie
house which it primarily is but   theater. because has a stage. she is or isnt me. it
or she (do I still have to call my self a she) sweater and pants angora breasted pullover
and plaid slacks of the fifties. Yet at same time sense of leviathans whales cavorting
and sweeping about like in water So you are made trivial you vast thing. Beneath the
shattered glass was a trained girl but other now No I still dont know what   is and
I am as always in the space between the audience and the stage, in the walls, or in the
coincident fluid element of the leviathans, all night. you didnt know it was wonder

because you feared sinking drowning, the leviathans   might seem dismal to you
since they didnt wear the clothes of sex and eras but they are edgeless rather than
whalelike and everything is you. or I. you are everything, *the soul of a one / not of "a*
man" / is a leviathan / untrained to shatter / to matter wouldnt matter. And so I dont have to
have a face in any jubilee. Your strikingly soulful presence with its
edgelessness and soulful fluids body fluids went to the stairs now I remember that that

was tomorrow in some sort of spiral or whirlwind in the telepathy if I could only
remember more of being leviathan as big as all the sea I feel in my skin and heavy and
light with my many metaphysical fluids. Dont you remember?

       The same texture as wrath   is a stone   tear
to be like a stone is to weep stones
thats to be like oneself not a striking imbecile   I'm awake
no one is here—no one is ever here
the affect is very no the
affect permeates me deeply. thats why Im a rock   Never use the word 'is'
the therapys to move the rock, render the affect flexible Why bother Nothing
wrong with rock, sings a rock You are not stone not stone soul, sings another thing
Yes I am Dont cry youre not allowed to. I will cry stone
I'd rather be stone than their imbecile.

            tears are the slave planets
called moons of Jupiter. that big at least
as big as slave   planets   titans

I will cry and will cry for more than   us two or three or few
I dont have to be alive in this instant in the way of the
imbecile. No nothing happens. too nothing happens. too, no one is here
we are enslaved to a disease to a situation in which the first body. becomes any
     trained fools object
not just us but everyone
And all night leviathans of light and fluid reason and bulging ruby foreheads speak
and speak invisibly in this room now. All that makes things tolerable
those other bodies dont exist. I am the biggest leviathan just like you and no other
kind   will ever be here. weep speak sing and maybe its like a
singer you
cant understand but can   understand entirely

the whole to live is not quite to get it but to be exactly here No in fact   we are getting
it. I am in the process of getting it. the blindest willy or johns son big as leviathan
heavy with   metaphysical fluids don them the flowers for the watch train blue light
red light gone down and we bawl brown green and brow. all that water in the train I
mean the river   didnt   divide us. all that mud all that mud We are here in
the corrupt real worl because they named it, all you named it   but we're there in
the crystal element because its there. we are here because they named it but we're
there because its there. I cant dream because I dont exist here. And because I am stone

more women in slacks, I do remember that
first there was a vat
of white rice or ricelike stuff
thats the antarctic as food
thats the ice of no images as food
the vat was as large as a. I dont know what it was as large as
comparisons are stupid the queen soul and I
were walking later at night of course in our slacks as if we were being
slack, no thats   stupid.   into a theater space again
She is a silkyhaired brunette and
is dressed in a bright red sweater and pants tight sweater and slacks
we will die gendered or sexed   in your unknowing eyes
though it is only in your eyes or is it lexicon we will die (have you ever seen)
white Im wearing white because Im nothing now at all
white for nothing or white for ignorance the
ignorance of the meeting of leviathans all leviathans of light at night and not
remembering. never never remember
what we said in our core of light
cant remember what   we sing or say
we sing that light water light in   syllables we cant understand though
we understand each other
perfectly

Later there was the phrase "life support system" it would make you want to vomit.

there is nothing to tell me.
        tell me something to
nothing to tell me
no life, nothing to tell
soul has nothing to
because reason and the color blue are gone   *not for long not really*
reason gone. my red is along
just being scarlet red
reason is quiet because she doesnt have to speak now

Everyone and their excellent body parts their good looks their life support systems
how stupid can you get. they think they're their brains

you remem doctrine not doctor of ignorance it isnt a doctrine it is itself the
simultaneous nothing we are in where everything happens that doesnt happen but is
the only thing that counts. it counts up to one. ive gotten to this place. im in another
tubulous hospital room and a gaunt featured stranger a thin man runs happily
towards me thats the only image there are none usually in this doc but im not anyone else
and so i say and see what i please the gaunt featured stranger rushes towards me
wearing a gray suit

                because we will escape you you world ones into ignorance together
this is our heresy we can have the mystical experience together or we can have the
vision of the cave and the folk together we can unite with real together and if two can
cant all and isnt that really the doctrine of the crystal city.
                        I can't remember the rest of the night except that I
talked to him. that stranger I knew to be you.
I did nothing but talk to you

There are hardly any there are hardly any more images its like drug withdrawal
tell me the story of. there is no. I said to him, But I have never seen you I couldnt I
see something we've invented that stands in for you an image but I could never
see you or anyone. *You* are not visible the only visible things are the ones we manufacture
that we agree to the appearance of so that we can endlessly make them.
We did not originate ourselves only the way we look at each other
                                    in the great ignorant deep where I have a red in my forehead,
a ruby of depth of experience, we dont look at each other. the stone I am, the stone self
is changing but its still there often or maybe its ice it was usually ice in the images of
the past I mean my past though I dont have one I mean things I wrote before.

          this life has been carefully constructed
          to make most people suffer. they did it
          themselves. we did it

I was supposed to stay interested in the testimony of the great mystics as of the great
poets but I only care about my own now. It seems to me that I am in that deep state at
the same time as when I am angry or sad for example it doesnt preclude affect it contains
it. Thus I was able to conceive of the Crystal City, which has nothing to do with religion
or sainthood, but a little something to do with philosophy since it rescues sophia from its
male rules from games. I am in that City now and I am not in a trance. not tingling. I
may be dead I haven't accepted your sense of what is or isnt I am conscious and many of
you seem to be here. There are not images at this point but I still crave them. I would
describe the crystal as it doesn't exist in such a way that you would never want to be
elsewhere. But I can't find images. I wear and am in white.

buried images
all night forgotten again, hospitals   clusters of hospitals we   were driving
towards as into the movie screen at that same theater   at that theater that we
women/girls in slacks keep entering. Earlier   someone had said a leviathans a

monster and I felt pleased, I had thought it only whalelike but mythological or then too it is a ship a monstrously vast construction faintly outlined in gold light on the horizon distant at night. we drove toward hospitals all night   they had nothing to do with truth only a contrived necessity   They are images my only dreams, plus the women in slacks.

the codl that is cod code or cold   all codes hurt there is no real code. we're just like its dirt or snow to is it speak its communality all the dirt or snow we'll ever be all the blood in the river run. its just. it isnt a code. i hated being explained to and meditated at as well performed to formed at and made the object of anothers desire to seem to exist as a difference when any one is and there are no fools and we are all equal. and yet i did it too i cant avoid it its like the hospital all the hospitals, all there are are roads hospitals and also, i know, airports. but the world is really composed of hospitals smelling of profound brown-dark fluids collected and disposed of as cheap stuff the cheap.

> I will include the old dream I've already included twice
> Dec 24, 1998 I dreamed variously and in this dreams final
> transformation in which I lived under a theater marquee
> with another woman with whom I
> was always trying to find food: I am no longer on the sidewalk
> I am no longer in the dream as I. Audrey Hepburn
> perhaps in India, outdoors in a natural setting, a womans cloth over her
> head but a physician, is testing a member of her own family for
> cancer. The cancer is there. In the traditional manner of grief
> she paints her eyes red—red circles. She is riding on a cart,
> horsedrawn and heaped with things. A voice says to her
> that it is good to paint the whole body red. There is a reference to
> the figure of love, my love, and the color brown, which in my symbolism
> of color relates to reds spectrum and the soul, and in his to kindness
> I have the right to include this.

this is where love becomes the target of this poem its pure eye

stone or ice or nothing love nothing. at the bottom of the hole of images   is the
nothing of love   the ultimate image is the hospital   or the woman as
woman as if that were   at the bottom   of the hole of images is   love.
images of evolution transparent in their lie fly past my tired when it was only ever the
word love will do. it is white   and thats why my outfit of sweater and slacks is as
pale as love a hospitals   is a urinous paleness different from that its a bleaching
out of any image but its own. Love is white   because it has no shadings it
doesnt think, its selflessness is unimaginable   it has as a reality no image
whatsoever It is nothing and I have been reduced to it I am still praying for dreams
praying for images as others say they pray for the sick but who can understand that?
the soul I say is the second body or is it the first, first or second no difference Ive said
second so lets stay with second. Ive been left with nothing and thats where it is. the
second is here. red is here for the life, white is here for all that counts nothing, blue is
in abeyance here but not really is a surrounding skirt of element for the monstrous
whales who sing white they sing white im in what they sing. if i paint my body red
youll know whats happening but   I dont care if you do. not all the voices are
true. how is your own horse-driven cart of junk doing, speaking to anyone? The sun
rises over the red eyes of the mountain gods who have wept blood and stone for their
eons of lives so everyone says but when has anyone ever said what counted. they
were just more males. and in the deep and in the deep the whalish presences are
growing whiter and whiter and the deep itself is white icy white but fluid

          there is still the matter of the image beneath the shattered glass because
it is matter.

          It was like a circus but maybe that was the smaller one since I wont settle
for this circus down here. there was an image once born of love what was it? was it
simply a baby was it that same old baby. probably not or probably

[2000]

IPHIGENIA

who dares me out turn the

profits (poems) from burning but am the victim. I counsel you to listen for irrational
connection (undergrowth): I myself can't listen to a one unless it cries unsense in my
ear, for I've a capacity to transmigrate and be a shapeless thing, the hole of images
itself I *am* Iphigenia, forced to consecrate the humans sacrificed to Artemis on Tauris,
though there are no deities except as torn from the hole by kings nervous of their
power blood buying it without the least sacred presence I am sacred, un-Iphigenia,
and I've got a barrel in my lip crying someone's dead, another death overseen,
death of a lover, I'm waiting for my brother whom my voices said would help me,
yes, my, voices, my, dreams, I *am* a poet, and I have been sacrified in order. As if I
could only become this if. If I watched their deaths consigned to deity a fetishy little
effigy. If in all image I could enter the image of the image, the hole the very one
that controls the godlike entities we discern with our senses as outlines we name and
worship, consecrating them to our interactions. Our ones. Our reasons. And so if I
could become Iphigenia, I could unbecome her, and destroy this need for her — but
being her now, babe of the contagion, (centuries, the money which requires our
allegiance to our gods)
        she who consecrates deaths:
my brother not quite Orestes will save me from carrying the contagion. He will do
this in my imagination, being dead: I will be saved by the dead. REPRISE: I was
removed from the altar as victim to the convention carried away in sequence by an
image will abolish the cult it's everyone's business to preserve on the money linger
pressing their learnéd desires, rest against a box, placating. No image will be
worshipped after my rescue, have become older than your deaths upon the altar of
chronology's ivory inlaid brochure. But the dead are looking after me as if only
they really love me, because they are love and because I *am* that old, the image
Iphigenia was torn from my own body-country, if someone cared to see, but care is
capacity for schedules not love, which I find as *I* keep it:
because I'm weaker

not
'Losing it.'
The voices, that is
the Dead are really with me—
because they
love me.
Because I'm weaker
the dead find me
and teach me more.
Use me to destroy the gods.
     I FOR
the premise that the brother like a terminator, broken by war, has tornout face, but
he's supposed to. He looks like that to keep *him*. And I for Iphigenia whose
motions are few,
the touching of the hair before the sacrifice, my brother will save me because he
killed,
that's how he comes to find me is it,
poised on my pain, so like his?
I still don't understand the story I'm caught in
the whim of the wind
to obligate one   to story or act
REPRISE she didn't die but yet was sacrificed yet lives on metallically. My brother
doesn't owe me. He searches for connection, in the wind the breath of the afterlife.
Will he put his face back together to come see me?
No, I am invisible but you can hear me
Tell me what you know
What can I know?
But you're transparent you must know
I'm down on parent. I'm own parent,
I'm transmuted by the love I cast down
on the ground where the parent eye
closed, and love for him glistens in my,
own destroyed eye, I still

love him in guilt. . .Iphigenia. . .is it, guilt, an

effigy? (To come to you I become that again)

It *is* becoming illusory, the

sky is a web of fine grey pieces it's breaking:

He isn't someone you killed

But I felt I   didn't I   kill everyone?

But didn't *I*? I watched

Why are we still in this one

       story?

Because there's a clause in it, a legality

the talons of the stale order.

You endured, I was endured.

When you died you were just going to tell me . . .

You endured, I was endured . . .

I got the talents, you got you, oh lucky. But take me down into the glass so it can

cut me so bad I don't care

Where is the glass?

Anywhere. I don't know the difference between anything, anyone. I whirl in the

hole of images, the dead mixed in as they should, and I awake as I should. And I

stood in front of the hospital again where my love had died, but the pain can be felt

anywhere, and coursing through words. We will command it to enter these words,

a frightening potential. We will command the pain to enter my words, sufficient

time forever in the cut-glass era oh exquisite object ambulance out there breathing

the *was* breath I am cut, or was I burned, or is it portray me, name me. Fold it into

the snakelength scarlet air, any portrait, fast to the corrupting dispersal . . .

Let me accuse: I gave you, my, to say.

It is too painful.

I give you my.

You give me your. I don't know if these words are the name for what happened.

No one would read your childish poems, if no one will read another's poems—then

the president will not read another country. And you were such another country.

Now I tell your story, though it is mine too, and I give you mine.

We command the pain to remain in the words. not in us.

And now we change the order. how we your reconstruct face.
Mine it shouldn't, no face
Then not a god it, no. will the pain find, if order not in, the words.
It is nearly a god, order. destroy it.
Order the now we destroy.
born red sound can plentiful scope it along
it slides glass in, cut and bleed I.
Iphigenia will I say I'm dead, because no order's on,
a fact broken
dark start down the hillside the ship and brought us
when.
      In the play.
Out of it?
      Destroy the cult
president, your need unsupposed they take, dine.
I killed in war
I watched
others die   and another—
     the
pain is entered, and words hold it.
I'm over,
so my no body
holds it, the effigy.
face? that part is dead—
Dead part that is
order now the destroy
spell
      Destroy order the effigy
      the effigy order destroy
      destroy effigy the
      gods and their order (he repeats it while
                     she speaks:)

The effigy must be shattered or I'll live this yet another kitchen forever, not
mice in the walls, children, a dirty boy, for scraps. You? Runs away so
shatter the effigy now. The spirit can no longer support what her object asks.
Taking me to free in ship of torn sail shadows blackened, escape protector the
fortified reasonable patina face. The spirit cannot support. Why not? If I
Iphigenia never happened. Why this pain then? The spirit can no longer, this
is yours or how much is mine? Iphigenia never happened, this island never
was, there is no goddess. The spirit can no longer, support what her object
asks. That object, must be destroyed. A squat vicious statue. But all the gods
alive with their maddening demands are the object. Sail the boat through
glass, the harbor is full of cut body. The spirit can no longer support.
I have said the spell. Sister, we will protect you, the dead, not the gods. Soon the
boat will leave the harbor
She still mars me but don't founder, I am inviting a lower body, more and more internal
I am crawling inside towards my
woman orange light flame
soul ostracized by an idea. Such as a superior power
      lower body   that is, soul   I consciously become . . .
      I stand here to forget   godly themes, names.
      Every effigy collapses   if you find the lower place,
      the primitive body undetectable,
      lower than remonstrance
      I automatic.
      Killing of the victim usage prescribed as impunity itself,
      the holy massacre of the real and made time by not knowing how to fly.
      Lower body is untaught and isn't precisely talking now it gets
      a whistle or then because I am like the phoebe bird or any winged forensic
      evidence, a blade that cuts through nouns, so damning. I'm dead I'm
      often dead. I don't even woo the outward it's too nar-row. I am low and I fly
      in no order. You I will become, as leaves the ship, wherefor, no for. The free
      to be mind, as it finds its own way, past all the dead gods. Cast away, across
      the water, with one whose primitive body is in death, another soul. Is he,
                                                 are you calling?

It's ready. The object is sinking, as we leave . . . .

HOW DID I COME TO BE IPHIGENIA THEN?

(Rational voice speaks)

Faced a certain internal construction no one approaches. It is of whatever story applied to the weight, lifts it. That is a simple. What is a feeling? It is all this matter I am not, pressing in, but never as low (or flying high) as I. Matter is emotion, time is emotion, death is emotion, frozen, by the rational system invented from exactly within that miasma, where did emotion come from, where and echo it nothing, so the question designs its answer, emotion moved.

I called him and he wasn't there, my love. he becomes the reasonable dead who love without effigy.

If the good one is stronger than sound, we can update

You are the good one and you can update, brother

but what does that mean?

That now I can be meaningless: and END IT!

in the growth waves spark the

fortunate—that is no word—strength to change the order.

The cut blood burns and I am still on fire a sort of new order

the one low she   no effigy   I am signalling

with sparks, that's all

                Inside care as a

bitter talent still but towards no wanting

> I dreamed myself tatooed with all the history I had been, those stories, and
> the worst displayed where my vagina was torn and deformed, the worst
> story told, was where my sex was mangled, and I watched her then turned
> away. I couldn't bear to see the unveiling of the lower part of her torso; not
> precisely Iphigenia,   she was more native to me

CHANGE THE ORDER NOW

of her unhealed

body.

> She I was revealing herself so END IT AND CHANGE ORDER. All because in
> sex, you tatooed of Iphigenia the story. Was written on myself. Intuition but
> burning body is more, the low soul who knows no order. The soul, in you it:
> Into it. Listen only for the irrational

So is there an ending?

As you and I who know, are

equals. Finally, and that, is, the final disorder

Equality is disorder?

Our bodies are both,You didn't kill him. Is that their name? The name of our

bodies?

father who died of his excess and

why not?

> I told you the last time I saw you, that if you needed someone to forgive
you, for the war, I did. But you wanted *him* to forgive you, who was already dead,
who approved of the war and whose excesses you thought you'd caused. Always a
man, now not. But now would you let me forgive you?

In the play, it would be a god.

Because I've always forgiven you, before I even knew

The effigy's pieces are shouting that they are betrayed

The order is out. If I can forgi

But   with no god

forgiveness is

destroyed, is meaningless too

you are trying to

tie things together that have been freed

as I am now freed of the fathers.

I am try for the audience

never requested, this story, poem

who ever asked for it?

THIS WILL NEVER END.

> It is

ending, has ended, is not in

order.

So we broke

every rule except.

That one must kill in time of war

Primary rules we broke:

That one must not know more

That one must not be amid an actuality of

repeated death. if not in war.

My love died in the poison blue of spring. The flowers were all a polluted blue in

my dreams, and you have been dead for so long that to tell you is

Meaningless?

Contrariwise, you are that one. It was nearly a year ago ravage, all that drama out

of order. Contaminate changes to a sacrificial body, tatooed with blue

so one would know where to fire the radiation

Sacrificial to?

Labor, the work of men

it won't be sense now I know

a benjamin of dust, a private referral to sweet james infinity, the cooling board. I

saw him on it last year, is this part in its disorder? Are you really here? I am telling

you because it was a year ago, I'm telling you, to appease the Furies who sang to me

your coordinates, but the Furies are shattered

and I keep going on and that's mine. You are fading

and will never speak enough. And I am the one

And I

(To the audience) Do you know this story?

[2001]

FROM *ALMA, OR THE DEAD WOMEN*

RADICAL FEMINIST

Alma speaks of the arrogance of countries, by shooting up into the worldmap on her head arms thighs and feet, each place requires a drug so she can forget it and dream the true again. innocents scream in her sleep though no one over 20 is innocent but who needed to die for the megalomanias of a man, men, their works together a tumor the size of this planet. they all beg me to care to care, she mutters, caring as at any historical time makes warriors appear, the stupid little fuckers, and the male leaders' faces—oh the old shit of it, the tastelessness of it and their reactions, their psychotic mugs, their being "up to it." she cries in her sleep because the numbers of dead women, and of dead men have been added to, but to take action is for patriots adherents of a father, sure i piss on flags she mutters piss on them all altogether, that would be a fine new kind of ceremony, wouldn't it Sonny? the annual pissing on all the flags of the world. but he wants to go out and kill, he wants to join up again, he hates it when his own momma talks that way, it's just the drugs. who are the real heros he asks? don't make me puke she says, and the hippy will write her poem anyway because that's what she does skinny and all with snappy high eyes. Sonny demonstrates to her how properly to use a knife, he has just bought a great big stabbing knife, he learned how to stab in the army and he keeps showing her, leaping and jabbing at the air it is the most boring demonstration he's ever made her witness but he has a way of keeping her in place by staring directly into her eyes, she squirms, she wants to go write a poem and forget about the deaths of thousands, globalization, international capitalism have taken their first sizeable American sacrifice—the mouth of that god drips red as the good cant is spoken.

i don't like Myra's name, i will change it to Ryma, no i see Mary in that, i'll change it to Mira. look. the poem is a Chinese poem perhaps of the 13th century, translated into English badly, sometimes it becomes a poem by a known man, of course it's a poem by a man because it's old. a dead man asks me to read it so he can appreciate it, we are lying on the grass of a high promontory overlooking the meeting of two rivers and out of one arises a black coach drawn by many black horses with red plumes on their heads, they are in the poem too, it all belongs to you doesn't it? you have created sorrow. who? you who lead of course, you who act for others, you who bathe in the blood of the rightness of taking action. i don't want to see your faces they are everywhere.

how will we dead women avenge ourselves now when there will be nothing but vengeance transpiring. oh these distractions says one. we intend that you keep on the subject says another. keeping on the subject is part of our vengeance. i am touched by men's love says the third but it isn't a world. men have died too someone says. they can take care of themselves someone else says but don't let one come near me again in the name of care. i want a chance to care for myself, perhaps i finally have that being a dead woman.

BELOVED EARTH RESTRAIN THEM

the furies were before Apollo Anyone was. i bind Bush and Cheney and Rumsfeld, and their tongues and words and deeds; if they are planning war for today let it be in vain. Beloved Earth restrain them, and make them powerless and useless. Beloved Earth, help me, and since i have been wronged by them, i bind them. says Mira.

i hand them over to Hekate eater of what has been demanded by the dead women. of the underworld of the crossroads of negative space. not Hekate but Alma. are we the furies asks Mara. i am the fates Moira says. but i am light and Apollo is not Luz says.

i went to the widow's store to buy food for my love. i bought him chard and courgettes, small, hanging from orange-flowering stems. i called them tender vegetables, but i had forgotten my keys, because he's no longer at home to unlock the door to. do i have a home. the coffee is weak. his paintings are not yet dry, embedded into the long table along the auditorium wall. they communicate his love in abstract shapes and transparent colors. the paint is still wet, does he come from the dead, at night, to paint them?

it's morning it's the same, i can't remember sleeping. i last remember walking in this corridor last night. i've forgotten the intervening time, it's as if i'm still walking from then. because nothing happens? can i forget you? "the U.S. servicemen are still at risk." Newsweek. "an unprecedented, real-time glimpse at an ongoing Green Beret mission." is it as dangerous as my love's cancer was? "the team spotted a campfire." etcetera. "Team leader Dean quotes Shakespeare from memory." yes but my love *was* a poet. "The men slowly made their way down the narrow road etc." bloody accuracy of attacks. "Atta could see the bodies of Taliban soldiers blown into the air. 'We wanted to show him we could help him beyond boots and clothes,' says Dean." Beloved Earth restrain them all and make those fighting anywhere powerless and useless. i can't remember what happened in between because he died that year, between walking at night and walking in the morning. i forget that there was a wheel-chair here, and a hospital table; forget the scars on his back from the vertebral surger-ies, the pain and the changes of pain medication, bathing him and how it hurt. scars still in the wall from where the backrest chipped paint. and how at every description of physical invasion of another person, whether surgical or criminal or military, he cried out in protest and empathy—because he too has been invaded. wants no one else to suffer so.

DISCREDITED

are we not only dead but discredited? asks Cosette. after all i've only been a fetus and a baby. do i prefer which state, fetus or baby? i prefer baby probably. it's called going on, which might be discredited too; anything is discredited which refers to how one survives the rigors of enslavement to the vacuous male-money world . . . discredited words because now said too often? but not as often as, "war on terror."

[from *Alma, or The Dead Women*] **319**

not until it's said as often as "war on terror" will i stop saying "vacuous male-money world."

i am discredited says Cherokee for i am a cliché—that's why i don't bother with a name.

we are all discredited, Mara says, because we exist in, and speak in sentences that come from, negative space. i am discredited by age says Mira. i am discredited by lament as well, to be middleaged and grieving, a woman, dead here, is utterly discredited "for he's gone to Bonny Scotland to bring home his new queen," and she is Death the discredited. oh hu hu says Alma and then nothing. comb Cosette's yellow hair with an ivory comb sings Carmen who has never and Carmen who has never ever been credited; for he was illiterate caustic love. for he was as illiterate as light is. light says Luz is so discredited that you may not say the word in any but a scientific document oh my curse on you sleep down you foolish, she is drowned who all of us and Sonny too is happily discredited. and i'll range over mountains flying till i find my discredited love. i dreamed of him yet again but he was afraid to be alone with me for would have to leave again being deceased. speak Anna are you discredited?

someone someone discredited speaks: i see thou and the mounted antlers, love me? bequeathed by a stallion quest watch it joke and you are steadfast my love— quandary? quarry. the axe for your head my head (they cut it off to mount it) what do we win beats in the tract-home vistas aerated girls?

Anna says, if a sense, if a sense tricks you. but this is discredited.

whatever is broken Mara speaks we are running through to get to if you make it this far it's still no. for we are still the dead women, and have never had credit. what do you want? i ask her. i want you to whisper the truth so slowly i can make it. are we going to make it? i don't know, no, why i say these for kindred followed her home past all the Atlantises there isn't anything just rearranging those same Chronos strip warriors. do i want the erotic once more as if integral to creation any older and older one's creation for it is credited eros always sing on to the money and the war, eros money and war singing laddy aye and laddy oh. this sect Pyramid Same, worshipping the top.

he is afraid to be alone with me, because of later leaving, and my grilled lettuce is inadequate or uneducable, back to the stories they prefer, i prefer these discredited. my lowlands away. down in the basement. i am trying to heal for no other man will find me fair my love lies drowned away my John, sings Anna no sings i. i am finding the discredited underneath the moratorium it is the same that i love still.

    what
    put it away, what
    then what's left
    nothing was remanded
    or shelter.
    and i was learning how to think
    when war covered over the mental
    you will never get a better
    not you prize, neat packet of genital area.

    thank you Carmen that was the old, forehead, you. how can you bloom so fresh. he never answers does he. you break my heart you warblin departing joy. discredited.
    what can they possibly know then, the credited? WHAT DO YOU KNOW? YOU CREDITED? NOTHING AT ALL.
    how can you bloom so fresh and fair? what blooms? where? i bloom, says Cosette. and i have my own songs, from my own hole in forehead, because my head opened in the womb and has not has not yet closed. i will see

    with the biggest eyes
    you've ever seen
    eyes large
    eyes large
    doctor.

    afraid to talk to me touch me. because he must return to the dead. it was before a composite of two Universitays, where there was a combination food and entertainment trailer/wagon, as if that was all one needed for a true universitay. two women and i, inside, placed food on the grill, but there was also enough room to learn, at least to learn to perform your own medicine show. but i only had lettuce and cherry tomatoes that's not enough food for you they said those two dead women. for they knew they were dead women, for if one is discredited one is dead, and most women are they? he entered to speak of the conflated Universitays as "we"; and then i understood he was afraid, to be alone with me, to talk to me, to touch me. for he knew he was dead and would have to return to the Universitays which were death. are Universitays death? all human organization, schematized and adhered to, is. and causes death as the conflated organization did not knowing that the medicine show was always there to feed and heal and be discredited. do you still want to heal others? i am beginning to heal the dead women, aren't i Alma? but i know she will probably only say hu hu.

OATH

by the little daggers of my dear, the very legitimate tendernesses of his spirit/body i
        swear.
to go on before the courts and flowing lectures, to animate the light with furious
        weight.
i needed to take the oath to go on in the previous torment but there was nowhere
        to swear it
i am taking it before dead women in an appeasing silence, their sorrowful calming
        negativity
that requires nothing but solitaire and the pretenses of an imprudent, feathered
        cosmonaut.
i then swear it, i will go on; by all the psalms and psychic pulleys connecting me with
        you, for their no reason
no interment of tantamount to sorrel, oxalis that means another word. i have blood
        for this, is it mine or his
my progenitrix name bears the substance, in obsolescence fading from even
        my memory but red on

the tooth cannot be brushed off; you have left a bloody corpse in my
             bed, and that is
again, says the man to the woman who is somehow the man, dark people—black
             undemolished lilies
she is wearing rhinestone embellished sunglasses in this funereal repartée, and
             he/she is transiently
irritated: which one has left the other the body created it conjured the death in
             bloom?
survivor then am i, the violent the needle handle hand outstretched from hooded
             figure taps me again
i am its best friend, a doormat to its subtractions. love has his own car and drives
             away
swifts in conference high above the tainted ground or pond it isn't even a
             story. i am not
undercover professor long in the quotidian papers here i dim my veins, terribly
             killer
to go on terribly killer to dispose. by every equal height we attained swearing by
             the tenants of our two souls
kneeling, somewhere to carry the oath to, somewhere to play it, across the
             endangered actress tablet
i cannot imagine how you felt. i am highlands point culminant. respecting the
             glasses they are older than this one
death. one wears them soliciting a battery of non-caressive trials, before entering the
court wornout. swear swear excuses, not blood but strawberries redcurrants.
             by too much life's red you'll never
and again there are no rights if i live instead of you. i swear to go on, no right to. i
             swear to go on. no right to.

AND WHO IS CRYING

And who is crying
And why
And why am i crying?

for myself or for the dead women? i dreamed that they, we, had blonde-haired selves that ate other such ones for food. long crinkly golden hair. but says Cherokee not i for i am Cherokee. and maybe you did anyway Mara says. and the dead Afghan woman says i am back, and why and why am i crying since the Afghan women have been liberated? so to speak. because you are dead says Mira, and so you are dead and not vindicated, since you are dead. dead dead. that is our meaning we forget for the writer is bound up in herself. crying. and who is crying. and why and why am i crying. she moved the tent house which they had boarded up and covered with corrugated sheet iron on roof and sides. they bought lumber and materials to build a structure onto the former one. it was partitioned into a small bedroom and a living room, with a screened-in porch. she lived there until her death in 1945. but i can't find the rest of this part of her story; my grandmother, three times widowed, died ten days after my birth. selves that ate other such ones for food?

but says Cherokee not i for i am Cherokee. or yes. on the Trail of Tears due to the discovery of gold, and so who was liberated and from what? that i am a woman is it part of anything even my events as a woman, erased by the large tribal death? is woman a tribe or only for you? i am here because (for i am the one who keeps questioning why) your deaths cry out so loudly? my death is tears of negation, and i am in negative space because i am too hurt to occupy the ancestral spirituality—am i also too "modern" that is ruined? and who is crying, and why, and why am i crying. dead Afghan woman says, can we be more dead than others? who can be certain of who is most dead? but i had not thought such grief could continue, These were tough years for our mother, who was frail in health and no financial income, with five children. the salvation army helped us, and we received help from the county until i went to work at woolworth's in 1925. the men were lovely too Carmen is one. D's blue eyes and blond hair, was black at the time of her demise. she had a mental breakdown and suffered for about ten years (her lobotomy and death are not recorded in this document.) are you here too? and your mother? if i try to hear your voices i will cry. and who is crying and why? i am crying because i never knew you. and because Cherokee though part of me is voice so difficult and hurts still; and the Afghan woman whom one saw die on tv. there are no complete thoughts. i know we are all here together. i am not dead but my death is my soul, who is crying.

the humane treatment of prisoners is a treaty stipulation and not a moral obligation. the United States has always done as it has wished, says Cherokee, with regard to treaties. ask any Cherokee. because it is not important to get along with anyone except for the powerful and rich. as none of us have ever counted. every single person mentioned on the front page of the international herald tribune today is a man except for the bits of the blownup Palestinian woman the first terrorist of her kind. every column on the op ed page is by a man. there are photos of a male tennis player and of the male premier of Bavaria, there is a photo of an israeli woman weeping, because the tears of women are politically exploitable. (and why am i crying?) inside the newspaper are three photos of soldiers including one of a general, a photo of many male Afghans, a photo of a male journalist who has disappeared, the Palestinian leader Yasser Arafat posing with two young boys, a photo of four Macedonian men in their village, a photo of some men involved in the Enron scandal, a photo of a man head of the SEC, a photo of a wireless computer screen in Tokyo with a Japanese worker, a man, nearby, a photo of a man who works for Apple, a photo of men from a rugby match, another photo of the male tennis player, a photo of two football players after a match.

i am not dead but will die in this world and my death is my soul, who is crying. as none of us has ever counted. do you know what your existence was—that is a discredited kind of question. if everything i know is from my body. where i am and my soul is. was i alive only to be aware of that fact. was i alive only to love and be hurt by that. was i alive to be told over and over by people, not just men, that i "had so much going for me." was i alive to give the men a justification for their obscene machinations pervasive throughout the details of my own life even into my body and causing the crying of my soul. so you might say this is to go too far, but it is not. we have all been invaded, we the dead women, and that is why we are together in negative space.

about 450 U.S. troops have already arrived in the Philippines, Pentagon officials said. Alma is an owl and she will terrorize you in your future dreams when you wake up knocking your head against the headboard of your bed, trying to get out of your past actions, for i know things about soldiers, but no one would ever listen. because your body in its privacy in its veritable intimacy of you—and why am i crying?— knows it has no right to kill, except for food, and even that is sticky. but all of this is discredited. Alma is your omen, god is your omen, beware of her. if you see her you will know, that before your death the privacy of your body will be filled with the wings of your guilt; for you will know that anyone's self is as intimate to that one as yours is to you and you negated that, you deleted yourself. the death was yours and it was the worst thing you could do. you will know this from exactly within where god's wings have come.

CHEROKEE

i didn't see you on the second the next ghost dance day. i waited for you and the others, to take over the real earth again. with the animals.

the president comes into this part   and stops it   my husband is not my husband is not at home   the president comes into every part   and stops it. marching through georgia   we are secretly holding the ghost dance   in the air beyond the partition   which divides the violent public world from our souls.   comes into this part, stops it   and signals with his infant finger   his gleeful hand   of self   the vast construction of callouses: we the american people are constructing   callouses wherever we may   upon the world which we conceive of as our own skin, isn't it ours   isn't the whole world ours and we will harden our flesh to possible blows from   usurpers.

i didn't see you on the second the next ghost dance day.   if they cover the earth with american materials   will the ghost dance work? you fountain of disappearances   you maker of power   to no one but you   he comes in the second ghost dance, who?   an image of the rattler of keys   to take me

home to my senses of old   but that was a dreamed wish   even in the dream
it was seen so   no one there   no one is here but men like presidential
figures and their ambitious   dogs.   i didn't see you on the second ghost
dance day   Cherokee chants   on the second ghost dance day   when i
have vanished into my version   of the pankisi gorge   where escaped
wild people   starve and take drugs bargaining   with the third day of a
ghost dance   you unholy barter   you ruby not   you so poor
yes i am poor   yes i am so poor i can't live on the american earth   yes i
am so poor you can't feel me through the callouses   on your senses
poor poor   my miracle comes upon me   on the subsequent days of the
ghost dance still   don't need me who needs me   a president needs his money
sometimes he needs to wear the poor   but i won't be worn for an hour.

    i didn't see anyone   on the third ghost dance day   was i the only
one there   ready   mist surrounding me   am i the dying   senses beneath
the callouses of ambitious non-native men   carry some more door   there is
only a door   to mist   and it is no mist of love   it is a cloud of knowing
i know   what you're doing   to my earth

DECOMPOSITION

and intone inside the spell   am i inside it with the dead
we will not distinguish ourselves from the nuances of speaking
do you remember anything?   you had a tenderness of rubies
what you bled to the tone of it, speaking
you need to know the name of the law: magic
if you're mental you'll know that, even as stench of corpses below
am like a bullet or ballot   i am the bullet you cut out
shot who shot us   ballet you cut out   where was art in the
whole floor space of war where was art in the plan? no

your owl eyes are mandalas BURNT
burnt into my eyes   i can't find my own home
he has trimmed my work   down to his size, cut it   and made the
misshapen long-legged star more "regular"
if you're mental you'll know the tone of it bleeding
i am bleeding only to intone and see through mandala eyes
is it for you i intone, or for the tone itself   as a smell is the tone of its own
corpse, the corpse flesh sings it

                                        *

strokes my abstract wound   in abstraction my nothing hurts
and i start and cry out.   intone the real pain imaginary
will you ever stop   making each other so unhappy
will you EVER stop   making each other so unhappy
but it was he who did such and such for one   on all night this sort of thing in
the basement of the big   department stores where you're sold
no i am   an un-faced spirit   associated with   fidelity
on the horizon without a mosaic of doves
i walked into a white shape, a sort of person hollow
you are a person thing, finding other things, of stores
how will you get back, leaving ruined
they can't leave the ruins   who can speak now they say   there is no our kind
how will i get back by leaving ruined as i am
you won't get back and you are ruined but you can leave
what   walk out on it
MAN   because he is a hunter and fisher. because he cannot speak
except in regulation   if he could speak as i can he would be in ruins too
to speak is difficult dangerous and   what a spirit might do, in times
or within a spell intoning outside of them stay outside of them
stay away just stay away in ruins

*

hear the rush to evening   on the fallen street, see your own
genocide   on the reservation (worldwide, they pattern)   pushed on further
an abandoned skirt, patterned with roses, fallen full
this genocidal expansion of ours   but the underground still   belongs to the dead
and your name is? . . . surcease, he said
but he really said   my name is cyanide.
as if he and his magic or medicine   were Now's suicide pill
press you further away from the surface we have need of above the dead and the
tones pressed from the head   which is meat, they say   so
here are the diagrams why shouldn't we   disconnect you from our evolution
i am no one on a small reservation   your owl eyes are mandalas BURNT
i see the unholy patterns you have placed   upon our surface of genocide
rhymes with cyanide the blue of reason   as if i could die of it,
reason   take it and die.   are you really cyanide?   no,
see through your mandalas   into my fluid eyes, tones
black to brown i won't desert you   because i am   moving, in your mind and
elsewhere   where   one still smells the corpses
everyone is defending a self against   their faces charred   the broken enemy

*

has to kill those people   why   the rules for taking over the room
except that i   am watching because   someone is usually there when they
kill them, who are dressed   in costumes as performing bears
he lines them up   pretending to choose   who will dance for circus pleasure
dressed as a brown-furred animal   but he is going to shoot them all and i'll
we are watching, nations founded   on the genocide of who was there first
a minuet for the more   expensive animals at court   i can't hear
it now i do   your dreams are boxes keeping it separate so i'll

get up and go on   can you hear he has to kill those people   why
in order to take over the room   am watching because   anyone's eye
is now never closed though she try   anyone's eye   sees the blood that they
must build on they say   and call them animals   if the tears
trail down of who was   you say, anyone   anyone but you   anyone
anyone but you   i will fight to make it you   who bleeds, will we
and   your audition   is not relieved   you will continue
to hear the bullet dance   from the last   century
i am here for the love of my incursion   we want you to know how we feel
as   decomposition   gone down and why   am i intoning?
because you bear the charge   of this ground

BALLAD

Cheney has used his power and authority unrivaled by that of any vice president in modern times to help set the course of the administration's war on terrorism look at him in his black glasses among organized gangs.

i must have been calling to you for you arose from a pond alive but i knew you were really dead and when you shone a small flashlight on my legs to see "my beautiful legs" within the dark theater of my psyche it was because before you died you no longer walked.

Cheney's impact on the Iraq debate or his influence on the president cannot be overstated officials and experts say. he's an oil ghoul and a war ghoul, Mara says.

you took out a pen-sized flashlight and shone it on my legs i was wearing some sort of front-slit skirt "i just wanted to see your legs again." we were in the darkened aisle of the movie theater.

foreign ministers including 17 presidents or prime ministers this year have learned they must schedule a visit with Cheney as they make their rounds. one of the planners of the secret bombing of Cambodia and Laos.

[from *Alma, or The Dead Women*]

then you and i were to make love with an emaciated dark woman. but she and i did so first she was so thin with scar tissue all over her torso. she was myself my emaciated soul.

Cheney's position about the importance of confronting Iraq over its weapons of mass destruction has changed significantly since september 11 both because of a new sense of vulnerability and increasingly alarming intelligence, according to administration officials. the liars.

get on a train the outside of a train riding a ladder there. then i'm in a town for the night waiting for the next train tomorrow. this is a train song this is a train song i'm on the train leaving you. do i really have to ride the train. can't i be an owl too.

Cheney's office in effect is an agile cruiser able to maneuver around the lumbering aircraft carriers of the departments of state and defense to make its mark.

what is your story owl? i was drawn on the night in charcoal but my eyes were alive because they were windows with golden light pouring through. and behind them everyone was gone everything was done. every little war was done. in the haunted future.

in the haunted future now, for how many millions of people. and. i am one. Cheney is done. a meeting with him is so highly prized that when the vice president recently canceled a meeting with the foreign minister of Kazakhstan because the government had not released a Turkmen dissident the Kazakh government quickly decided to set the man free. there are major oilfields in Kazakhstan, Mara says.

and in my eyes i keep something of you. i do. is that what they are for. for keeping you there, when everything was gone. when every little war was done. when i still had legs and eyes and wings. in the haunted future.

[2003]

1 4

My childhood was held on my own, beyond any wheel.

Somewhere like ancient Assyria. How near Assyria is!

I waded in the shallows. I never wore shoes on the road. Over the fields, where I breathed.

This is a heavenly tree. And the world is open windows. Who needs angels? If they speak, I'm not even going to listen.

How near the ancient culture is! I see the carved foundation, at the foot of the green hill. Designs in stone.

Has anybody seen my love? Oh, I don't care.

This is the morning of the age I was, six, when she died in the state mental hospital. There was never an official cause of death for her.

If I've brought back my soul, have I brought back hers too, even if she couldn't leave?

Have I brought back yours too?

She and I are both innocent in the photo, the man says. The man on the bed says.

Anyone's transparence, I want you to be here with mine. I'll keep it with mine.

My purpose is to return with your soul. The last fair deal, for you were fair.

✳   ✳   ✳

I ride the exactitudes of pitch, the tune, in words alone. I wouldn't be able to take the journey, if I couldn't hear the poem.

Could you voyage without the register of changes?

Who do you serve? Do you serve somebody?

I serve the poem, no one.

As they are taking down the tent, as if there were no more poetry. See the ghosts of it; woman chanting, blind man sings. Like no one. This land, condemned, endures. I could never be ashamed of my life.

Hearing that old owl sing.

I was born to be your poet. I am the woman, your poet. All that I am.

And I know one thing. No one. Is the poet. I am.

She just did what she had to do.

Who else can do this? No one. Any no one who cares to, and the eyes above, where I have been, approve.

I don't think you had a choice except to be a poet, he said. But this world still can't stand long. He was already sick.

There's an enormous pine beneath which she lies. Momma, in the pines and of all the pines, this one above, with some of its needles gone yellow, is the most beautiful.

It can't stand long, can it? More and more parts of us die, covered up after, by the long black coat of his preference, ignorance.

I prefer the live versions. The performance of the search for the soul.

> The scratches in this
> recording
> are due to a perfect technique,
>
> beauty's intransigence.
> Them that don't like it
> can leave me alone.

Take care of the pines where we sleep.

I never do anything else.

The photos of the dead women, too, were faint and silvery, scratched. I knew who they were, my relations, and I still longed to help them. Though they were dead and I would become one of them.

Never got what we should have had
Never got what you should
Equality is a poor word
For life.

You can't have what they had, their loss.
Or else the rich would live and the poor would die.
She don't have no where to go, wandering round from door to door.
She's travelin' through the land. Don't you hear me calling?
I remember when Momma dreamed of her crying outside her bedroom window, trying to get in. She was, at that time, far away, in the hospital for the defective. She for whom I had often played a song.
Don't you lie to me. Tell me where did you sleep last night.
She couldn't lie. She never grew, never spoke.
Beneath the great pine tree, I think all this, in my high old bed, Momma said.
I do whatever you do.
Momma, I keep trying to find her soul.
But she has it. Don't you know?

*   *   *

In the boughs where the shamans come to life. Boughs where the poems' dark eyes hang.
It's such an old function I've forgotten everything that I know.
Except how to do it again.
He still knew how as he lay, mostly blind, dying. He just didn't do it anymore. He was it.
Kiss him goodbye in the hospital for the moneyless. There's another poet, lying over in another ward.
Which one? Which poet? Do you know him?
I know one thing, nobody can sing the blues like Blind Willie McTell.

I am your poet, Momma said. I gave you everything I had. Though you thought I was wrong sometimes.

I didn't give you genes, I gave you poems.

It's all the same being, wrapped up.

Beneath the tree on the river bank. Wrapped up with Black Jack Davy.

       Divided, spreading their wings
       they fly up from the tree.

       Though tonight they'll lie on the
       cold cold ground in his arms.

I gave you everything you know.

This world tree is patterned but unconditioned; because you never know. If you'll make it or not to the heavens and bring back your soul in this song.

There's no because.

Who do you serve?

The tree, she said. The tree with golden needles, never barren.

But nobody could sing the blues like you could. Singing his/her/your song, all wrapped up one. In the arms of the old infirmary.

I'm gazing out the window, all the windows.

Everything's in motion, he said. At least that's all that I see. I only see movement now.

I'm its audience. He may have said. Still interested, though he hadn't walked for months.

              *   *   *

       If I'm not your poet, who is?
       If you don't want a poet
          then don't say so.
       Baby, please don't go.

[from *In the Pines*]   **335**

I gave up my long blue gloves and shoes of finest leather. But I never left my babies. I bore them in the great pine tree and we lived there together. In the tree of shamans. We still do.

Don't lie to me. Who are you? Just who are you?

I am the poet.

Made the words around him ring. How old are you my pretty little miss, a long time ago and now.

You never will want for money, because you never will want it.

What will you forsake?

I'll forsake everything but the tree. The pilgrims call it the tree of life.

[2003]

FROM SONGS AND STORIES OF THE GHOULS

There was power in that room. I saw
it, because my eyes were crushed out

It's my judgment   on this almost face
holding the mouth   so.

The scars on my right side won't fail.
I've come back wearing them
instead of a conscience or a guide

in order to cause
                    a breakaway culture.

trembling white   vertical lines
in black sky   above sea. they
spell what it   might be; the

emotional   tone of the old
universe   was vicious.
it had no   care for me

~

The ghoul-girl. There was one to care for, but I can't remember the name.

The ghoul. Care about the bodies again.

You will always be the ghoul-girl now.

To stagger and live; a moonstone will fill the head.

I see their thoughts. They are round and white and constitute the power. If you drop your thought, you fail. And if you let some fall, and if you let some spill, you are facing it.

It leaks out and faces you dead. But I keep loving myself she said.

She will walk me to sleep.

She walks me to sleep.

I bore a child said she and cruel to see it perceived as I. Walking here where the city's open to ghouls.

You find that magic is dreadful.

It's all that I have.

You are the ghoul-child.

It was carved on all the walls: no one sees it. No one sees me.

This is a luminous quality. I'm the ghoul; because it's what I say.

Because it's what I say, I'm in love with that.

~

What she reports against you isn't
what she reproaches you for
Building presses through windows,
faces of who you betray. It's all
in a store front now, everything is.
When you protest, you're no
longer a civilian: they can kill you.

[from *Songs and Stories of the Ghouls*]

I've come back without anyone to
snitch to, I must really be dead. You
can't bribe me if you can't see me.
"I've killed hundreds in honor of
you." Cooking the books so alive
was that way. Coin after coin in the old
pay phone to hell. "Listen to my music . . ."

~

The city I founded I will found again. Running through the cards, you've used all

the cards up. The city I founded I will found again. These are the new ghoulish cards

with their own magic lice made licit. Suit of blood, suit of crania, suit of viral oblig-

gatos, suit of blunting salt. The city I founded I will found again. And as in those days

was there not found so false a lover going on the ground as whose power I will slay

this new city's burning into my forehead. I can't see it, give me something, you can

have dread. Can I have justice? Never, what can I have this new city burning into

my forehead.

~

What were you doing when I thought you were dead, weren't you dead? The history

of Carthage has been related by numerous ancient men but the Tyrian princess Dido

founder of the city cannot be mentioned except in relation to her tragic passion for

Aeneas; an important production of little masks characterizes the Punic world you are

hellenized you worship Demeter and Kore. The young woman is dressed in a skirt of

[from *Songs and Stories of the Ghouls*]   **339**

folded wings upon her sarcophagus our knowledge of the religion is lacunar but it is possible that one worshipped nothing except for untrue but powerful images and symbols perhaps 'worship' means 'use' as it should. Was there once again but this time I knew he was really dead there is a poem in the scars on my liver a written history or map which is beautiful but only covers me I must be the child who isn't listening so I'll hear. Destroyed in 146 B.C. your poetry is dreadful, vacant and inept and ours will survive as long as our empire lasts: every present writer says. Towards changes hands of configuration each small mask is a word to cover your lack that is where language stands on no foundation but the wars it has always upheld for if your ways were destroyed and your poems broken and ploughed into the salted earth what would you be? The ghoulishness of this project is affirmed by any style and there is no way forward but your empire's way.

~

If you meet me here I was Lady
if I meet you where you were killed
then I'm no longer a civilian if I was
your drug. There's nothing to replace what

you need from the soil; salted it's perfect
your Lady. If you meet me here. (say the scars)
If I met you as Lady, the senses of
where you are now; if I met you without

a conscience: why should I have one
when you're asking me to assuage yours?
The gas is always free when you're dead.
There's no money where you meet me, too bad.

~

Walking away turns to look over shoulder in black dragging power out of time pursed
lips less disapproving in the tornout robe along the strand. Someone decided, for you,
to destroy Carthage or Corinth, make you weak a beautiful invention of the owners for
you. Where the beauty is, take some and use it against them. If they invented it take
some. Is she willful though right away a compiler of fates I will use, who can't get a
job at the bureau. She's pulling power away from his torso, leaving. I'm inclined to
use you myself, motivated mask. It was my city first, and I found it before you could
rule, because your secrets were mechanical. You'll have to beg for it from me, you'll
have to come backwards behind your own words because there's no picture of you.
A curse was invoked with great solemnity upon anyone who might attempt to rebuild
the city. Is that a picture? You were so barren you couldn't hear the beauty in the
scratches when twigs dragged against the panes on the other side of old records.
I lived with whatever you said because I could sing it, the sources say. The ruins
ploughed to express final destruction I WILL tell in the recitative of misery and
fury what you do to me still. Even backwards can she know different word if the
salt's ploughed in. But all words are different without their masks.

~

Black sequins compression. Only the pressure is certain, lay this next to another. She'll turn around on initial discomfort. The sequins are appealing, beside the violets that are paper seals. At first it was too compressed, so I've diffused it she says. I'm looking back at the future so it won't hurt with its depravity, dead man. And no one went with me that smooth because these jewels when nothing cost. Don't you see that once there was no cost, because there wasn't really a compression, because there were shiny sequins. There's something I have to destroy. Place the humble sequins next to the light waves I'm in struggle takes the eyes. She takes a mask to use its eyes I remember this—have eyes for light posed a given. You needed to see, if you were a maid. She took the light and broke it as hard as she could so you couldn't tell it. The black disks scattered deaths of details to place there all the change I had.

~

I stand here in whose eyes
the name of light is audience
burning into my forehead
waitresses' voices along the spine
if what was once light
    isn't
    my audience
what are you doing to me?
who was I broken for
was it worth it to be?

If I'm a shade
          acting
what once will occur
it must be for the song I wore
hear what they all said to you
a gesture or tone: someone lies
in the intentional tongue
betraying you again and again
          the one
          or the many
whose thoughts I stand here before

Because there's no light, what an
          outrage
was made of the science
of definitions
like what happened to me
performing here in a mad scene
          not
          and never mad
I hadn't seen clearly until I enacted her

~

Woman with antlers, deer-headed antlered woman in black against black lace,

black-headed deer woman, Lady of the mountains whose antlers melt into lace.

Lady of the mountains, emerges from my right side and all the lacy scars there, why

is she a deer? Because I'm not anthropomorphic, soul of the mountain night. This

is my echo from before, from what I had made for you vocally, and from before we

[from *Songs and Stories of the Ghouls*] **343**

acceded to the time line never like lace. Lady the mountain middle of no spatial universe. I have the antlers she says which extend from the deer head in the middle of our echo. Lady of Wild Animals, for whom the animals return, the deer with the heart or breath line, through the mouth to the center echoing. Do you hear the words of the conquerors or do you hear the voices of deer? echoes, can you find a center in an echo. I'm finding, with the finder, the antlers paths leading from my head. I am the center of it, the center of the lady.

~

If there's change you put it into this sculpture's slot the room where once before Carthage we're not in the named light, soldier. In this gold the other side of a word like bear or not to be borne unless you make up nerves for it but in the shadow-nerves this song. For that breakthrough into the Shadow, we the dead and mutilated the defective dip our hands. Let Mavis in, without obligation face most all the beautiful face. I am the most beautiful face said a ghoul one down, you have promoted the whore until it's still. Every whore in the history collection come forward with his face of a woman to find if he were beautiful so Mavis sing. He had shaved skull to make a shape under the wind but there's no real wind. I would have been placed wherever you wanted to kill some, for I have long use and no signature; am I glad you'll be dead too, nameless no-record or no-document; put to head hard-liner calls for a shoot, always calling. But there is no bloodfill of ticks here of wisdom so say what they took from you in order to keep their own mien with mine they'd say to any linguistic heiress or bird. This is the shade of that thrush leave it alone. I can't calculate

the arrows in time you thought you were whole but didn't know now there's only

narrow to a single expansion your little death as viewed by the times bolstered by

them successful with one's death the real shadow Mavis sings, that's what the power

called it till I took power we the shadow I saw heads and fingers, hands, push up

through the soil. That was us, so Mavis sings.

~

Justice may appear in the
guise of a hard, devious mother
I want shoes for my baby
son my werewolf son

None of you can sing a song
The best you can do is breathe
every breath opining
following the prescribed instrument

which is now a hatchet
Justice has Egyptian hair because
you'll be dead; she wants ten
dollars from you; I've offered mine

None of you sing; you beg for each
other's love in chopped-up phrases:
every breath opining a duty to
the gods of the times, whose times

Justice isn't a pleasant woman
Her baby has a wolfish face that only
I could love; the Egyptian gods
have animal heads don't they: the

dead man loves Justice's baby
Having had his soul weighed by her
Take your backpack off, it's in the
way, she says gruffly; he plays

with her hairy baby. I'm trying
to tell you, the Law knows you're
as wise as a wolf; only the baby
is important; only I can sing

the Law that hard and devious woman
says that this is just. You have
given birth to another wild hybrid
like yourself. I'm following you to your

heights: I'm the only intellectual
Justice says—she's worked in peep shows—
You'll never figure me out; but
you owe my baby, and you owe me.

~

No world is intact
and no one cares about you.

I leaned down over
don't care about, I care about
      you
I leaned down over the

world in portrayal
of carefulness, answering

something you couldn't say.
Walking or fallen and you
      were supposed
to give therapy to me—

me leaning down
brushing with painted feathers
to the left of chance your operatic,
      broken

book.

[2005]

Poems in *Grave of Light: Selected Poems* 1970–2005 are listed below under the titles of the books in which they found initial significant publication—that is, in finished form and not as extracts.

165 MEETING HOUSE LANE
NEW YORK: 'C' PRESS, 1971

Nos. 1, 4, 16, 22

PHOEBE LIGHT
BOLINAS: BIG SKY, 1973

Dear Dark Continent

INCIDENTALS IN THE DAY WORLD
NEW YORK: ANGEL HAIR, 1973

Dear Dark Continent
Incidentals In the Day World

FOR FRANK O'HARA'S BIRTHDAY
CAMBRIDGE, ENGLAND: STREET EDITIONS, 1976

Your Dailiness
But He Says I Misunderstood

ALICE ORDERED ME TO BE MADE
CHICAGO: THE YELLOW PRESS, 1976

"Alice ordered me to be made"
"The Virtue of Uncreatedness"
Endless Day; 30th Birthday

A DIAMOND NECKLACE
NEW YORK: FRONTWARD BOOKS, 1977

Little Egypt
Sonnet ("The late Gracie Allen was a very lucid comedienne")

SONGS FOR THE UNBORN SECOND BABY

LENOX, MASS.: UNITED ARTISTS, 1979

Extract from I

WHEN I WAS ALIVE

NEW YORK: VEHICLE EDITIONS, 1980

Poem ("St. Mark's Place caught at night in hot summer")

When I Was Alive

After Tsang Chih

Today

You

The Goddess Who Created This Passing World

Untitled

"If she says that she's the goddess Fortune"

The World, All That Live & All That Occur

HOW SPRING COMES

WEST BRANCH, IOWA: TOOTHPASTE PRESS, 1981

January

How Spring Comes

A California Girlhood

Bus Stop

Jack Would Speak through the Imperfect Medium of Alice

September's Book

A True Account of Talking to Judy Holiday, October 13

Poem ("You hear that heroic big land music?")

The Prophet

WALTZING MATILDA

NEW YORK: KULCHUR PRESS, 1981;
REISSUED, CAMBRIDGE, MASS.: FAUX PRESS, 2003

Untitled ("Clouds, big ones oh it's")

Flowers of the Foothills & Mountain Valleys

World's Bliss

Waltzing Matilda

MARGARET & DUSTY
ST. PAUL, MINN.: COFFEE HOUSE, 1985

Untitled ("All my life")
Postcards
Margaret and Dusty
Congratulating Wedge

PARTS OF A WEDDING
NEW YORK: UNIMPROVED EDITIONS PRESS, 1986

"Corpus Sagrada"
"in this Paradise"
I the People
"in the dark I"
"*More important than having been born is your city*"

AT NIGHT THE STATES
CHICAGO: YELLOW PRESS, 1988

La Mort
The Ten Best Issues of Comic Books
Poem ("Why do I want to tell it")
Love
It Would
Weekend Weather
At Night the States

HOMER'S ART
CANTON, NEW YORK: THE INSTITUTE OF FURTHER STUDIES, 1990

[This chapbook was reprinted in *The Scarlet Cabinet*]
Homer's *Art*
Mother Mask
White Phosphorus

THE SCARLET CABINET with Douglas Oliver
NEW YORK: SCARLET EDITIONS, 1992

[See note above for *Homer's Art*]
Homer's *Art*

Mother Mask

White Phosphorus

Beginning with a Stain

    "Beginning with a stain, as the Universe did perhaps"

    "I will never not make a sound not have made a sound"

    "Some people refuse to remember, & I"

    "Against all agony a bunch of flowers in the chest"

    "born in beauty born a loved one, before history"

    "They say something ruinous & tragic happened soon after"

    "Speaking firstly forever"

'*You haven't saved me any time*'

'*What does she think?*'

THE DESCENT OF ALETTE

    [This long poem was subsequently published as

    The Descent of Alette (New York: Penguin Books, 1996)]

        BOOK ONE

           "One day, I awoke" "& found myself on"

           "There was a woman" "in a station"

           "We couldn't find" "our fathers—"

           "A mother" "& child"

           "'When I was born,' "I was born now"

           "I once" "found an exit"

           "A car" "awash with blood"

           "I stood again" "on the platform"

        BOOK THREE

           "'It's time to go,' he said" "'Go where?'"

           "As I stared down" "into the black lake"

           "The horizontal" "black void"

           "Talons tore me," "tore my flesh"

           "When I awoke I" "was in darkness"

           "'We will be silent" "& wait'"

           "I looked into the light" "directly"

DISOBEDIENCE

NEW YORK: PENGUIN BOOKS, 2001

Circorpse

Help Me Corpus Sagrada

The Islanders Remember That There Are No Women And No Men

Red Fish

Enuma Elish

IPHIGENIA

BROOKLYN, N.Y.: BELLADONNA 36, 2002

Iphigenia

ALMA, OR THE DEAD WOMEN

NEW YORK: GRANARY BOOKS, 2006

Radical Feminist

Beloved Earth Restrain Them

Discredited

Oath

And Who Is Crying

Cherokee

Decomposition

Ballad

PREVIOUSLY UNPUBLISHED WORK

Love Poems

"2/?   Saturday"

Friday Midnight Exactly

Cold Poem

I Hope I'm Not Here Next Year

The Locket

White Evening Primrose

Memorial Day

So Much

Reason and Other Women

Amid These Words I Can Know

Parable of Christian

Moses and the Burning Bush
Jone Jonah
Leaves
Grave of Light
Where Leftover Misery Goes
Benediction
City
Love
In the Pines
14
Songs and Stories of the Ghouls
"There was power in that room. I saw"
"The ghoul-girl. There was one to care for, but I can't remember the name"
"What she reports against you isn't"
"The city I founded I will found again"
"What were you doing when I thought you were dead, weren't you dead?"
"If you meet me here I was Lady"
"Walking away turns to look over shoulder in black dragging power . . ."
"Black sequins compression. Only the pressure is certain . . ."
"I stand here in whose eyes"
"Woman with antlers, deer-headed antlered woman . . ."
"If there's change you put it into this sculpture's slot . . ."
"Justice may appear in the"
"No world is intact"